Ob

Objective-C

Jiva DeVoe

WILEY

Wiley Publishing, Inc.

Objective-C

Published by
Wiley Publishing, Inc.
10475 Crosspoint Blvd.
Indianapolis, IN 46256
www.wiley.com

Copyright © 2011 by Wiley Publishing, Inc., Indianapolis, Indiana

Published by Wiley Publishing, Inc., Indianapolis, Indiana

Published simultaneously in Canada

ISBN: 978-0-470-47922-3

Manufactured in the United States of America

10 9 8 7 6 5 4 3 2 1

For general information on our other products and services or to obtain technical support, please contact our Customer Care Department within the U.S. at (877) 762-2974, outside the U.S. at (317) 572-3993 or fax (317) 572-4002.

Library of Congress Control Number: 2010943062

For my wife, Dawn, and my children, Robert, Alex, and Izzy.
You are, and always will be, the most important people in the world
to me.

About the Author

Jiva DeVoe has been writing software for nearly 25 years, starting with his Commodore VIC-20 using BASIC and assembly language, and gradually working his way through C, C++, Python, Ruby, Java and finally Objective-C. In 2001, he founded Random Ideas, LLC, a software company dedicated to building great applications for the Mac. When the iPhone SDK was announced, he was honored to be selected as one of the earliest developers to have access to the SDK, and using it, he developed several applications that were available in the iTunes App Store when it launched on July 11, 2008. Since that time, his iPhone applications have received several awards, including being chosen as among the Top 100 apps and games in the App Store, and been featured as Apple Staff Picks and in Apple Advertisements. Today, Jiva continues to work full time for his company, Random Ideas, developing great iPhone and Mac applications. He lives with his wife, three children, and two basset hounds in the dusty desert of Arizona.

Credits

Acquisitions Editor
Aaron Black

Executive Editor
Jody Lefevere

Project Editor
Beth Taylor

Technical Editor
Brad Miller

Copy Editor
Beth Taylor

Editorial Director
Robyn Siesky

Editorial Manager
Rosemarie Graham

Business Manager
Amy Knies

Senior Marketing Manager
Sandy Smith

Vice President and Executive Group Publisher
Richard Swadley

Vice President and Executive Publisher
Barry Pruett

Project Coordinator
Katherine Crocker

Production Specialist
Carrie A. Cesavice

Quality Control Technician
Melissa Cossell

Proofreading and Indexing
Laura Bowman, Evelyn Wellborn,
BIM Indexing & Proofreading Services

Preface

Objective-C gets a raw deal in the IT industry. Though it's a powerful and dynamic object oriented language, it doesn't get nearly the amount of recognition that C++, Java, and others get.

When I wrote Cocoa Touch for iPhone OS 3, I knew that it needed a companion book, one which helped people over the hump of learning Objective-C before moving on to the higher level frameworks, Cocoa, and Cocoa Touch.

So when the opportunity came to write a book dedicated to Objective-C, the language, I jumped at it!

In the end, I feel I have been given an opportunity to contribute to the foundation of new Mac, iPhone and iPad developers knowledge through this book, and I'm tremendously excited by that. I love the idea that this book might be a catalyst to helping Objective-C grow, not just on these, but across many different platforms. There's no reason that Objective-C shouldn't be used more on platforms such as Unix, Windows, and so on.

As a reader, you are expected to have only a limited knowledge of computers. I have tried to approach the subject from the absolute bare essentials, but you will need at least a basic background in how to navigate around a computer.

If you already know some programming languages, that won't hurt you here. Some of what I discuss will be review for you, but don't worry, there's plenty of specifics for Objective-C that you will pick up.

If you already have a background in Objective-C, I hope that you will find some nuggets of information you didn't know in this book. I've tried to keep it in an accessible form so that you can look up specifics that you're looking for. You may not read it cover to cover, but it should give you the ability to jump to specific parts and gain insight into how to do what you are looking to do.

With regard to conventions used within this book, I've tried to be reasonably consistent, and also tried to generally err on the side of Apple conventions when prudent. The only notable exception has been in my use of the phrase "method" to indicate functions on instances and classes. Apple generally prefers the term "message." This is in part due to the influence of Smalltalk on Objective-C.

When referring to keyboard shortcuts, I opted to use the term "Command-Key" to indicate keyboard shortcuts using the key directly to the left of the space key on most Apple keyboards. You may also know this as the "Apple" key, since prior to only a few years ago, it included a small Apple logo on it. Additionally, the key next to the Command-Key, has been called the "Option-Key" and the key next to that, the "Control-Key". These should all be consistent with Apple documentation conventions.

When referring to variables which store objects in them, I will often refer to them as "instance variables". Some books like to use this term, or it's abbreviation, "ivar" to refer to variables that are part of a class. For these, I prefer the term "member variable." To me, member variables can be instance variables, but not all instance variables are member variables.

When referencing methods in the text, I have used the standard apple convention of referring to them using the method name, but without parameters. So, for example, the method:

```
- (void) someMethodUsingParam1: (NSString *) param1 andParam2: (NSString *)
param2;
```

Would be written in the text as: -someMethodUsingParam1:andParam2. If it's a class method, the leading hyphen is replaced with a +, just as if you were writing the method in your class definition.

With regard to sample code, in chapters where I have instructed you to build specific full-on projects, I have generally tried to include full listings for the code. In cases where I have not, you can always download the projects, complete with artwork and other supporting files from the book's website. There are also chapters where it didn't really make sense to make a full-on project to demonstrate a technology. In these cases, the code listings are more snippets that you can use as a basis for your own code. Since these snippets don't comprise fully functional projects, there will not be example projects for these on the web site.

I hope that you find this book as enjoyable an experience to read as I had writing it. To me, the mark of a good technical book is that it doesn't sit on my shelf. It holds a place of honor on or near my desk because I keep returning to it, time and again. I hope that this book holds such prestige in your library, and that it becomes a dog-eared, cover-torn, page-scribbled-on reference that remains useful to you for years to come.

Jiva DeVoe

book@random-ideas.net

Acknowledgments

Writing this book has been both rewarding and challenging, but I could not have done it without the aide and support of some specific individuals whom I would like to thank.

First and foremost, I have to thank Brad Miller, of Cynical Peak Software who has been one of the best Technical Editors in the business. His careful attention to detail and his tireless tenacity in helping me correct my mistakes has been amazing. Thank you for your efforts. You rock.

For his help and advocacy at Wiley, despite a few bumps in the road, I want to thank Aaron Black. Your patronage and assistance has been much appreciated.

For teaching me to marvel at the wonders of technology and encouraging me to pursue my dreams in computers, I'm thankful to my father, Robert A. DeVoe.

To my son, Alex, who spent many hours formatting the pages of this book, thank you. Your efforts and assistance were key in making this book a reality.

Finally, and most importantly, I'd like to thank my wife, for her unerring support, not just in this project, but in all my work. Without her, this book could not have been finished. You lift me when my spirits are low and tired, and inspire me to keep reaching for new accomplishments and goals. I can't thank you enough.

Contents

Part II: Exploring Deeper Features 137

Chapter 5: Working with Blocks 139

Chapter 6: Using Key Value Coding and Key Value Observing 163

Introducing Objective-C

Introducing Objective-C

The year was 1986. Halley's Comet was the closest to the sun that it had been in 75 years. The United Kingdom and France announced plans to construct the Channel Tunnel. Polaroid was all the rage and had just recently forced Kodak to leave the instant camera business. The C programming language had been in use for about 15 years, but C++ was a newcomer to the field, and barely known. The Smalltalk programming language had been making the rounds in the technology industry and getting people excited about a new concept in programming called object-oriented programming, or OOP for short.

Two developers, Tom Love and Brad Cox had been exposed to Smalltalk while at ITT Corporation's Programming Technology Center. Cox thought that it would be interesting to add object-oriented features to the C programming language, enabling object-oriented programming in C. In fact, he called his extension to COOPC, which stood for object-oriented programming in C. Eventually, the two formed a company to commercialize these extensions and market them as a language to developers. The name of this new language was changed to Objective-C. A few years later, a tiny startup headed by Steve Jobs, called NeXT, licensed and standardized Objective-C as the primary language that they wanted to use to develop a new operating system called NeXTstep. NeXT computer was eventually purchased by Apple, resulting in the absorption of the NeXTstep operating system, and its eventual evolution into Mac OS X.

Few people realize that Objective-C is as old as it is, and that it has in fact influenced many other programming technologies. For example, the Java programming language shares a great deal in common with Objective-C. The reason for this is that early in Objective-C's history, NeXT computer partnered with Sun Microsystems to develop the OpenStep platform. The language that they used to develop this technology was Objective-C. When NeXT computer did not do as well as they had hoped, and the company began to fail, Sun decided to develop their own language and cross-platform development kit, Java. The engineers that worked on Java were intimately familiar with Objective-C because Objective-C is the language that they had been using prior to developing Java. As a result, they copied many of the better features of Objective-C to the new language they created.

In This Chapter

Learning about Objective-C history

Exploring Xcode for writing Objective-C Code

Configuring your development environment

Today, Objective-C is the language of choice for developing both on Mac OS X and iPhone OS. It has evolved to become an elegant solution, fitting just right between fully statically typed languages and dynamically typed languages. It is one of the few languages that is typically compiled, thus benefiting from the compile time syntax checking of languages like C and C++ while at the same time benefiting from a dynamic runtime, which enables dynamic object typing.

In addition to Mac OS X and iPhone OS, Objective-C has grown quite a following on other platforms as well and can be used to develop applications on Linux, Windows, and anywhere else that the GNU compiler collection has been ported. Its use on the iPhone OS has especially increased the popularity of this language, and brought many new developers to it. It could even be argued that Objective-C is experiencing a new renaissance today — hundreds of thousands of new developers are flocking to this language, making it one of the hottest new sensations in technology today.

In this book, I hope to introduce you to Objective-C and show you why I think it is a first-class language deserving a place among the best programming languages in the world. I like to say that a good programmer needs three languages under his belt. The first is a workflow automation language. Typically, this is a scripting language. One that he can use to automate his workspace and to build ad hoc tools to help optimize his workflow. The second is an editor macro language. As developers, we spend 99 percent of our time crafting text into software. Having a tool that helps you to manipulate your editor is amazingly valuable. The last one is a language for building systems and applications — one that can be used to deploy applications that require high performance and high reliability. Usually these languages are compiled so that you can squeeze the most performance out of your platform of choice. Their most important feature, however, is the ability to leverage system libraries to their fullest extent.

My hope is that by the end of this book, Objective-C will become your application language of choice. There is no task that this language cannot perform as well as or better than any other compiled language out there.

Using Xcode for Development

In this book, I assume that you will be using the Xcode development environment for your coding. Xcode is an excellent IDE provided by Apple for free by simply signing up for the Apple developer program. It supports C, Objective-C, C++, Java, and several other languages natively, but we're only going to use it for Objective-C here.

Starting a project

When you first start Xcode, you are given the choice to open a recently opened project or to create a new one. For the purposes of our discussion here, choose to start a new project at this time so you can follow along. This brings up the New Project dialog box, as shown in Figure 1.1.

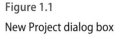

Figure 1.1

New Project dialog box

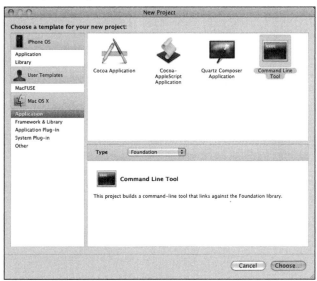

In this dialog box, you can choose to create various kinds of projects, including command line applications to desktop graphical applications. You can find templates for virtually anything. Additionally, if you have the iPhone SDK installed, there are also project templates for various kinds of iPhone and iPad applications. Because you are primarily interested in simply understanding the Objective-C language, choose the project that is the simplest of all of these.

1. From the Mac OS X group, choose Application and then choose Command Line Tool.

2. Under the Type drop-down list, choose Foundation.

3. Click the Choose button, choose a location to save your new project, and click Finish.

Over the next few sections, I'm going to give you a brief introduction to the Xcode development environment so that you can become familiar with it. To begin with, look at the Xcode window. It is shown in Figure 1.2.

Figure 1.2

The main Xcode window

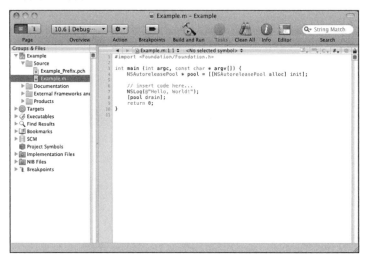

The main Xcode window consists of two panels. The first one, shown on the left, contains all the files in your project. Selecting one of these files brings up that file in the Editor panel, located on the right-hand side of the window. Project files can be grouped in Xcode by moving them into folders within your project. For the most part, these groups are strictly for your benefit during development and have little or no impact on the final completed project.

In addition to your source files, the frameworks that you are linking your project with are also shown.

Below the project files are a set of Smart groups. These encapsulate things such as the targets that your project will make, search results, and breakpoints.

The Targets group contains the targets that your project will compile. By modifying the settings on the objects within this group, you override the project-wide settings for your compilation. This is also where you can add and edit custom compilation steps for your projects. Figure 1.3 shows the build settings from this group.

Figure 1.3

Build settings

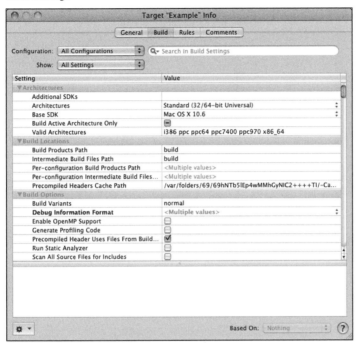

Exploring the files in your project

In this simple project, your source files are contained within the source group. You should see that you have only one source file, which will be named the same as whatever you named your project. It will have an extension of .m. Click this file and it should display in the Editor panel in Xcode, as shown in Figure 1.4.

NOTE

Although I said that there's only one source file, you may see another file with an extension of .pch; this is a Pre-Compiled Header and not a file you need to edit or work with. It's automatically generated by the compiler.

Don't worry right now about understanding everything that's in this file. I go over the syntax of a basic Objective-C program in the next chapter. For now, the important part is to focus on understanding Xcode and how it works.

NOTE
If your source file does not display, you may need to drag the divider from the bottom of the Xcode window to show the source editor.

Figure 1.4

Editor panel in Xcode.

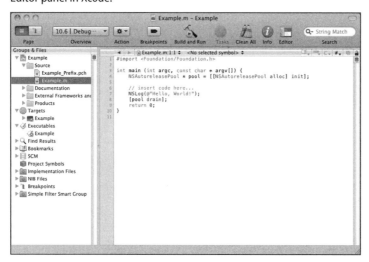

Other files included in the default project include a documentation file for your program in the Documentation group, the frameworks that are linked with your project in the External Frameworks and Libraries group, and your actual executable, which is located in the Products group. Your executable will be shown in red. This is because you have not yet built your executable. If you click the Build and Run button, it will build the executable, run it, and display its output in the console window. Be sure to familiarize yourself with the console window and what it looks like, because you will use the console window quite a lot in the upcoming chapters to examine the output of the programs that you will be writing.

Adding source files

To add new source files to your project, you simply select the source group in the file organization panel, and then go to the File ⇨ New File menu, which shows the New File dialog box, as shown in Figure 1.5.

For the most part, you'll be using the Cocoa Class selection and the Objective-C class template when adding files in this book, so familiarize yourself with this window.

In some cases, you may have multiple targets in your project, and, as a result, you may have different source files which are compiled for the different targets. To explicitly include or exclude a file from compilation in the currently selected target, click the file, and then find the detail view in the source panel. The small Target column contains a selected check box when a file is configured to be compiled for the current target. When it is deselected, it will not be compiled. An example is shown in Figure 1.6.

NOTE

If you don't see the detailed display, go to the View ⇨ Zoom Editor Out menu to display it.

Figure 1.5

New File dialog box

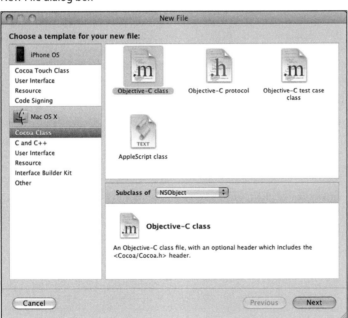

Figure 1.6

Showing the Target check box

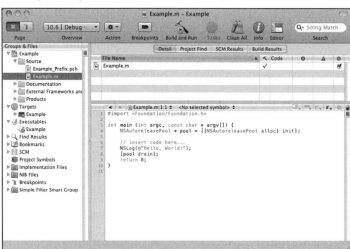

The main Xcode window

Now that you're somewhat familiar with basic file management in Xcode, you'll want to familiarize yourself with the main Xcode window. This is where you'll do the majority of your work in Xcode. The main Xcode window is shown in Figure 1.7.

When you look at this window, you can see that the left-hand side is the File Browser panel and the right-hand side is the detailed display panel, or as I alternatively refer to it throughout the rest of this text, the Editor panel. Selecting files in the File Browser panel causes them to display in the Editor panel on the right. Additionally, the Editor panel has several different modes. The detail mode shows a summary of the files that are selected in the File Browser. The Project Find mode shows a find panel that enables you to do a search through all the files in your project for an arbitrary text string. If you enable the All-In-One layout for Xcode, you also have a build results mode for the Editor panel. This mode enables you to see the build results for your last compilation.

At this time, look at the strip at the top of the text editor window. This shows you several interesting informational items related to the file that you are currently editing.

The first item you see in this top strip is the filename and line number of the file you're currently editing. This is actually a drop-down list, and you can click on it and choose from a list of recently opened files. Next to this, another drop-down list shows the function declarations of the methods in the current file that you are editing. If you choose one of these methods, then the editor will automatically jump to that declaration in your existing file.

Figure 1.7

Main Xcode window

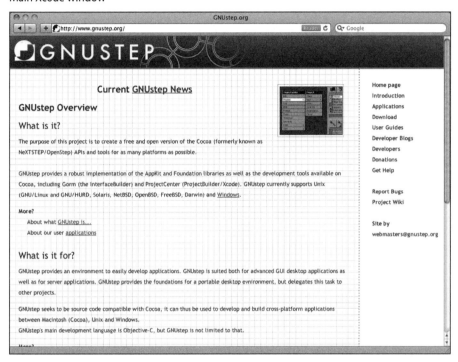

Figure 1.8 shows a typical file showing this drop-down list in use.

NOTE

You can also add arbitrary labels to this drop-down list by using the pragma directive in your code. In the case of this file, you can see that there is already a pragma directive for the interface builder action methods.

Above the text editor and the File Browser is the main toolbar. You can configure this with various buttons, but typically the default ones are perfectly fine. They enable you to launch builds, to stop the current build, and so on.

Finally, in the lower-right corner of the Xcode window, you can see a summary of the last build results. If it was successful, you see Succeeded. If it was unsuccessful, you see an account of the number of warnings and errors occurred during the last compile, as well as a yellow icon for warnings and a red icon for errors. If you recently ran the static code analyzer, you will see a blue icon for any warnings generated by it.

Figure 1.8

File Navigation drop-down list

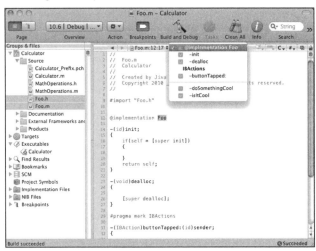

Understanding the Compilation Process

Before we can begin a detailed introduction of the language features of Objective-C, you must have a thorough understanding of how the compilation process works. The process of compilation is the process by which the computer turns your typed code into instructions that the computer can actually execute. At the end of the day, computers are really only able to execute instructions in their native language. That language is typically extremely verbose and difficult for humans to understand and work with. Therefore, for humans to write instructions for the computer, we use higher-level languages, such as Objective-C. We write our programs in text editors, save the file to disk, and then run a compiler over the text file. The compiler then takes the text and turns it into instructions that the computer can execute.

Most of this is Computer Science 101. If you are already familiar with programming, perhaps in another language, then you already know all this information. You can probably safely skip the next few sections. If, however, you are brand-new to programming, then this information will be useful to you. It's instructional to understand this process even though, in practice, the process of compiling your code is very short.

The first step in understanding the compilation process is in writing code.

Writing code

As I said before, as a programmer, you will spend 99 percent of your time crafting text into software. All software development requires that a programmer enter the instructions for the computer into a text editor before it is compiled. This is typically referred to as writing code.

Essentially, this involves nothing more than typing instructions and saving those instructions as text files. Those text files, and the instructions in them, are usually referred to as source code.

Many programming languages include the concept of interfaces and implementations. An interface is typically the methods and properties that your module exposes to other modules. An implementation is the actual instructions that the computer must execute in order to perform the duties that it has promised to other modules in the interface. So to put it another way, the interface is the promise to other parts of the system of what a particular module can do, and the implementation is the instructions to the computer about how to fulfill that promise.

Most programming languages fall under one of two categories when it comes to interfaces and implementation. The first are languages that do not separate their interface from their implementation. They use one file to declare both their interface and implementation in one location. The second are languages that do separate their interface from their implementation. These languages use two different text files to represent interface and implementation separately. Objective-C falls into this latter category.

Objective-C is an object-oriented programming language. This usually means that developers divide a program's different components into objects and classes. A class is a collection of data and the methods that operate on that data. An object is an individual instance of a class. Objective-C classes, then, include an interface and an implementation.

The names of the text files used to store Objective-C source code typically have an extension of .m in the case of implementation files and .h in the case of interface files. So, for example, imagine a case where you wanted to create a class called `MyClass`. In this case, you would create two text files to hold the instructions for the computer for that module. Those text files would be called `"MyClass.h"` for the interface, and `"MyClass.m"` for the implementation. Listings 1.1 and 1.2 show what those two files might look like. For now, don't worry about understanding what's in them. I'm including this so that you can get a feel for what you will eventually be implementing.

Listing 1.1

Interface File

```
@interface MyClass : NSObject
{
    int foo;
}
@property (nonatomic) int foo;
-(void)someMethod;
@end
```

Listing 1.2

Implementation File

```
#include "MyModule.h"

@implementation MyClass
@synthesize foo;

-(void)someMethod
{
    NSLog(@"some method got called");
}
@end
```

Again, there's no need to worry about understanding this code right now, but I will take this opportunity to point out a few interesting features of these listings.

First, notice that the interface file clearly states the fact that it is an interface by including the @ interface directive. The @interface directive delineates the entire interface and continues until you see the @end directive. Within these lines, there are several subsections.

The first subsection is delineated by the curly braces ({}) at the top of the interface. This is the member variable declaration area. Member variables store data related to your module.

The second subsection is where properties and methods are declared. Properties document and allow access to state and data in your objects. Methods are instructions to the computer for operating on that data. The code shown above is typical of an object-oriented module. You will learn more about object-oriented programming, classes, member variables, properties, and methods in Chapter 3.

NOTE

Objective-C retains its C programming language roots. Therefore, creating modules in Objective-C that are pure C is impossible. In these cases, the modules might have had file extensions of .h to indicate the interface and .c to indicate the implementation. Additionally, Xcode can compile C++ if you name your implementation with a .cc file extension and Objective-C++ (an Objective-C/C++ hybrid) if you name your implementation with a .mm file extension. In this book, you're here to learn Objective-C, however, so we won't be doing this.

You can use any text editor that can save plain text files to write Objective-C code. However, Apple provides the excellent Xcode integrated development environment on Mac OS X expressly for the purpose of creating applications for Mac OS X, iPhone, and iPad. It is a superb tool, and one that you use in this book. On the other hand, if you are developing on platforms other than Mac OS X, you need to find a suitable text editor for your platform of choice.

Turning source code into compiled code and compiled code into an executable

After you have created your source code, you need to have the computer turn your source code into the instructions that it can execute. This part of the process is called compiling the source code.

Compiling the source code actually involves several steps.

The first step is called *preprocessing*. You can think of the preprocessing step as the computer preparing your code to be compiled. During this step, the compiler removes any code that will not result in executable code such as comments and so on. It also expands parts of the code and rearranges certain directives so that the second step of the compilation process can be more efficient. The end result of the first step of compilation is an intermediate state of the source code. You typically will not see or deal with this intermediate form of the code though there are compiler switches that will cause the compilation to stop at this stage if you wanted to look at the output for whatever reason. Some developers who utilize advanced techniques will sometimes use these compiler switches so that they can look at the intermediate file and see exactly what the compiler is doing. You will probably never have to do that in your normal application development.

After preprocessing, the second step is where the compiler actually turns your source code into what's called an object file. Object files have an extension of .o. Compiling source code can be a relatively lengthy process, involving many different modules and many different source code files. As a result, if you can avoid rebuilding a particular module in the case where it and none of its dependencies have changed, then this can be a big win in terms of reducing compilation time. Because of this, the object files are typically stored on disk in your build directory. In the case where a source code file did not change since the last time the compiler was run, this enables the compiler to simply skip recompiling that source code and instead reuse the object file that was left from the last run of the compiler. Typically, you will have no need to look at these files in day-to-day use. They are there for the compiler's use only. The final step of compilation involves a process called *linking*. Linking means taking the object files produced in the last step and connecting them together to form an executable. In addition to the objects themselves, libraries and frameworks are also linked into the executable as well. The end result of the linking process is your actual application executable. In the case of a command line application, this will be a single binary file which you can run from the command line. In the case of a desktop application, this will usually be what's called an application bundle that actually is a directory on disk containing an executable and all the resources such as graphics, sounds, and so on that are necessary for running the application. You learn more about application bundles in the next section.

In Xcode, compiling your app is as simple as hitting the Build and Run button. If you do this with your example project, it'll launch the application in the console and display it's output. While doing so, Xcode switches to debug mode and allows you to debug the application as well. Debugging is an advanced IDE topic; see the Xcode documentation for information on how to use it for debugging.

The end result of the compilation process is your executable. If at any point the compiler detects an error in your source code (a very common event indeed), then it will halt the processing of the file in question and display the error to you so that you can correct it. Sadly, the compiler is pretty picky. Computers are not nearly as good as we are at inferring meaning from words. As a result, the compiler, rather than guessing at what you meant to type, simply gives up and displays the error to you. These errors can be as simple as a missing semicolon, a missing space, incorrect capitalization, or any number of tiny things. Be prepared — by embarking on a career as a programmer, you will be dealing with errors like this hundreds if not thousands of times a day. Even the best programmers rarely write code that compiles perfectly the first time.

Exploring application bundles

In the previous section, I mentioned the term application bundle — what may be a completely new term to you even if you are an experienced programmer. You may be wondering what that is. An application bundle is really more related to being an operating system construct than it is to an Objective-C construct. The Objective-C language itself does not require or produce application bundles. That said, however, application bundles are an important and integral concept to programming on almost all the platforms on which Objective-C can be used, and, as a result, they are important concepts for you as an Objective-C programmer to understand.

An application bundle is simply a directory on a disk containing a grouping of files. In Mac OS X, application bundles are used for applications to group together all the files necessary for an application to run. This includes items such as executables, graphics, sound files, and user interface resources. Additionally, when building graphical applications for Mac OS X, the user interface definitions are typically done in an application called Interface Builder. This application also produces bundles called NIB files. NIB files usually have an extension of .nib and are stored inside the application bundle.

NOTE

NIB stands for NeXTstep Interface Builder and is a holdover from the NeXT days. Recently, the format was changed from binary to XML, and the file extension was changed from .nib to .xib. During compilation, XIB files are still compiled to NIB files, so when you look in an application bundle, you'll see .nib and not .xib.

Listing 1.3 shows a typical application bundle directory structure. In this case, it's a partial listing of the Xcode application bundle.

Listing 1.3

Contents of an Application Bundle

```
Xcode.app
`-- Contents
|-- CodeResources -> _CodeSignature/CodeResources
|-- Info.plist
|-- Library
|   |-- QuickLook
|   |   `-- SourceCode.qlgenerator
|   |       `-- Contents
|   |           |-- CodeResources -> _CodeSignature/CodeResources
|   |           |-- Info.plist
|   |           |-- MacOS
|   |           |   `-- SourceCode
|   |           |-- _CodeSignature
|   |           |   `-- CodeResources
|   |           `-- version.plist
|   `-- Spotlight
|       |-- SourceCode.mdimporter
|       |   `-- Contents
|       |       |-- CodeResources -> _CodeSignature/CodeResources
|       |       |-- Info.plist
|       |       |-- MacOS
|       |       |   `-- SourceCode
|       |       |-- _CodeSignature
|       |       |   `-- CodeResources
|       |       `-- version.plist
|       `-- uuid.mdimporter
|           `-- Contents
|               |-- CodeResources -> _CodeSignature/CodeResources
|               |-- Info.plist
|               |-- MacOS
|               |   `-- uuid
|               |-- Resources
|               |   |-- English.lproj
|               |   |   |-- InfoPlist.strings
|               |   |   `-- schema.strings
|               |   |-- Japanese.lproj
|               |   |   |-- InfoPlist.strings
|               |   |   `-- schema.strings
|               |   `-- schema.xml
|               |-- _CodeSignature
|               |   `-- CodeResources
|               `-- version.plist
|-- MacOS
|   `-- Xcode
|-- PkgInfo
|-- PlugIns
```

continued

Listing 1.3 *(continued)*

```
|     |-- BuildSettingsPanes.xcplugin
|     |    `-- Contents
|     |         |-- CodeResources -> _CodeSignature/CodeResources
|     |         |-- Info.plist
|     |         |-- MacOS
|     |         |    `-- BuildSettingsPanes
|     |         |-- Resources
|     |         |    |-- Built-in Build Settings Panes.pbsettingspanespec
|-- Resources
|    |-- AskUserForNewFileDialog
|    |-- CreateDiskImage.workflow
|    |    `-- Contents
|    |         `-- document.wflow
|    |-- DevCDVersion.plist
|    |-- Document-Cert.icns
|-- _CodeSignature
|    `-- CodeResources
`-- version.plist
```

Note that the directory Contents/MacOS contains the Xcode executable. This executable is the same as one that you would produce if you were making a command line application. The difference here is that it is packaged inside of an application bundle and contains code to load the resources from that bundle. Some other interesting directories inside this application include the PlugIns directory, which has bundles inside of it as well. The Spotlight directory also contains bundles in the form of the SourceCode.mdimporter and uuid.mdimporter directories. The Foundation framework, which we will visit in Part II of this book, includes methods that enable you to read application bundles, and it allows access to these sorts of embedded bundles.

The important thing for you to know at this time is that when you create a graphical application for Mac OS X, iPhone, or iPad, Xcode creates an application bundle for your application. In the future, if you have the need to include compartmentalized groupings of resources within your application, you may want to create an application bundle yourself. Xcode also gives you the ability to do exactly that. For now, however, you don't need to worry about that.

Working with build settings

There are two locations in Xcode where build settings for your projects are configured. The first and primary location is the project information window, which you access by choosing Project ➪ Edit Project Settings. In this section, I cover these windows in detail because the information is useful and instructional. Because of where this is falling within the book, you may not understand many of the things that I'm going to talk about. I suggest that you skim through this section to begin with and then return to it later after you've worked through Chapter 2. The first panel of the Project Settings window, shown in Figure 1.9, shows the general settings for the project. Most of these you won't need to change, with the exception of configuring your source code management by using the Configure Roots and SCM button.

Figure 1.9

Project settings

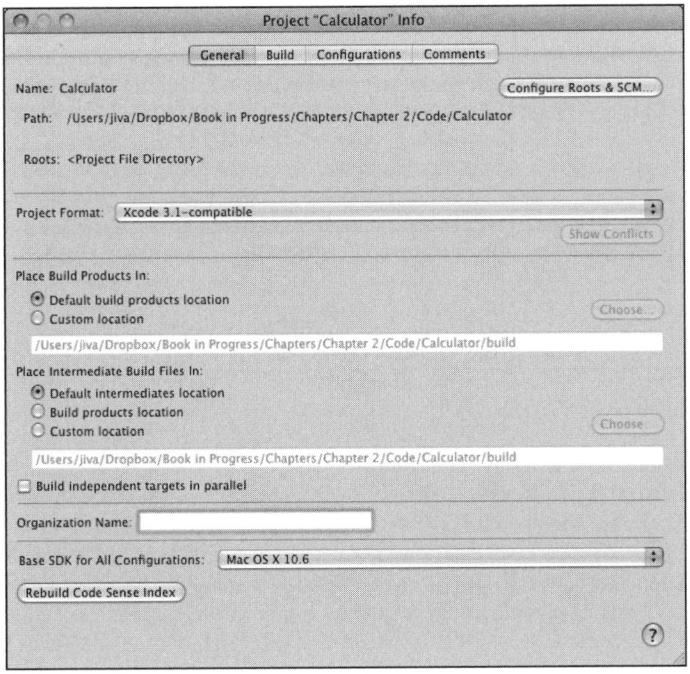

The Place Build Products In settings configure where in your project your executable will be placed after it is compiled. Again, this is another setting that you probably don't need to change, but it's useful to make a note of it at this time to be aware of where your executable will be placed. This directory is where you will find your executable.

The setting beneath this setting, the Place Intermediate Build Files In setting, configures where the object files for your source code will be placed while your application is building.

The next setting, Build Independent Targets in Parallel, affects how the compiler builds targets for different independent platforms, for example PPC and Intel. If it is enabled, the separate targets will be built in parallel. If not, they will be built serially — one after the other.

One of the most frequently asked questions about Xcode, is "How do I change the organization name that's placed automatically in my source code headers after my copyright notice?" The next setting, Organization Name, is for exactly that purpose. By configuring an organization name here, when you add new files to your project, the copyright listing will list the organization name that you put here as the owner of the copyright. Configure this to be the name of your company or your name.

The next setting, Base SDK for All Configurations, configures the SDK that your application will be compiled and linked against by default. The SDK used defines the code completion and frameworks available for your project. For the purposes of this book and the projects that you will work on while going through it, you can configure the base SDK for your current Mac OS version. However, if you are doing development for other platforms, such as iPhone OS, and so on, you should configure this setting appropriately. You also should modify this setting in the cases where you may want to compile your application for an older version of Mac OS.

NOTE

The term SDK refers to Software Development Kit. An SDK is a collection of libraries, tools, documentation, and source files which is used to build applications for a specific platform. Xcode comes with SDKs for Mac OS X and iOS.

The final setting on this panel relates to rebuilding the Code Sense Index. You may encounter some rare cases when the Code Sense Index can become corrupt. In these cases, you may want to choose to rebuild the Code Sense Index by using this button. These cases are rare, but if you ever need it, this is where you'll need to do it.

There are two primary locations where all build settings for your projects are configured. The first is at the project level, and the second is at an individual target level. If you can think of your project level settings as being the base settings for building your application, then the target level settings are the items that you want to change for specific targets. For example, you may have a project for a given application that has both a debug target and a release target. In this case, you would have all your project level settings the same for both targets, but you would vary a few things, such as whether you want to strip your executable and so forth on a target-by-target basis. Xcode supports this by having the project level settings and the target level settings as two separate windows. You can configure the project level settings, which cascade down into your targets unless you make a change on a particular target's settings. When you make a change to the settings for a particular target, this change overrides the settings from the project level. Figure 1.10 shows an example of how this works.

In this example, you are looking at both the project level settings and the target level settings. The example application being shown has configured two different targets that share code but build different executables. As you can see, the items that are different between the project versus the target are shown in bold on the target-level settings. If you choose to delete that setting, then the bold goes away, and the default value, which it gets from the project level settings, take its place.

The drop-down list at the top of the screen allows you to choose what configuration you are editing, for example, whether you are working with a debug build versus a release build, as well as to filter the list for specific settings. The configuration options shown are set by using the Configurations tab at the project level. Figure 1.11 shows a typical project in which a debug and release build are configured.

You can think of the configurations as being different builds of the same target. Besides debug and release, another typical example might be a case where you have different architectures that you want to build for, for example PowerPC versus Intel.

Figure 1.10

Target versus project settings

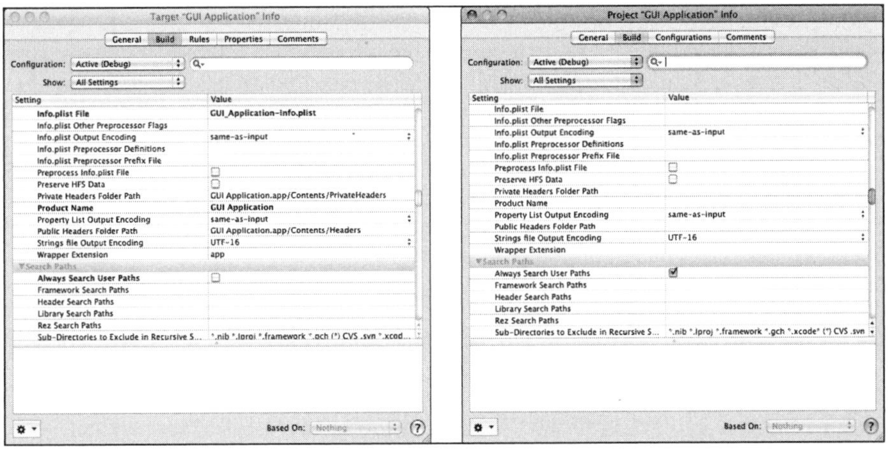

Figure 1.11

Build Configurations

It is possible to use the command line utility xcodebuild to build your projects. This can be handy when automating builds. If you do this, the option at the bottom of this screen, "Command-line builds use," controls which configuration will be used if you do not specify one.

Most of these settings are things that you will typically not be changing for most of this book. That said, you can scroll through the settings, click on each of them, and view the information that it shows at the bottom of the screen describing each of the options if you are curious what they do. The third tab under the target build settings is the Rules tab, which enables you to configure the default compilation behavior for different types of files within your project. So, for example, if you have a particular kind of file that requires special processing as part of the build process, you can add that file here by pressing the plus button. Then configure whatever type of custom behavior you require. Additionally, if you want to change the default behavior for any of the built-in files, you can also do that here by simply changing the drop-down list options.

For the most part, you will not need to make any changes to the settings. When building graphical Cocoa applications, one additional tab under the target build settings is the Properties tab. This tab allows you to configure options such as the executable name and the main bundle identifier for your project. Typically, you want to configure the identifier to match your company name as opposed to using the default. Additionally, if you have files that your application saves that you want to be able to double-click to launch, you can register and configure a document type for those files here. When your application is built, Mac OS X will detect the file type that you specify as associated with your application, and it will list your application as one that can open that particular type of file. This behavior is shown in Figure 1.12.

NOTE
For command line applications, you will not see a Properties tab. The Properties tab is actually configuring the information in your App bundle, which doesn't exist in command line apps.

You can also configure an icon for your application if it's a graphical application. You do this by including the icon file as part of your application bundle and specifying its name in the Icon File setting.

Again, for most of the development that you do in this book, you don't need to change any of these options, but it's good to know where they are for future reference.

NOTE
Xcode 4, which is still under development as this book goes to print, has moved the build settings around a bit, but the settings themselves remain mostly the same. See the Xcode 4 documentation for the latest information on this feature.

Figure 1.12

Application bundle properties

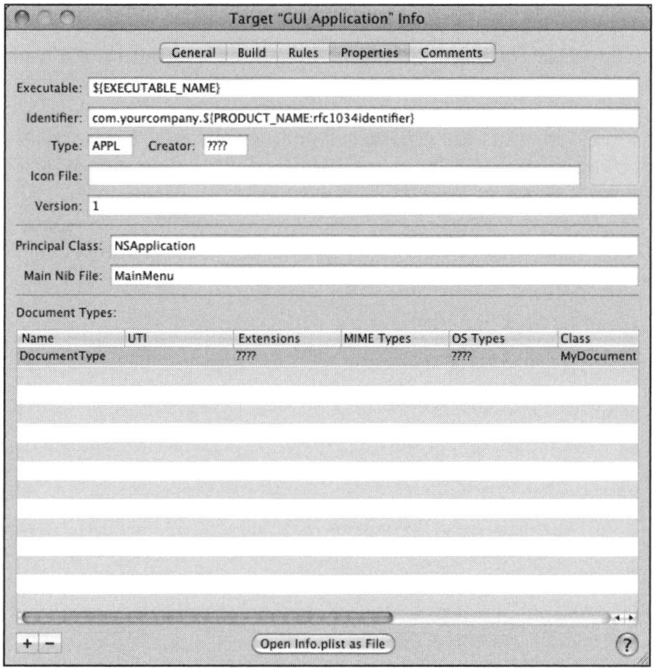

Using the Xcode Static Analyzer

One of the biggest improvements to compiler technology included in the Xcode development environment over the last couple of years has been the inclusion of the Clang Static Analyzer. The Clang Static Analyzer is a tool for analyzing source code to detect common errors. Though compilers are good at detecting some errors, they generally tend to err on the side of speed and forsake the detection of some conditions that are more complicated to find. As a result, some otherwise detectable errors, errors that one might detect through code review, often go undetected and result in bugs in your application. Examples of these kinds of errors are failure to release allocated memory, infinite loops, and use of uninitialized variables, to name a few. Typical compilers are unable to detect most of these errors. The Clang Static Analyzer was created specifically to fill this gap.

To run the Clang Static Analyzer on your source code, you simply choose Build ➪ Build and Analyze. This will cause your source code to first be built using the compiler, and then the static analyzer will be run.

The errors detected by the analyzer are displayed just like regular compilation warnings. However, when you click on an error in your source code, you get additional contextual information in the form of graphical code flow arrows. These arrows show you the predicted code path that the analyzer expects will be used when your code is run. This information can help you to understand in greater detail the exact circumstances that the analyzer is considering when detecting your error.

Take a look at how the analyzer handles some common coding mistakes. Again, much of what I'm discussing here is an advanced topic that you learn more about in later chapters. For now, skim over this section, but return to it later after you see these kinds of errors in your own code.

Listing 1.4 shows a sample program with a common mistake. In this case, memory which is allocated is not being released.

Listing 1.4

A Program with a memory leak

```
#import <Foundation/Foundation.h>

int main (int argc, const char * argv[])
{
    NSAutoreleasePool * pool = [[NSAutoreleasePool alloc] init];
    NSDate *date = [[NSDate alloc] init];
    NSLog(@"The time is: %@", date);
    [pool drain];
    return 0;
}
```

In this case, the `NSDate` object that is allocated is not being released. The static analyzer output from this code is shown in Figure 1.13.

Note that the error is displayed both in the build results panel at the top of the screen, as well as in-line in the code. Not only does the Clang Static Analyzer catch errors that most compilers do not, its output is also much clearer than most compiler errors. If you expand the disclosure triangle on the error message in the build results, it will show you the two separate messages that are associated with this particular error. Clicking on either of these messages shows you the exact location where the memory is allocated and shows you the program flow as the program was analyzed. You can then follow the arrows through your code. Figure 1.14 shows the same code with the errors expanded and the full output of the analyzer displayed.

Figure 1.13

Output from the Static Analyzer

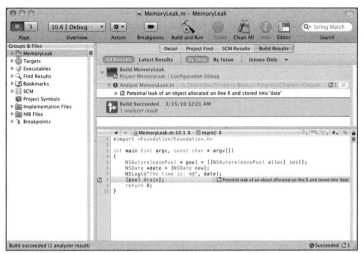

If you correct the code by modifying it to look like Listing 1.5, you will find that the error disappears and you get a clean compile.

Figure 1.14

Detailed Analyzer output

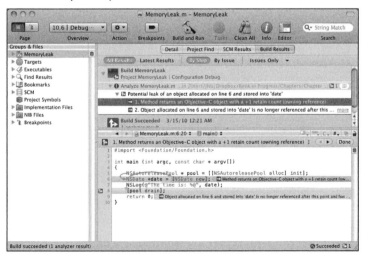

Listing 1.5

Correct Code

```
#import <Foundation/Foundation.h>

int main (int argc, const char * argv[])
{
    NSAutoreleasePool * pool = [[NSAutoreleasePool alloc] init];
    NSDate *date = [[NSDate alloc] init];
    NSLog(@"The time is: %@", date);
    [date release];
    [pool drain];
    return 0;
}
```

NOTE
If you recompile the app, you see that the Clang Static Analyzer no longer flags the errors.

Understanding the Objective-C Runtime

The first and most basic idea to understand about Objective-C is that Objective-C is a compiled language with a dynamic runtime. What this means is that the language is compiled using a compiler, enabling static, compile time type checking, but it is also linked with a runtime, which enables dynamic dispatch of methods. This dynamic runtime gives you the ability to do many things that are only found in scripting languages such as "duck typing" and introspection of objects.

NOTE
Duck typing refers to a type of language type safety where it is assumed that if an object "looks like a duck, and quacks like a duck, it must be a duck." This is as opposed to *static typing,* where an object must be the type that it is declared to be in order for the language to resolve methods on it. There are advantages and disadvantages to both techniques, but in the case of Objective-C, duck typing enables many of the cool features in the language.

There are actually two primary Objective-C runtimes. The "modern runtime," which is used on 64-bit machines and on the iPhone, and the "legacy runtime," which is used on 32-bit Mac OS X and everywhere else. There are several features in the "modern runtime" that are very advantageous for development, but because of its lack of widespread use, the code samples that I show in this book will be written for the legacy runtime. The modern runtime is completely backwards compatible with the legacy runtime, so this will not present any problems for you in writing code. In cases where there are significant advantages to the modern runtime, I will try to make a note in the text for your reference.

The Objective-C runtime is automatically added to your application when you compile it. Using it is completely transparent, unless you need to use some of its advanced features. For now, however, the important thing to understand is simply the capabilities that the runtime gives you in terms of dynamic typing and static typing. This is a unique capability that Objective-C has in comparison to other programming languages.

One of the side effects of this capability is the introduction of the `id` data type. The `id` data type is a special type of object in Objective-C that can actually be any type of object. I discuss more details in Chapter 3.

Summary

In this chapter, I've introduced you to the Xcode integrated development environment, which you use throughout this book for developing your applications. I've shown you how to configure it to your tastes, how to organize your files within it, how to build your applications, and how to read its output to find errors in your code. I also explained the compilation process and the format of application bundles, as well as explained a bit about the Objective-C runtime.

Understanding Basic Syntax

I n this chapter, I show you how to write a basic Objective-C program. This very simple command line application will print a short message to the console. Using this basic program, you will explore some of the essentials of Objective-C, beginning first with how to actually write the code, moving into working with variables and functions, and finally, controlling the flow of your program by using conditional statements and loops. These concepts are fundamental to learning the language, and you should study this chapter thoroughly before moving on to the next one.

Go ahead and type in the code from Listing 2.1 into the Xcode project you created in Chapter 1. This code should be entered into the source file which is named after your project name, located in the Source group.

Listing 2.1

Your first program

```
#import <Foundation/Foundation.h>

int main(int argc, const char *argv[])
{
    NSLog(@"Hello from Objective-C");
    return 0;
}
```

In This Chapter

Writing your first program

Declaring variables

Working with functions

Using flow control statements

Using loops

I'm going to jump around in this code a bit because it makes it easier to explain that way.

Start with line 3, which is the declaration of the main function. All Objective-C applications have a main function. Typically you don't see it because it's usually created by your template when you create your project; when working with graphical applications, it's rare that you have to edit this code at all. I want to teach you also how to write command line applications, so that's why I'm showing you this code here.

NOTE

What is a function? A function, essentially, is a subroutine in your program. It's a branch to another piece of code that executes some task and then returns. You send data to your function by including arguments when you call the function (the things in parentheses). You get data back from your functions in several ways, but the primary way is by receiving a *return value,* which is a value returned from the function back to your calling code.

All Objective-C applications have a `main` function. The `main` function is also where your program begins and ends. Your program begins executing by calling the main function from the operating system. The two arguments shown, `argc` and `argv`, contain the parameters given on the command line to your application. Your application begins executing each of the lines inside of the main function one after another, until it reaches a return statement. In this case, our return statement is simply returning zero. This indicates that our program has exited successfully.

Line 5 contains a call to a function called `NSLog`. This function causes whatever string is passed to it to be printed to the console when the application is run.

The curly braces on lines 4 and 7 indicate the scope of the `main` function. You see these used frequently. The semicolons at the end of lines 5 and 6 indicate the end of those statements, and they are used by the compiler to separate one statement from another. Statements in Objective-C can be split up over multiple lines. As a result, the compiler needs to have some indication when a statement has ended so that it can parse that statement. Knowing when to place a semicolon at the end of a line can be confusing for many beginners. Remember that any statement inside a function block, except for flow control statements, requires a semicolon at the end of the line. Additionally, declarations also require semicolons. Line 1 is an `import` statement. Import statements allow you to load code from other files in your current file. In this case, we are including the interface declarations for the Foundation framework. (You can read more about the foundation framework in Part II of this book.) This line of code is required in order to load the code that will allow us to use the `NSLog` statement in line 5.The unusual `@"Hello from Objective-C"` is known as a string. Strings are literal text in your code; they are stored in a variable in your program and can be accessed later. In this particular case, this string will be sent as an argument to the `NSLog` function which will then display it on the console.

Go ahead and compile and run this application and view the output. You should see something like Figure 2.1.

Figure 2.1

The output of our application

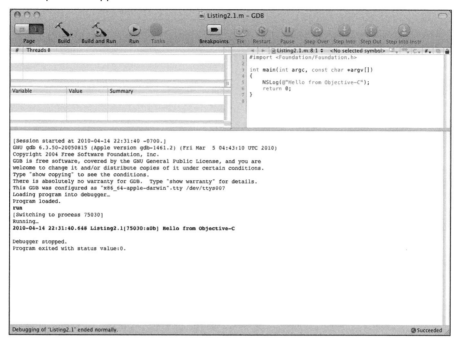

Working with Statements and Expressions

All Objective-C programs are made up of statements and expressions. Statements are lines of code that exist strictly for the purposes of executing an action. Generally speaking, statements do not have return values, and so therefore do not change the state of the current line of execution except in ways that are side effects of calling the statement. In other words, the statement can branch into another line of code, and in that other line of code it can cause things to occur that have side effects (such as printing something to the console or displaying a dialog box), but it does not return a value to the current line of code that the statement is in.

Expressions, on the other hand, do return a value to the calling code, and therefore can be used to change program flow.

For the most part, the distinction between these two is minor enough to not be something to be concerned about. I use these two terms interchangeably.

Declaring variables

So you've seen the basics of how to write a simple Objective-C program. Now you can go further. Change the code you've written to look like Listing 2.2.

Listing 2.2

A program with Variables

```
#import <Foundation/Foundation.h>

int main(int argc, const char *argv[])
{
    int aVariable = 5555;
    NSLog(@"%ld", aVariable);
    return 0;
}
```

This new change illustrates the next concept — variables.

As you can see, I've added a variable and have assigned a value to it; then I output the variable by using the NSLog statement. A variable is a place to store data. Variables have memory associated with them that is allocated to store the thing that you want to store. In this case, I am storing the value 5555 into the variable aVariable, and then passing that variable to the NSLog function. Interestingly, several other variables have been in our program from the beginning. These are the argc and argv variables. Just like the aVariable variable, they store values that can be referenced elsewhere in our program. For example, you could also change the code to look like Listing 2.3.

Listing 2.3

Working with argc as a variable

```
#import <Foundation/Foundation.h>

int main(int argc, const char *argv[])
{
    NSLog(@"The argument count is: %ld", argc);
    return 0;
}
```

In this case, you've changed the program to print out the number of arguments that are passed to it. The `argc` variable stores the number of arguments passed to our application. By passing a variable to the `NSLog` function, we are able to print it out.

Variables can be declared within a given scope, also known as a stack frame, or they can be declared outside of all stack frames, in which case they are a global variable. Stack frames are defined by the curly braces in your code. For example, look at Listing 2.4.

NOTE
Global variables are generally considered a bad programming practice and should be avoided.

Listing 2.4

Different stacks

```
#import <Foundation/Foundation.h>

int main(int argc, const char *argv[])
{
    // this is the first stack frame
    int aVariable1 = 5;
    if(aVariable1 > 4)
    {
        // this is the second stack frame.
        int aVariable2 = 10;
        NSLog(@"aVariable1: %ld", aVariable1); // this is OK
        NSLog(@"aVariable2: %ld", aVariable2); // this is OK
    }

    NSLog(@"aVariable1: %ld", aVariable1); // this is OK
    NSLog(@"aVariable2: %ld", aVariable2); // error, aVariable2 does not exist
    here.
    return 0;
}
```

In the above code, the variable `aVariable1` is declared in the first stack frame. This frame exists all the way to the end of the second curly brace. We say, "`aVariable1` has scope within the first stack frame." The variable `aVariable2` only has scope within the second stack frame which exists from lines 7 through 12. Therefore, when we reach line 15, `aVariable2` no longer exists, and will cause an error. We say, "aVariable2 goes out of scope at the end of the second stack frame which is at line 12." Earlier in this chapter, I mention that variables store data in memory. The memory they use can be allocated on the stack, just as you see in this example. The memory associated with those variables is also freed when the variable goes out of scope. That is, when the variable no longer exists. However, memory for variables can also be allocated on what's called "the heap," which is a pool of memory that your application can allocate data from by itself and which your application has much greater power over. However, as they said in *Spiderman*, "With great power comes great responsibility." You have to also be sure to free any memory you allocate on the heap. Listing 2.5 shows an example of allocating an object on the heap and then freeing it.

Listing 2.5

Allocating memory on the heap.

```
// this allocates the memory
SomeClass *aVariable = [[SomeClass alloc] init];

// do something with aVariable

[aVariable release]; // this frees the memory.
```

The code in this listing is demonstrating a concept that I spend a great deal of time on later, when I look at objects. For now, simply understand that the variable aVariable is having its memory allocated on the heap. This means that if we didn't release that memory at the bottom of this listing, that memory would stick around and it would be what is commonly referred to as a *memory leak*. One of the key ways to tell if a variable has its memory allocated on the heap versus the stack is by looking to see if it is a pointer. The * operator in the declaration of the aVariable variable in the prior example indicates that this is a pointer. A pointer is a variable that points to another memory location.

Note that previously, all the variables we have worked with so far have not had the * operator before their names. This has meant that their memory was allocated on the stack. Although you can use the pointers that are strictly allocated on the stack, most often when you see pointers in Objective-C, it will be for variables that are allocated on the heap. The key is to look for some kind of allocation function like that shown here.

Pointers are a tough subject to get your head around, but I have a section coming up that delves into them in detail.

Earlier in this chapter, I describe global variables. Similarly, another word for a variable that is allocated on the stack is *local variable*. Local variables are ones that exist only within the local scope. The *local scope* is another phrase that means "the current stack frame." Some other types of variables that you encounter include *member variables,* which are variables that are members of a class, and *instance variables,* which are variables that store a particular instance of an object. I cover both of these in Chapter 3 when I discuss objects.

When working with variables in Objective-C, they first must be declared, which means that you have to tell the compiler you're going to use them. When you declare them, you have to give the type. There are three broad categories of types — scalars, pointers, and structures. It is these three categories that we talk about in the next sections.

Using comments

Listings 2.4 and 2.5 introduced another bit of syntax, the double slash (//). In Objective-C, lines that are preceded by // are comments. They are ignored by the compiler, and can contain anything you want. Usually, they're used to give some kind of human-readable documentation in the code, but they can just as often be used to temporarily remove code, or simply for the purposes of making the code pretty. The important thing to know is that whenever you see // in code, everything on that line until the end of that line will be ignored by the compiler.

In addition to the // style comments, there's another syntax for comments delineated by the characters /* and */. In this case, rather than commenting everything to the end of the line, it only comments the text contained within the /* and */ characters.

Which of these commenting techniques you use is entirely up to you. I prefer the // style commenting, so that's what I use throughout this book.

Exploring scalar types

The first and most basic form of variable is scalar variables. A *scalar* is a type of value that can hold only one value at a time. Examples of scalars are integers, floating point numbers, and characters. Scalars have different defined sizes in terms of their memory footprint and the size of values that can be stored in them. You should be aware of these limitations when deciding what type to define your variables to be. Table 2.1 shows the size of the most commonly used scalar types in Objective-C.

Table 2.1 Commonly used scalar types

Type	Description
int	An integer value between +/– 2,147,483,647.
unsigned int	An integer value between 0 and 4,294,967,296.
float	A floating point value between +/– 16,777,216.
double	A floating point value between +/– 2,147,483,647.
long	An integer value varying in size from 32 bit to 64 bit depending on architecture.

continued

Table 2.1 Continued	
Type	*Description*
long long	A 64-bit integer.
char	A single character. Technically it's represented as an int.
BOOL	A boolean value, can be either YES or NO.
NSInteger	When compiling for 32-bit architecture, same as an int, when compiling for 64-bit architecture, +/− 4,294,967,296.
NSUInteger	When compiling for 32-bit architecture, same as an unsigned int, when compiling for 64-bit architecture, value between 0 and 2^64.

Most of these scalar types are also shared with C and C++, but there are a couple here that are unique to Objective-C.

Apple has been very good about supporting 32-and 64-bit architectures with their operating system and libraries. Doing so, however, is no easy task from a programming point of view. For example, some values, such as array indices, may benefit from the increased upper limit of 64-bit integers. As a result, in an ideal world, we want our code to be able to seamlessly transition between 32-bit and 64-bit platforms. Therefore, Apple provides us with the NSInteger and NSUInteger types, which automatically will be either 32- bit or 64-bit depending on the architecture they are compiled under.

Using scalar types is very straightforward. To declare a scalar variable, you simply tell the compiler the type and the name of the variable. You can also give it an initial value. For example, Listing 2.6 shows how some typical scalar variables might be declared.

Listing 2.6

Declaring Scalar Variables

```
int foo = 10;
double bar = 500.0;
float baz;
unsigned long n;
NSInteger x;
char a = 'a';
```

NOTE
Notice the variable a has been initialized with the value 'a'. Using single quotes around a character tells the compiler to take the value of that character as a char. This should not be confused with a string, which I will discuss later, and which is designated with the @"" construct.

Using special variable modifiers

In addition to the variable type and the variable name, there are also a number of keywords that are used to modify the type of variable that you are declaring. The most important of these modifier keywords, and the ones that you will see in this book, are the `static` and `const` keywords.

As I mention earlier, when declaring local variables, the memory for your variable is normally allocated each time the scope of the local variable is entered by your program and deallocated when you leave the local scope. This class of storage is called automatic, or, by the default modifier keyword, `auto`.

The `static` keyword modifies the memory allocation of the variable being declared so that it will be allocated only once during the run of your program. Subsequent accesses of the same variable in your application will in fact access the originally allocated memory. This is important, because it gives you the ability to specify a local variable which will maintain its contents indefinitely. This makes it ideal for storing local variables which take a lot of resources to create, but for which the contents of the variable do not change often. Listing 2.7 shows how you might use the static keyword in association with a function to optimize an expensive operation such as initializing a variable.

Listing 2.7

Using static

```
void someFunction()
{
    // x will be created and initialized only once,
    //no matter how often you call this
    static Expensive *x = [[Expensive alloc] initWithData:...];
    // do things with x here...
    [x doSomeOperation];
}

int main(int argc, char *argv[])
{
    someFunction(); // x is created up in someFunction
    someFunction(); // x already exists and will not be created again.
    return 0;
}
```

Global variables, because they are global in scope, by default, behave similarly to static variables. That is, they are allocated only once, and they maintain their contents throughout the run of the application. When you apply the `static` keyword to a global variable, however, it modifies the scope of the global variable so that it can be accessed only within the file in which it is declared. This is in contrast to the normal behavior of a global variable. Normal global variables are in scope anywhere in your program.

The static keyword is known as a storage modifier. There are several of these types of modifiers available in Objective-C. There is the register modifier, which can be used to provide a hint to the compiler that the data being stored will be accessed often and so could benefit from being stored in a register on the CPU. This keyword is rarely used. Another, more commonly used, keyword is the extern keyword. This modifier indicates that a variable or function declaration is referencing an actual variable or function that is defined or allocated in another compilation unit in your application. You'll see the extern keyword in use later in this chapter when I talk about functions.

The const keyword similarly modifies the memory behavior of the variable being declared, but in the case of const, the variable is made to be read-only. This means that once the variable is initialized, its contents cannot be changed. This is useful in cases where you are declaring variables that should never be modified, such as constants. By declaring such variables to be const, the compiler will enforce that behavior. If you accidentally later attempt to modify one of these variables, this would be a bug, and the compiler would generate an error. Listing 2.8 shows how the const keyword can be used to avoid overwriting a constant.

Listing 2.8

Using the const keyword

```
int main(int argc, char *argv)
{
    const NSString *foo = @"MY_CONSTANT";

    // do things here....

    foo = @"SOME_OTHER_VALUE"; // this will generate a compiler error.

    if([foo isEqualToString:@"MY_CONSTANT"])
    {
        // take action here...
    }
}
```

Understanding structures

Structures, or *structs* for short, are types that you yourself define, which can contain multiple subvariables within them. For example, if you wanted to declare a variable which grouped x and y coordinates together to represent a point, you might declare that variable using a struct. You do this using the struct keyword.

Declaring a `struct` is a two-stage affair. First you have to tell the compiler about the `struct` itself, and then you can use the `struct` to declare variables that are of the type of the `struct` you have defined. Continuing our example of declaring a variable for a point, Listing 2.9 shows how this structure might be initially defined. Again, this is the first step of the process — defining the structure.

Listing 2.9

Declaring a struct

```
struct Point
{
    float x;
    float y;
};
```

In this case, I've defined a `Point` structure that contains two member variables, `x` and `y`, which are both of type `float`. Now, after you have the point structure defined, you can then declare your variable, which will eventually actually hold the individual point you're referring using. Listing 2.10 shows how to do that.

Listing 2.10

Declaring a struct instance.

```
struct Point p;
```

Structures can even be made up of composites of other structures. For example, Listing 2.11 shows a structure that defines a line by combining two points.

Listing 2.11

A composite struct.

```
struct Line
{
    struct Point start;
    struct Point end;
};
```

Tie these together to show some code that actually uses a `struct` to store and displays some points. This is shown in Listing 2.12.

Listing 2.12

Working with point structures

```
#import <Foundation/Foundation.h>

// declaring the point structure.
struct Point
{
    float x;
    float y;
};

int main(int argc, const char *argv[])
{
    // declaring the point variable...
    struct Point p;
    // assigning values to the struct's members...
    p.x = 20.0;
    p.y = 50.0;

    // ... then to use the point...
    moveCursorToPoint(p);

    return 0;
}
```

Objective-C and Cocoa use structures for storing things such as points, rectangles, and so on. The nice thing about using structures is that they are a very lightweight way to store groups of related variables. In Chapter 3, you see how to use objects to also group related variables and the methods that act on those variables. However, objects can have a fair amount of overhead associated with them. Structures, on the other hand, have no more overhead than the variables that make up their members. Therefore, they can sometimes be used in performance-sensitive areas where objects would be too heavy.

Using typedefs

Naturally, typing `struct Point` every time you want to declare a point can quickly become tedious. Fortunately, Objective-C provides another construct that can help with this. This construct is called `typedef`.

The word `typedef` comes from the words *type definition,* and essentially allows you to define your own types. Using it in conjunction with structures enables you to define a custom type that represents your structure. You can then use this custom type anywhere you'd normally have used your structure definition. Listing 2.13 shows the `typedef` version of the `Point` structure example.

Listing 2.13

Working with point structures and typedefs

```
#import <Foundation/Foundation.h>

// declaring the point structure.
typedef struct
{
    float x;
    float y;
} Point;

int main(int argc, const char *argv[])
{
    // declaring the point variable...
    Point p;
    // assigning values to the struct's members...
    p.x = 20.0;
    p.y = 50.0;

    // ... then to use the point...
    moveCursorToPoint(p);

    return 0;
}
```

As you can see, by simply adding the `typedef` keyword before the `struct` keyword, and by moving the `struct` name to the end of the structure, it does something amazing; it allows you to declare your p variable by simply doing `Point p`. Essentially, `Point` becomes a first-class type, and you can use it anywhere you would be using any other type.

The syntax to use the `typedef` keyword consists of `typedef variable-definition new-type-name`. Where `variable-definition` is the actual type you want inserted when you use the new type, and `new-type-name` is the new type name that you will use in your program.

Due to the way typedefs allow you to use type names that more clearly describe the type of data that will be stored in a variable, typedefs are a nice addition that makes your code more self-documenting than code that doesn't use them. I touch on using typedefs again in Chapter 5 when I discuss using blocks.

Using enum

Another way to define a custom datatype is to use the enum keyword. Enum is short for enumerated type, and it allows you to create a datatype, which has a restricted list of possible values that can be stored in it. Enums are often used in Cocoa and Cocoa Touch for parameters and return values where the list of possible values falls within a specific limited set.

To define an enum, you use the enum keyword, followed by a tag for the enum you are declaring, then followed by {}, which contain a list of the possible values for the enum separated by commas. Listing 2.14 shows an enum definition.

Listing 2.14

Creating an enum

```
enum MyEnum
{
    Value1,
    Value2,
    Value2
};
```

To use an enum in your code, you must declare a variable to be of type enum, followed by the tag that you specified when defining your enum. Then, to assign a value to it, you simply use one of the allowed values from your enum definition. Listing 2.15 shows how this is done.

Listing 2.15

Using an enum

```
enum MyEnum foo;
foo = Value1;

// or for a function
enum MyEnum myFunction();

// as a parameter to a function
void myFunction(enum MyEnum foo);
```

The actual values of the enums themselves are determined by the compiler, but they default to integers, starting at 0 for the first value, 1 for the second, and so on. You can force an enum to assign a specific value to one of the values by simply providing that value as part of the enum definition, as shown in Listing 2.16.

Listing 2.16

Assigning values to the enum options

```
enum MyEnum
{
    Value1 = 20,
    Value2 = 13,
    Value3 = 155
};
```

This can be useful when dealing with legacy code that expects a specific value.

Typing out enum whenever you use an enum can be inconvenient. So enums can be typedef'd just like structures can. Listing 2.17 shows how this works.

Listing 2.17

Using typedef with an enum

```
enum MyEnumType
{
    Value1,
    Value2,
    Value3
};
typedef enum MyEnumType MyEnum;

// Now this allows you to type...
MyEnum foo;
foo = Value1;
```

Cocoa and Cocoa Touch use enums quite a bit. The nice thing about enums is that they allow you to have a compile-time check to verify that the parameter passed to your function is one of a limited set of values. If you accidentally pass the wrong value, the compiler will generate an error.

Understanding pointers

The third type of variable I'm going to discuss are pointers. Pointers can be a difficult concept to wrap your head around, but fortunately, in Objective-C, the more complex aspects of pointers are rarely used. However, understanding them is important.

Recall that a typical variable stores data in RAM. The computer looks up the variable by using an address in RAM. Metaphorically speaking, if you can imagine a variable as being a house where people (data) live, the street address of the house is the address of that variable.

A pointer is a variable that contains the address of another variable. Declaring a pointer is similar to declaring a variable of whatever type it is that you want to point to except that you also include the pointer operator as part of your declaration. The pointer operator is an asterisk (*). You can get the address of a variable by using the address-of operator (&).

Listing 2.18 shows an example of declaring a pointer to an integer.

Listing 2.18

Declaring pointers

```
#import <Foundation/Foundation.h>

int main(int argc, char *argv[])
{
    int x = 5;
    int *y = &x;

    NSLog(@"X:%ld - Y:%ld", x, y);
    return 0;
}
```

In this code, you are declaring a variable, x, which is an `int`. Within this variable, you are storing the value of 5. We are then declaring another variable, y, which is of type pointer to an `int`, and within it, we are storing the address of x.

Pointers can be used just like regular variables, but when you access them directly, such as what we are doing on line 8 of this program, the value you get is a memory address. In this case, when you run this program, you should see output, as shown in Figure 2.2.

Your value for y will probably vary from mine because your computer may be storing your x value at a different address from mine. This is normal. The asterisk operator (*) is also the pointer-dereferencing operator. The process of dereferencing a pointer allows you to access the value of the variable that the pointer points to. So in other words, in your program example, you want to print the value that the white pointer was pointing to, in other words the value of x, then you could rewrite your program to look like Listing 2.19.

Figure 2.2

Output of the pointer program

Listing 2.19

Dereferencing pointers

```
#import <Foundation/Foundation.h>

int main(int argc, char *argv[])
{
    int x = 5;
    int *y = &x;

    NSLog(@"X:%ld - Y:%ld", x, *y);
    return 0;
}
```

Notice that we are now dereferencing y, which means that when you run this application, you should see something like Figure 2.3.

Figure 2.3

Output of the dereferencing example code

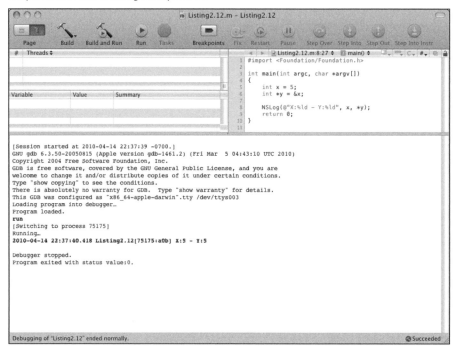

The interesting thing about pointers is that they can be manipulated just like regular variables. This means that you can increment them, you can decrement them, you can add to them, and you can subtract from them. You can do all these things, but what you're really doing is changing the location in RAM where the pointer is pointing. Consequently, you can then dereference the pointer at the new location and access a different value than where it was originally pointing.

Most of this discussion of pointers is relatively advanced subject matter. In day-to-day Objective-C, you typically don't have the need to dereference many pointers. (There are a couple exceptions to this rule, and I will point them out as we go through this book.) For a deeper understanding of low-level pointers, I suggest picking up a good book on the C programming language.

Typical Objective-C use of pointers is primarily limited to the declaration of objects. Objects in Objective-C are in fact pointers. Fortunately, for the most part, even though they are pointers, you rarely have to think of them in that way. The most important thing that you do need to remember is that anytime you are declaring an object, it needs to be declared as a pointer. For example, look at Listing 2.20.

Listing 2.20

Pointers with objects

```
#import <Foundation/Foundation.h>

int main (int argc, const char * argv[])
{
    NSAutoreleasePool *pool = [[NSAutoreleasePool alloc] init];

    NSString *foo = [NSString stringWithString:@"Foobar"];

    NSLog(@"foo: %@", foo);

    [pool drain];
    return 0;
}
```

Again, if you compile and run this program, you should see something like the listing shown in Figure 2.4.

Figure 2.4

Output of the object pointer example

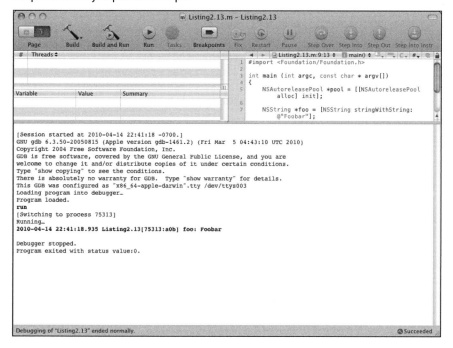

NOTE
Ignore the code that references **NSAutoreleasePool** here. You learn about that in a future chapter.

Another unusual pointer situation that you will run into in this book centers around the use of pointers to objects, such as in the case of using an NSError object to get an error message back from a failed call. When I discuss this in Chapter 10, I cover this in more detail.

Using operators

Like mathematics, programming languages typically support operators. An operator is a function that "operates" on variables and values. For example, the expression "5 + 4" contains the values 5 and 4 and the operator +. In this case, the + operator is said to be a binary operator. Therefore, it operates on two values, one on the left and one on the right, the 5 and the 4. Another type of operator is the unary operator. A unary operator only has one value that it operates upon. For example, the address-of operator, &, is a unary operator. It gets the address of the value that it operates on.

Table 2.2 shows most of the typical operators in Objective-C.

Table 2.2 Typical operators

Operator	Purpose
() [] -> .	Parentheses, array operations, dereference
! ~ - + * & ++ --	Not, add/subtraction (unary), dereference (unary), address-of (unary), increment (unary), decrement (unary)
* / %	Multiplication, Division, Modulus (binary)
<< >>	Bitwise Shift (binary)
< <= > >=	Comparison Operators (binary)
== !=	Comparison Operators (binary)
&	Bitwise AND (binary)
^	Bitwise XOR (binary)
|	Bitwise OR (binary)
&&	AND (binary)
||	OR (binary)
= += -= *= /= %= &= |= ^= <<= >>=	Assignment Operators (binary)

Typically, operators return some kind of result, and that result is either assigned to a variable or used in a control statement to affect program flow. For example, enter the example program in Listing 2.21 and check out the output.

Listing 2.21

Working with operators

```
#import <Foundation/Foundation.h>

int main(int argc, char *argv[])
{
    int a = 10;
    int b = 3;
    int c = a + b;
    int d = a - b;
    int e = a * b;
    int f = a / b;
    int g = a % b;

    NSLog(@"a: %ld", a);
    NSLog(@"b: %ld", b);
    NSLog(@"c: %ld", c);
    NSLog(@"d: %ld", d);
    NSLog(@"e: %ld", e);
    NSLog(@"f: %ld", f);
    NSLog(@"g: %ld", g);

    return 0;
}
```

In this code, we assign the values 3 and 7 to a and b, respectively; then we add them together by using the + operator, subtract them by using the - operator, multiply them, divide them, and so on. Run the program to see the output shown in Figure 2.5.

Notice that the program prints out the results of each of the mathematical operations. Now I threw a bit of a monkey wrench into this program. If you notice, the value for f is wrong. This is because the result of dividing 10 by 3 isn't a round number, it's a fraction. Or, on a computer, it's a floating point number. Normally, you might want to store this into a float or a double, both of which can represent floating point values; in this case, we're storing it into an int value, which means that the decimal portion of the value will be truncated, resulting in just the whole number portion of the result. Even if you store the value in a float, it's possible to still get a truncated value from the division operator if both the operands are integers. The takeaway here is that you have to remember that if you are working with integers, you should convert them to floats before doing any mathematical operations that might result in floats. That said, the next value, g, demonstrates the modulus operator, which returns the remainder value from a division operation. So, in cases where you want to work with fractions, and represent them as a real number and a remainder, you can use this technique to do so. f and g can be taken together to mean 3 with a remainder of 1.

Figure 2.5

Output of the operator program

Operators have an order of precedence, just like in mathematics. This order is also shown in Table 2.2. Sometimes it can be difficult to remember the exact order of the precedence. Rather than risk confusion, you should try to remember that parentheses have the highest precedence of all; they are free syntactical sugar you can sprinkle into your expressions to make certain they are clear. Use them at your discretion.

The ternary operator

In addition to the unary and binary operators that I've already shown you, there's also a ternary operator. This operator is `? :` and can be used in place of an if/else statement. I won't cover this operator here, because it really belongs more in the "Controlling program flow" section of this chapter. Therefore, look for more information in that section.

Working with Functions

So far, I've shown you how you can feed instructions to the computer so the computer will execute those instructions sequentially as it goes through your program. However, as your programs grow in size and complexity, you'll quickly find that putting all your instructions sequentially one after another in your program will become extremely laborious. You want to reuse portions of your code, and cutting and pasting is a very poor method of reusing code.

Fortunately, you can use several mechanisms to solve both of these problems. The first of these mechanisms, and the one I'm going to explain in this section, is the concept of using functions. Before object-oriented programming, procedural programming was the preferred method for breaking your program up into smaller chunks that could more easily be reused.

Objective-C, of course, is a fully object-oriented programming language, and you will for the most part use object-oriented programming in your application development. However, procedural programming is a fundamental building block that is vital for you to understand because there are still parts of Objective-C that are procedural in nature.

Understanding functions

The first question that you may be asking is, "What is a function?" And the answer is that a function, essentially, is a method for declaring a subroutine in your application. A function enables you to encapsulate a portion of your program's instructions into something that can be named and then used as many times as needed, anywhere in your application.

Look at an example; Listing 2.22 shows a program that calculates 5 factorial (it should yield a value of 120). It's using a `for` loop to do the calculation, a concept I discuss in the next section, but you can ignore that for now and just try to understand that it's doing a calculation, that's all.

Listing 2.22

Calculating a factorial

```
#import <Foundation/Foundation.h>

int main (int argc, const char * argv[])
```

continued

Listing 2.22 *(continued)*

```
{
    int a = 5;
    int result = 1;

    for(int i = 1; i <= a; ++i)
    {
        result = result * i;
    }

    NSLog(@"%ld", result);

    return 0;
}
```

Now, the interesting thing about this program is that we're doing a fair amount of work here to do this calculation. What if we wanted to change the number we're calculating the factorial for? Perhaps it would be better if we could isolate that bit of code in a function so that we could reuse it over and over again. Perhaps we could make a function that simply takes an int as a parameter, and then returns the factorial of that int.

Listings 2.23 shows a program where I've done exactly that.

Listing 2.23

Extracting the calculation to a function

```
#import <Foundation/Foundation.h>

long int calculateFactorial(int value)
{
    long int result = 1;

    for(int i = 1; i <= value; ++i)
    {
        result = result * i;
    }

    return result;
}

int main (int argc, const char * argv[])
{
    int a = 5;
```

```
    long int result = calculateFactorial(a);

    NSLog(@"%ld", result);

    return 0;
}
```

Where I previously had the code to calculate the factorial in our main function, we're now calling this our `calculateFactorial` function. The variable that contains the value we want to calculate is declared in the local scope of our main function, therefore our `calculateFactorial` function doesn't know about it. In order to get the value from our main function to our `calculateFactorial` function, you have to pass the value through the function call to the `calculateFactorial` function.

If you compile and run this program, it should give you close to the same output that you got before. Now you can reuse that code to calculate a factorial for a bunch of different values. This is shown in Listing 2.24.

Listing 2.24

Demonstrating use of the function

```
#import <Foundation/Foundation.h>

long int calculateFactorial(int value)
{
    long int result = 1;

    for(int i = 1; i <= value; ++i)
    {
        result = result * i;
    }

    return result;
}

int main (int argc, const char * argv[])
{
    NSLog(@"5!: %ld", calculateFactorial(5));
    NSLog(@"10!: %ld", calculateFactorial(10));
    NSLog(@"15!: %ld", calculateFactorial(15));
    NSLog(@"20!: %ld", calculateFactorial(20));

    return 0;
}
```

As you can see from some of those larger numbers, calculating these by hand would be pretty time-consuming. Your computer can do it very quickly.

NOTE

I used a `long int` to hold the value of the result because the numbers can get large very quickly.

Defining functions

In order to create a function, you have to define it. The process of defining a function consists of telling the compiler what types of arguments the function takes and what type of value the function will return, and then placing the code for the function within curly braces.

Listing 2.25 shows our example function again. Notice that I have highlighted the sections of the function definition that correspond to the return value and the argument for the function.

Listing 2.25

The function in detail

```
long int calculateFactorial(int value) // function declaration
{
    long int result = 1;

    for(int i = 1; i <= value; ++i)
    {
        result = result * i;
    }

    return result; // return value here
}
```

The first line of the function definition is called the function signature. It must be unique within your application so that the compiler can find your function.

When you define a function, you put the parameters that are passed to the function in parentheses after the function name. Each of the parameters is specified with a type and a variable name. In cases where you have more than one parameter, the different parameters are separated by commas. These parameters become available within the scope of your function just as if they were declared locally within the function itself.

The return value type is specified to the left of the function name. The return value does not have a variable name associated with it as part of the declaration. You define what value is returned from your function by using the return keyword inside your function body. This should be the last statement of your function.

In Objective-C, parameters and return values are passed using what's called "pass by value." What this means is that when you pass a parameter to a function, the runtime will actually make a copy of the value that you are passing. This means that changes made to those values inside of your function will not affect the value in the calling function. If, however, you pass a pointer to your value instead, then changes made to the dereferenced variable will be sent back to the original variable in the calling function.

Listing 2.26 demonstrates this concept.

Listing 2.26

Working with pointers

```
#import <Foundation/Foundation.h>

void myFunction(int a, int *b)
{
    a = 20;
    *b = 20; // de-reference the pointer to access the original
}

int main(int argc, const char *argv[])
{
    int a = 10;
    int b = 10;

    myFunction(a, &b); // using the & operator changes b into a pointer

    NSLog(@"a: %ld", a);
    NSLog(@"b: %ld", b);

    return 0;
}
```

Similarly, when returning values from functions, you have to be careful to not return pointers or references to variables that will be out of scope when the function exits. For example, if you return the address of a value inside of your function, when the calling function tries to access that value, that variable will have been deallocated and therefore will no longer be available — this causes a crash.

When I talk about objects in Chapter 3 and memory management in Chapter 4, I will show you how you can return pointers created in your functions to other functions. For now, however, stick with simple values.

Understanding implementation versus interface

Collections of functions can be grouped together into separate source files so that you don't have to clutter your main source with all your programming logic. These source files are typically called units.

When you separate your source code into units, a unit consists of two files: One of them contains declarations of your functions, the other one contains definitions for those declarations. Understanding the difference between declarations and definitions is an important concept that you need to understand.

You've already seen function definitions. The functions that you've worked with so far have all been fully defined. A *function definition* is where you actually write the code that makes up the function itself. A *function declaration* declares the function signature for your function including the return type, the function name, and its parameters. It does not include the actual definition of what the function does.

Function declarations can be said to be declaring the interface to your function. This is a loose definition, but later, when we discuss object-oriented programs, you will see that this concept of interfaces is heavily used.

Extending this idea, the function definition can therefore be said to be the implementation of the interface that you declared.

To declare a function that can be used in other units, you use the `extern` keyword and then the function signature just like your function definition. Because a function declaration is a statement, just like declaring a variable, you also need to include an additional semicolon at the end of your function signature. Knowing when to place the semicolon and when not to is a common mistake new programmers make. Be sure to remember that the semicolon comes after the declaration but not after the definition.

So, imagine that we wanted to encapsulate our factorial calculation method in its own unit.

To do so would take three steps. The first step would be to create the interface file for our unit. Typically, interface files in Objective-C use a .h extension, which stands for "Header." Create a new Header file in your Xcode project called "`Factorial.h`" and add to it the code in Listing 2.27.

Listing 2.27

Function declaration

```
extern long int calculateFactorial(int value);
```

This is the function declaration for the `calculateFactorial` function. The next step is to create an implementation file. The implementation file has as .c extension. Create a new C source file in your Xcode project called "`Factorial.c`" and modify it to look like Listing 2.28.

Listing 2.28

Function definition

```
long int calculateFactorial(int value)
{
    long int result = 1;

    for(int i = 1; i <= value; ++i)
    {
        result = result * i;
    }

    return result;
}
```

Finally, you have to modify the file that calls your function to include the interface file for your unit. Modify your own source file to look like Listing 2.29.

Listing 2.29

Calling the function

```
#import <Foundation/Foundation.h>
#import "Factorial.h"


int main (int argc, const char * argv[])
{
    NSLog(@"5!:  %ld", calculateFactorial(5));
    NSLog(@"10!: %ld", calculateFactorial(10));
    NSLog(@"15!: %ld", calculateFactorial(15));
    NSLog(@"20!: %ld", calculateFactorial(20));

    return 0;
}
```

The definition of the function is now removed from this file and replaced with an import command.

Import statements are used to include other units' interfaces in your current unit. The import statement works by searching through the directories of your project and through the frameworks associated with your project for the interface file that you want to include. When you use angle brackets <> to enclose the filename, as in the case with the Foundation framework, it searches the system paths for the interface file. When you use quotes, the statement only searches the current directory of your project and any of its subdirectories.

The rules concerning the search directories for interface files can be difficult to remember, so I suggest you simply remember these two rules of thumb: If an interface file is part of your project, and something that you created, then you want to use quotes when specifying it in an import statement; otherwise, if the interface file is part of a third-party framework or part of the frameworks provided by Apple, then you want to use angle brackets.

Linking with implementation files

After you split your code into units and use those units in your code, you still have one more thing that you need to do. You need to ensure that the implementation file is linked to your executable. An executable is made up of multiple implementation files linked together with the Objective-C runtime. As you add more implementation files to your project, you have to make sure that they are also linked with your executable. Typically, when you create a new file, Xcode asks you if you want to include it in your project. In Figure 2.6, notice the check box indicating that this file will be added to the Listing 2.6 target.

If, however, you forget to do so, or if you add another target and need to include an existing implementation file in that target as well, then it's important for you to also know how to manually link an existing implementation file with your current target.

To do so, simply select the implementation file that you want to include in your current target, click on the Detail tab above the editor, and ensure that the check box under the bull's-eye column is selected, as shown in Figure 2.7.

Again, notice the bull's-eye check box, which is unchecked for our "NewFile.m" file. To include this file in your current target, select this check box.

Now that you know some of the basics of syntax and program organization, take a look at how you can control flow in an Objective-C program.

Figure 2.6

Adding a file to your target

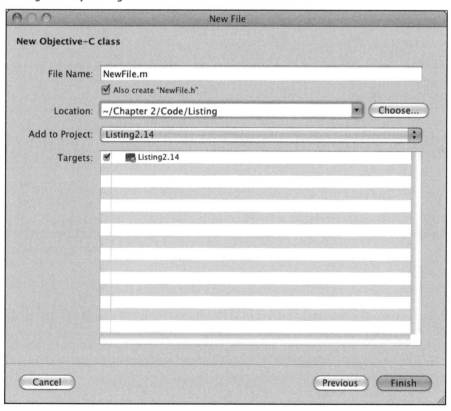

Figure 2.7

The target check box

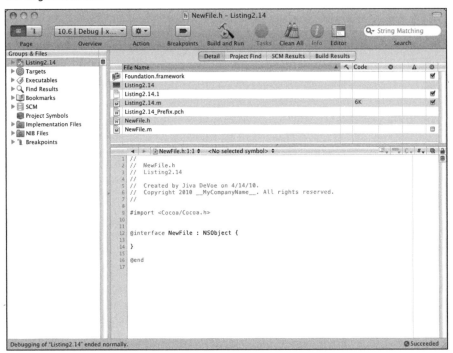

Controlling Program Flow

Applications would be pretty dull if they could only do one thing. If you couldn't have them branch and make decisions based on conditions at runtime, they wouldn't be very useful. Fortunately, we don't have to worry about that, because Objective-C provides us with a rich toolkit of flow control mechanisms.

These flow control mechanisms fall under two broad categories.

The mechanisms in the first category, conditional statements, enable you to change the execution path of your application based on runtime conditions. You can have a fork in the road, essentially, in the middle of your application. Which path your application takes can be determined based on the variables. Those variables can be set based on the parameters, user input, or any other condition that you want.

The second category of flow control mechanisms is that of loops. Loops enable you to perform some set of operations repeatedly until some condition is met. This enables you to do things like iterating over items in a list, doing something for some set number of times, and so on.

We will spend the remainder of this chapter discussing both of these categories and seeing how you can use these in your applications to drive the flow of execution.

Using conditional statements

To reiterate, conditional statements enable you to branch execution in your code between two or more different paths. Conditional statements consist of three constructs.

Using if-else

The first construct is the if-else construct. It is shown in Listing 2.30.

Listing 2.30

If statement

```
if (n > 75)
{
    NSLog(@"%ld is greater than 75!", n);
}
```

The syntax for this construct consists primarily of an `if` statement which is followed by the conditions for the `if` statement in parentheses, then a code block to execute if the conditional statement is found to be true. If the conditional statement is found to be false, an optional `else` block can also be provided. This is provided after the code block for the `if` statement, as shown in Listing 2.31.

Listing 2.31

If with an else

```
if (n > 75)
{
    NSLog(@"%ld is greater than 75!", n);
}
else
{
    NSLog(@"%ld is less than 75.", n);
}
```

The else statement can also be followed by an if statement on the same line as the else statement. In this case, the else block will be executed if the initial if statement is false, but it will be skipped if the if that is currently being evaluated is found to be true. In this case, you can have multiple else-if conditionals one after another. Typically, this would be followed by a final else statement which is executed in the case where none of the if conditions have been met. This is shown in Listing 2.32.

Listing 2.32

If, else-if, and an else.

```
if (n > 75)
{
    NSLog(@"%ld is greater than 75!", n);
}
else if(n < 25)
{
    NSLog(@"%ld is less than 25!", n);
}
else
{
    NSLog(@"%ld is between 24 and 76.", n);
}
```

If the code block to be executed after an if-else statement is restricted to only a single statement, the curly braces may be omitted.

The conditional statement after the if or the else if can be any statement that returns a Boolean value of YES or NO. Additionally, for functions or statements that return something other than a strict Boolean value, a return value of zero is considered to be a negative, or NO, value, and a return value of anything else is considered to be positive, or YES.

CAUTION

The fact that any statement can be placed into a conditional statement for an if statement can lead to a very common error in code where the programmer's intention was to check for equality using the == operator but instead they accidentally do an assignment using the = operator. In this case, the assignment will always return true. Be very careful about this case in your code.

Using the ternary conditional

I prefer to use the if-else construct for most of my conditional branching in applications. I find it to be clearer, syntactically, then the ternary operator. That said, however, the ternary operator has its place in certain cases, for example, in the case where you want to assign a particular value based on another particular value to a variable. This example is shown in Listing 2.33.

Listing 2.33

The ternary operator

```
int result = (x > y ? 10 : 20);
```

The ternary operator essentially works like a tiny if-else statement that's all on one line. You can break the ternary operator up based on its three components which are separated by the ? and the : on the line. The item to the left of the ? is the conditional statement. If the conditional statement evaluates to be true, then the result of the ternary operator is the value between the ? and the :. If the conditional statement evaluates to be false, then the result of the ternary operator is the value on the right-hand side of the colon.

So in the case of Listing 2.26, if x > y, the result will be 10. Otherwise it's 20. As you can see, using the ternary operator can be a convenient, terse mechanism for choosing one value versus another value for assignment and so on. Because of its terseness, however, I find the ternary operator to be difficult to read, and I prefer the greater clarity of the if-else statement. However, if you have a state where the ternary operator produces cleaner, clearer code, then by all means use it. It's another tool in your toolbox.

Using switch statements

The final type of conditional statement that I'm going to discuss here is the switch statement. The switch statement is ideal for branching among several different options. You can achieve essentially the same thing as a switch statement if using an if-else construct, but the switch statement can often be clearer and in some cases faster.

An example of a switch statement is shown in Listing 2.34.

Listing 2.34

A switch statement

```
switch(state)
{
    case 1:
        doStateOneAction();
        break;
    case 2:
        doStateTwoAction();
        break;
    case 3:
        doStateThreeAction();
    default:
        doDefaultAction();
}
```

As you can see, a `switch` statement is constructed by using the keyword `switch` followed by the value upon which you want to branch in parentheses. This value is commonly known as the *control variable.*. After the `switch` statement, a code block must be provided that contains the possible values that the control variable may contain and the instructions to execute for each of those possible values. These "cases" are written by including a case statement followed by a colon and then the instructions to execute in the case of that condition followed by a `break` statement.

The `break` statement, which is optional, will stop evaluation of the switch at the point of the break and jump the program execution outside of the switch. If one is not provided, the subsequent case statements will continue to be evaluated until a `break` is encountered or until the exit of the `switch` statement.

In addition to case statements being provided inside of the `switch` statement, you can also provide a `default` case. This is provided at the bottom of your `switch` statement, and is the case that occurs if no other cases have been met.

NOTE

In Listing 2.34, case 3 is missing a `break` statement, so if case 3 is entered, both case 3 and the default case will be executed.

It's important to note that the control variable of a `switch` statement can only be an integer value. This is not a case where you can, for example, use a string or something of that nature to determine the different cases. Additionally, new variables cannot be declared inside of a `switch` statement.

Choosing among conditional statements

Because of the additional constraints of `switch` statements, `switch` statements can be optimized by compilers to be more efficient and faster than if-else statements. However, for the vast majority of cases, if-else statements are probably going to be fast enough for most operations that you will need to perform. It is only in cases of extreme performance tuning that the difference between a switch statement and if-else statement become an issue. As is usually the case, you should measure your performance before prematurely optimizing for one type of conditional statement over another. Most of the time, you want to choose the conditional statement that best expresses the intent of the code that you are trying to write. Choose the conditional statement that is easiest for future developers looking at your code, including yourself, to read.

For me, I personally prefer if-else statements over `switch` statements because I find them easier to read. Some would disagree, citing long if-else blocks as being difficult to follow. As with most things, your mileage may vary.

Working with loops

Loops enable your program to perform a set of instructions repeatedly until some condition is met. As with conditional statements, you encounter three primary types of loops: the `for` loop, the `while` loop, and `do-while` loop, which is really a variation of the `while` loop.

With the introduction of Objective-C 2.0, and its fast enumeration capabilities, the `for` loop has become really the primary loop of choice when working in Objective-C. However, the `while` and `do-while` loops serve important functions in the language.

Working with for

The `for` loop is probably the most commonly used loop in Objective-C. Using it, you can count over a range of numbers, iterate over an array of items, and so on. Because of this flexibility, some variations in its syntax can be confusing.

Traditional for loops

The first variation of the `for` loop that I would like to introduce to you is the traditional form. In this form, a `for` statement consists of the statement followed by the conditions of the `for` loop in the form of three statements inside parentheses. These three statements correspond to the three operations that are performed on the control variable as the `for` loop executes. The first operation sets the initial conditions of the control variable, and it is typically used to initialize the variable to zero, or, in the case where you don't want to start counting at zero, to some other value. This first operation is only executed the first time the `for` loop is entered.

The second operation is the conditional statement that is evaluated upon each iteration of the loop to determine if the loop should be halted. If the conditional statement is evaluated to be true, then the `for` loop is interrupted and program execution continues after the `for` loop code block. If the conditional statement is evaluated to be false, another iteration of the `for` loop code block is executed.

The final operation is the counting expression. It is this expression that is used to actually change the value of the control variable for each iteration of the loop. During each iteration, the control variable can be incremented, decremented, assigned to, and so on at will in the counting expression.

Listing 2.35 shows an example of a typical `for` loop.

Listing 2.35

A for loop

```
for(int i = 0; i < 100; i++)
{
    Foo *foo = [array objectAtIndex:i];
    [foo doSomething];
}
```

In this case, the first time that the `for` loop is entered, the control variable (`i`) is created and assigned a value of zero. On each iteration of the loop, the conditional expression is evaluated to determine if the control variable has reached 100. If it has, execution will jump to the statement directly after the `for` loop code block. If it has not, then the counting expression is executed; in this case, the control variable is incremented by one.

NOTE

Your counting expression can be anything you want it to be. For example, to increment a loop that counts by twos, you could simply increment your control variable by two in each iteration of the loop instead of by one like we are doing here.

NOTE

The **x++** operator is the postfix increment operator. It increments the value of **x** and stores it back into **x**. When doing so, it also returns the value of **x** before it has been incremented. The **++x** operator is the prefix increment operator. It also increments the value of **x** and stores it into **x**, but the value it returns is the value of **x** after the increment. The same goes for the post/pre versions of the decrement operator, **--**. In some cases, you may want to assign the return value of these operations to another variable. When doing so, be aware of this behavior.

The control variable is available within the scope of the `for` loop code block and can be used, for example, to reference indexes within arrays or to drive conditional logic within the `for` loop code block. Additionally, a `for` loop can be aborted at any time within the `for` loop code block by executing a continue statement. The continue statement will stop execution of the `for` loop immediately and reset execution back to the beginning of the loop. An example of this is shown in Listing 2.36.

Listing 2.36

The continue statement

```
for(int n = 0; n < 100; ++n)
{
    if(n > 10 && n < 20)
        continue; // this skips 11-19
    // do something with n...
    Foo *foo = [array objectAtIndex:i];
    [foo doSomething];
}
```

Using for for fast enumeration

The second form of `for` loops is a new addition in Objective-C 2.0; it applies to enumerating over objects contained in collections. You learn about collections and objects in the next chapter, but I want to introduce you to the fast enumeration syntax here so you'll be familiar with it when we come to it.

In the previous form of the `for` loop, we had to use the control variable to retrieve an element of the array in order to operate on it. The fast enumeration form of the `for` loop obsoletes this mechanism by providing us with an ability to specify, as part of the `for` statement itself, a temporary variable to store the elements of the collection that is being iterated over. This is tremendously convenient, because the vast majority of `for` loops are written specifically for the purposes of iterating over the members of a collection and performing an operation on each of the members individually.

An example of a fast enumeration `for` loop is shown in Listing 2.37.

As you can see, a variable (object) is declared as part of the `for` statement itself. As the `for` loop is executed, each member of the collection (array) is assigned to the variable. It is then available within the scope of the `for` loop code block.

Listing 2.37

For loop with fast enumeration

```
for(Foo *object in array)
{
    // the Foo object is assigned to an element of the array
    // do something with object
}
```

You'll see a pattern with `for` loops in use a great deal when I describe collection objects in Chapter 13. For now, simply be familiar with the form of the `for` loop, and be prepared to return to this chapter again for review.

Working with while

`While` loops work similarly to `for` loops with the exception of the fact that there are not multiple statements inside the parentheses after the `while` statement. A `while` statement has a conditional statement which is checked upon each iteration of the loop. When the conditional statement is found to be false, execution continues at the next statement after the end of the `while` code block.

An example of a `while` statement is shown in Listing 2.38.

Listing 2.38

While loop

```
int x = 0
while(x < 10)
{
    NSLog(@"Value of x: %ld", x);
    x++;
}
```

The implication of this sort of control flow is that whatever condition you are checking within the while's conditional statement needs to, at some point, change to false within the while's code block. If it doesn't, your while statement will continue to loop forever. Whiles can also be interrupted with a continue statement just like a for loop.

NOTE

If the conditional statement is false upon the first run of the loop, the code within the while code block will never execute.

While statements are particularly convenient in cases where you have complex iterative logic involved.

Older versions of Objective-C did not have the fast enumeration capabilities that are available today. As a result, the while statement is often used to iterate over arrays using an NSEnumerator. An example of this is shown in Listing 2.39.

Listing 2.39

Old-style enumeration

```
NSArray *someArray = [self getArray];
NSEnumerator *enumerator = [someArray objectEnumerator];
while((NSObject *obj = [enumerator nextObject]))
{
    // do something with obj…
}
```

You rarely see this pattern used today, but because it is so ubiquitous in older code, familiarizing yourself with this concept is important. Each time the conditional statement is checked, the enumerator returns the next object from the array. When it reaches the end of the array, it returns nil. This causes the `while` conditional to return false. This, in turn, causes execution to jump to the next line of code after the `while` code block.

Using do

The final type of loop that we are going to talk about in this section is the `do-while` loop. This loop is similar to the `while` loop, with the exception of the fact that the conditional is moved to the end of the loop so that no matter what, at least one iteration through the loop is executed before the conditional is checked. An example of this kind of loop is shown in Listing 2.40.

This loop is one that is rarely used, but when it is, it's usually an ideal solution to the problem that you're trying to solve.

Listing 2.40

do-while loop

```
int x = 0;
do
{
    NSLog(@"%ld", x);
    x++;
}
while(x < 10)
```

Usually, this loop is used in cases where you are dealing with some type of control variable that is in a pre-existing state, which you do not want to change until the loop has executed at least once. You may also use this loop when calculating the control variable within the scope of the control block. Again, you might be doing some kind of complex logic in order to arrive at the value of the control variable. The `do-while` loop gives you an opportunity to perform whatever complex logic you desire inside of its code block before the `while` conditional is evaluated. Note, however, that the control variable must be declared outside the scope of the `do-while` code block in order to be within scope for the `while` conditional.

NOTE
Remember, when dealing with a switch, that it was possible to break out of the switch by using a `break` statement. This is very common in switch usage. However, `break` can also be used with `do-while`, `while`, and `for` loops. When used in these contexts, it causes the thread of execution to jump out of the loop to the next line of the program after the loop's code block.

Applying What You Have Learned

Now you can create a command line calculator program. Although you may not understand everything in this program, you will understand most of it, and the things you don't yet understand I explain in the next section.

This program takes a series of arguments on its command line. It should be in the form of numbers separated by operators. So, for example, you run the program as follows: ./Calculator '10 + 5 – 3'. The program then sequentially adds, subtracts, multiplies, or divides the numbers. When finished, it outputs the final result on the console. Just for the purposes of demonstration, I've broken the program into two units: the main unit, which contains the logic for the main functionality, and the MathOperations unit, which contains the functions for addition, subtraction, and so on. To enter the program, start Xcode and create a new Foundation-based Command Line application. Name it "Calculator."

NOTE

Don't worry about the calls to NSString, NSArray, and so on; those will be explained in the next chapter. After the project is created, open the Calculator.m file and modify it to look like Listing 2.41.

Listing 2.41

Calculator.m

```objc
#import <Foundation/Foundation.h>
#import "MathOperations.h"

BOOL isAnOperator(const char value)
{
    return ((value == '+') || (value == '-') || (value == '*') || (value ==
    '/'));
}

int main (int argc, const char * argv[])
{
    NSAutoreleasePool * pool = [[NSAutoreleasePool alloc] init];

    double result = 0;

    char operator = '\0';

    NSString *equation = [NSString stringWithUTF8String:argv[1]];
    NSArray *eqParts = [equation
                        componentsSeparatedByCharactersInSet:
                        [NSCharacterSet whitespaceCharacterSet]];
```

```
for(int n = 0; n < [eqParts count]; n++)
{
    NSString *argString = [eqParts objectAtIndex:n];
    char firstChar = [argString characterAtIndex:0];

    if(isAnOperator(firstChar))
    {
        operator = firstChar;
        continue;
    }

    double newValue = [argString doubleValue];

    switch (operator)
    {
        case '+':
            result = add(result, newValue);
            break;
        case '-':
            result = subtract(result, newValue);
            break;
        case '*':
            result = multiply(result, newValue);
            break;
        case '/':
            result = divide(result, newValue);
            break;
        default:
            result = add(result, newValue);
            break;
    }
}

NSLog(@"%.3f", result);

[pool drain];
return 0;
}
```

N O T E

I said earlier that `switch` statements only work with integers, and yet, here I am using chars. Recall when talking about scalars that chars are represented internally as integers. Using the single quote characters, ", the compiler automatically converts the character inside the single quotes to the integer representation of the value of that character.

Next, create a new C source file, name it `MathOperations.m`, and make it look like Listing 2.42.

Listing 2.42

MathOperations.m

```
#include "MathOperations.h"

double add(double value1, double value2)
{
    return value1 + value2;
}

double subtract(double value1, double value2)
{
    return value1 - value2;
}

double multiply(double value1, double value2)
{
    return value1 * value2;
}

double divide(double value1, double value2)
{
    return value1 / value2;
}
```

Finally, edit the `MathOperations.h` file and make it look like Listing 2.43.

Listing 2.43

MathOperations.h

```
extern double add(double value1, double value2);
extern double subtract(double value1, double value2);
extern double multiply(double value1, double value2);
extern double divide(double value1, double value2);
```

After you do this, compile the application and start your terminal program. You should be able to find the compiled application in your project directory under the subdirectory build/Debug. Enter that subdirectory, and run your new program, as shown in Figure 2.8. Be sure when you run it to enter the single quotes just as I have shown here. This causes the console to ignore the ' * ' character as a wildcard and to just pass it to your program.

This program combines all the information from these first two chapters: for loops, conditional statements, functions, working with basic types, and so on.

Figure 2.8

The output of the program

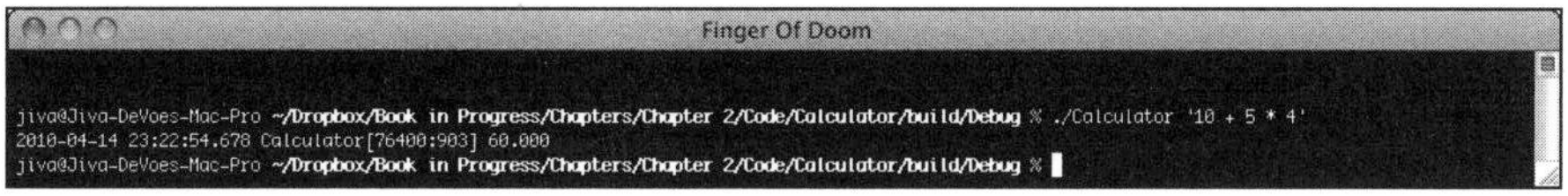

Summary

In this chapter, you've learned all the basic syntax for procedural programming in Objective-C. You learned how to declare variables and structures, how to use operators, and how to use functions. You've also learned about things like loops and conditional expressions for controlling the flow of your programs at runtime. Finally, you combined all this knowledge to make a basic calculator program.

In the next chapter, we're going to delve into the Objective part of Objective-C and see how Objective-C implements object-oriented programming.

Adding Objects

undamentally speaking, all software development technologies are ultimately aimed at solving one specific problem. The problem is that thinking about more than one idea at a time is difficult for human beings. So, all these technologies enable us to compartmentalize and encapsulate our ideas into reusable packages that can be mixed and matched in novel ways to solve new problems.

You've already seen how procedural programming — breaking our ideas out into procedures that we can reuse — enables exactly this kind of compartmentalization and encapsulation. Procedural programming was a revolutionary concept when it was initially introduced early in computer science history. However, it had one major flaw: Procedures have no mechanism for storing state within themselves. Typically, procedural programmers work around this limitation by either passing state variables into the procedures along with the parameters that are necessary for the procedure to do its work, or by relying on global variables to store their state instead. Both of these are not ideal solutions.

Passing state variables into the procedures can quickly get out of hand because, as your programs become more complex, they require more and more state to be preserved between procedure calls.

Using global variables is similarly complicated because excessive use of global variables can lead to excessive dependencies that are difficult to track in your code. For example, to determine what global variables a particular procedure relies on, you have to become familiar with the procedure itself. There's no way to know simply by looking at the interface of a procedure what global variables that particular procedure relies upon. This leads to variables not being initialized properly, or side effects, such as variables receiving values that you were not aware were accessed in that function.

As procedural applications became more and more complicated, these problems became more insurmountable by developers.

In This Chapter

Learning object-oriented terminology

Working with objects in Objective-C

Creating classes and class hierarchies

Defining properties

Writing class and object methods

Declaring member variables

A new programming paradigm that enabled developers to encapsulate both the data that they wished to operate on and the logic to operate on that data together in one package was needed. The name for this new programming paradigm is object-oriented programming. In the following sections, I introduce you to this technology.

Understanding Objects

The idea behind object-oriented programming is to allow a programmer to encapsulate the data that you want to operate on with the procedures that you want to use to operate on the data.

For example, imagine that you want to encapsulate the behavior of a cat. The first thing that you need to do is capture the attributes of that cat — its data. Figure 3.1 shows an illustration of this concept. You might want to capture the properties of the color of the cat. In this case, the color of the cat is black.

Figure 3.1

Encapsulating the properties of a cat

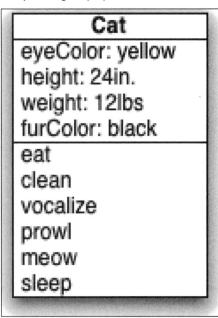

You might also want to capture the fact that the cat's eyes are yellow. Some cats have gray eyes, some cats have green eyes, but this cat's eyes are yellow. Perhaps you also want to capture the weight of the cat. All of these things are attributes of the cat. If you can imagine dealing with this in a procedural application, all of these properties would have to be stored in some sort of global variables. You could probably alleviate some of the problem by using structures for those global variables, but even so, after you move beyond one, managing bunches of structures would quickly get out of hand.

Using object-oriented programming, you can represent the state of the cat and its attributes using an object. In the same way that a given instance of a cat is a physical representation of the more generic, ideal "Cat" concept, you can say that there is a generic version of cats called, generically, Cat. This is called the "class" of the object. Another way to think of this is to think of this class of an object as sort of the platonic representation of the concept of a cat. This platonic ideal representation of a cat acts as a sort of conceptual template that you can then use to create instances of our actual individual cats. My specific, individual cat (named George) is the "object," or "instance," of a cat "class."

Putting this a different way, our Cat class represents the definition of all the attributes that make up what a cat is, including all the potential variety of different kinds of cats. Using that template, you can create an individual instance of a cat that describes your particular cat. The Cat class might define that cats are small, furry animals with pointy ears, sharp teeth, and a tendency for attacking their owners' legs. The class might also define that cats have eyes or fur of different colors. The fur color of your particular instance of cat would be a variable that you define in order to differentiate your cat from the generic concept of the cat.

In addition to defining the attributes of both the generic concept of a cat as well as the specific attributes of your particular cat, a class can also encapsulate the behavior of the cat. For example, it might be said that a cat vocalizes by meowing. You could create code in your Cat template that represents the instructions required to make that cat meow, this is called a "method." Similarly, you might have a method on the cat that represents the process of cleaning itself. The cat might have a temporary state that represents "dirty." The "clean" method might represent the behaviors necessary to change the cat from dirty to clean. In this way, the methods defined on the class Cat define the instructions necessary to alter the data in your particular instance of cat.

Moving away from our metaphor, and returning back to actual Objective-C, the takeaway here is that Objective-C defines programming constructs that give you the ability to define these concepts and relationships.

In Objective-C, a class represents the definition or template for a particular type of object. When working with objects, you create classes. In those classes, you define both the data that the object encapsulates and the methods that are used to manipulate that data.

An object is a particular instance of a class. Objects are also often referred to as instances, and I use these two terms interchangeably.

The data that is encapsulated within an object can be referred to as data, state, attributes, or properties. It's important, however, to be aware that there is also another programming concept called properties, which I cover later in this chapter. All data is not necessarily a property, nor are all properties necessarily data.

Finally, when talking about the behavior of an object, including behavior that changes its data, the instructions to the computer related to that behavior are referred to as methods. Objective-C developers also tend to adopt the Smalltalk convention of referring to methods as messages. This terminology is most often used when referring to using a method as an action. Some programming languages refer to this as "calling a method," but Objective-C programmers tend to use the phrase "sending a message." I, for one, happen to prefer to use the "method" oriented terms, but I may on occasion use the messaging terminology instead.

NOTE

It is vital that you understand the terminology that is used for describing classes, objects, properties, and methods before you move on to the rest of this chapter. If you have any amount of confusion, please reread the Understanding objects section so that you understand the distinction between these items clearly.

Understanding inheritance

Inheritance has two sides to it. One side represents the class design aspect of class inheritance, which affects how you design your classes and where you place behavior in your class definitions. The second aspect of class inheritance relates to how those classes look from an outside perspective and how you use the classes. (I cover this topic in the following section, " Using polymorphism.")

Returning to the Cat class, recall that the Cat class represents, sort of, the template for the creature that is your pet. You could also think of this as representing the species of your pet. Just like a species, the Cat class can be said to have descended from other species. In other words, the cat species is descended from, and inherits certain characteristics from, the classification known as mammals. Similarly, the classification mammals descends from and inherits characteristics from the classification vertebrates. Cats also have sister species, such as dogs. Each of these species has shared characteristics with each other as well as with their parent species. You can extend in either direction, becoming more specific (poodles, German shepherds, and so on). Or you can become less specific, moving up the inheritance tree to mammals, vertebrates, and so on. Figure 3.2 demonstrates this concept by roughly laying out the classification of several different creatures and how they relate to each other.

Classes in Objective-C have the same kind of capability. In fact, Figure 3.2 could just as easily be used to describe a class inheritance tree as a species inheritance tree. In other words, classes in Objective-C can have parent classes from which they inherit behaviors and attributes. Additionally, any class that you create can have child classes that inherit your class's attributes and behaviors.

Figure 3.2

A class inheritance tree

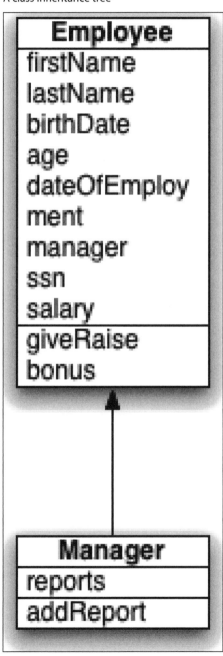

In our example, the cat class inherits from the mammal class. The mammal class specifies that all its child classes have fur, give live birth, eat, sleep, and have some kind of vocalization. As a result, it provides attributes such as the fur color, eye color, and so on. It also provides standard methods for eating, sleeping, and vocalizing. The child classes of mammal inherit all these attributes and behaviors automatically, but can override them in cases where it is required. For example, the particular vocalization that a cat makes is different from the vocalization that a dog makes. A cat's vocalization is a meow, and a dog's vocalization is a bark. To override behaviors in a parent class when implementing a new subclass, you simply define the method in your subclass. Your new version will replace the version in the parent class and will automatically be used by the runtime when the method is called.

All these same customizable capabilities are available when you are defining classes in object-oriented languages. In Objective-C, a given class can inherit from any other given class. However, it can only ever have one parent. The class itself will inherit all the attributes and behaviors of its parent and all its parent's parents, but it cannot inherit behavior from more than one direct parent. This concept is known as *single parent inheritance.* Some languages, such as C++, enable classes to inherit from multiple parents. This can result in ambiguity during compilation. As a result, Objective-C chooses to remove this ambiguity by only allowing a single parent inheritance. Our species inheritance tree eventually leads back to a single global great, great, great grandparent class that is the ancestor of all creatures; Objective-C also has a single class that all classes eventually inherit from. This class is NSObject. The NSObject class provides the most basic functionality that all classes in Objective-C require, such as memory management routines, copying routines, and so on.

NOTE

In Objective-C, you can do some things that simulate multiple parent inheritance without actually requiring multiple parents. I go over how you do this when we look at protocols and categories.

Using polymorphism

Earlier in this chapter, I introduced you to the concept of class inheritance. Polymorphism means that any object that is created from a given class can be assumed by users of that object to be an instance itself, or any of its parent classes. What this means is that your code can be written to utilize the bare minimum functionality required based on classes it inherits from. Because Objective-C classes all eventually inherit from NSObject, you can even create code that only requires NSObject in order to function. It might not be particularly useful, but it would be extremely flexible, in that you could pass any object to it and it would work just fine.

To extend this back into our animal analogy, you can imagine writing code that requires capabilities that mammalian objects provide, for example, vocalization. How the particular instance of mammal that you are currently working with implements the vocalization method can vary, but when you call the vocalization method, it will determine what type of actual animal you're working with and do the appropriate thing. For example, the dog would bark, the cat would meow, or the lion would roar.

This is a tremendously powerful capability, and one that you will leverage continually in your programming career. Polymorphism gives object-oriented programming its real power.

Using the id datatype

I want to introduce one more concept to you before we actually start looking at real code in this chapter. It is the concept of the id datatype. The id datatype is a special data type in Objective-C that essentially means any object. It can be used in any location where an object type would normally be used.

For the most part, you will not need to use the id datatype directly in your code. However, you will probably see cases where the id datatype is used in the Cocoa or Cocoa Touch libraries. Particularly, in areas such as arrays, dictionaries, and so on. In these cases, it is the use of the id datatype, and the fact that it can masquerade as any class at all, that give Objective-C its dynamic typing capabilities.

You might ask yourself, "Why not use id all the time? Then I don't have to worry about declaring my actual object types." Unfortunately, because the compiler can't know at compile time what type of object you're working with when you use an id datatype in place of a more specific type name, it opens up the possibility for errors within your code that could have been caught by the compiler otherwise. Also, the additional overhead required to look up the data type at runtime can cause method calls to objects declared as an id datatype to be slightly slower than those with more specific data types. Therefore, generally speaking, it is better for you to declare your objects to be of a specific type rather than using the id datatype. That said, however, it is important for you to understand the concept of the id datatype so that you can use it in those rare occasions when you need it.

N O T E
You use the id datatype for your initialization methods.

Creating classes

Now that I've introduced you to the general concepts of object-oriented programming, classes, inheritance, and polymorphism, in the following sections, I show you how to actually create classes and how to use them in your code.

Working with class files

Classes are defined by using two separate files. The first is the interface file. Interface files are created with an extension of .h. Within this file you declare the interface of your class. An example of this is shown in Listing 3.1.

Listing 3.1

An interface file

```
#import <Foundation/Foundation.h>

@interface Foo : NSObject
{
    NSString *someVariable;
    NSString *someOtherVariable;
    NSArray *someArray;
}
@property (nonatomic, retain) NSString *someVariable;
@property (nonatomic, retain) NSString *someOtherVariable;

-(void)someMethod;
-(BOOL)someOtherMethodWithArg:(NSString *)param andAnotherArg:(int)param2;

@end
```

As you can see, the interface is declared by using a special syntax of @interface Classname. Where Classname represents the name of the class that you are defining. If your class is inheriting from some other class, you place the name of the class you are inheriting from after your class name. In this case, you are simply inheriting from NSObject.

After the @interface line, there is a block of code bracketed by curly braces. Within these curly braces is where you define your class's data. Variables defined within these curly braces are considered to be within scope in any method defined as part of your class.

The older runtime requires that all your member variables have to be defined here, but the modern, 64-bit runtime, which is available in Mac OS X 10.6 and iOS, does not. You can declare your member variables by simply declaring them as properties. It doesn't hurt anything to declare them additionally here, however, so there's nothing wrong with being in the habit of doing so.

After the curly braces, you define the method signatures for the methods that are part of your class. Finally, you declare the end of your interface by using the @end directive.

After you have created the interface definition for your class, you must also implement it. The implementation of your class is created in a file with an .m extension. An example implementation for the class that we just saw is shown in Listing 3.2.

Listing 3.2

An example implementation file

```
#import "Foo.h"

@implementation
@synthesize someVariable;
@synthesize someOtherVariable;

-(void)someMethod
{
    // body of method
}

-(BOOL)someOtherMethodWithArg:(NSString *)param andAnotherArg:(int)param2
{
    // body of method
}

@end
```

Again, we have a special syntax that tells the compiler that we are creating an implementation. This syntax is the `@implementation` directive. Just like the `@interface` directive, you include the name of the class that we are defining after it. Between the `@implementation` and the `@end` directive is where we define all the methods that will be used in our class.

Jump back into the interface file and take a closer look at how we encapsulate data in our class.

Writing object methods

Object methods are methods that are defined as part of a class and that are only able to be called once an object has been instantiated. Typically, these methods are the methods that we refer to when we talk about the idea of methods operating on the data within an object. For example, methods that change data inside of an object or do a calculation based on data inside of an object are typically implemented as object methods.

Creating an object method consists of two parts. The first part is the method signature declaration in the interface file for the class. An example of this is shown in Listing 3.3.

Listing 3.3

Object method declaration

```
-(BOOL)someOtherMethodWithArg:(NSString *)param1
            andAnotherArg:(int)param2
```

All object methods are prefixed with a hyphen character to differentiate them from class methods, which are prefixed with a plus character.

NOTE

Class methods are methods that can be called using an uninstantiated class instead of an object.

The method's return type is specified within parentheses. After the return type, the name of the method and the parameters it takes are specified. Each parameter is specified after a colon. Its type is specified within parentheses and then its name is specified. Finally, the method must be suffixed with a semicolon.

After you have declared the method signature for the method that you want to create, you have to create its actual implementation. This is also known as the *method definition*. The method definition is placed within the implementation file for your class. When creating your method implementation, the first line of the method implementation should match your method interface declaration that you placed in your interface file. Following the method signature declaration in the implementation file, you then place the body of your method within curly braces. Listing 3.4 shows the implementation for the method that we declared previously.

Listing 3.4

Object method definition

```
-(BOOL)someOtherMethodWithArg:(NSString *)param1
            andAnotherArg:(int)param2
{
    // do something with param1 and param2 here
    if([someOtherObject doSomething:param1] == param2)
        return YES;

    return NO;
}
```

The method implementation specifies the instructions required for the computer to execute whatever behavior it is that you want to occur when this method is called. To return a value from a method, you use the return statement just like you did previously when defining procedures.

All the data members of your class are within scope and available to be used within any object method defined for that class. Additionally, any variables passed into the method as arguments are also within scope and available within the method as well.

Working with the special object methods

In addition to object methods that define behavior that you require for your functionality, there are also certain special object methods that you can optionally define as part of your class that have specific functionality and standard behavior. A variety of these methods exist, but I want to introduce you to two of them right now.

The first of these special object methods are in the generic category of initializers. Initializer method names always begin with the word init and always return an id datatype. Other than these conventions, the method signature of initializers is reasonably arbitrary. However, the body of an initializer method should follow a special standardized syntax. Listing 3.5 shows an example of a typical initializer.

Listing 3.5

A typical initializer

```
-(id)init
{
    if((self = [super init]))
    {
        memberVariable = [[NSMutableArray alloc] init];
    }
    return self;
}
```

The structure of the initializer method is very important. The first step is to call the superclass designated initializer. The initializer returns an initialized instance of the superclass object, and you must assign that to the special variable "self". If something fails during the initialization process, the contract associated with the initializer specifies that it should return a nil object instead of a validly initialized object. Because of this, after assigning the return of the super class initializer to self, you should check to see if self is nil. If it is, you should not initialize your own variables, but instead, simply return nil yourself. In the example shown above, we actually assign the variable to self and check it for nil at the same time in the if statement.

The real purpose of the initializer, aside from creating `self`, is to initialize any data members in the object. So, after you have verified that `self` is not `nil`, you can initialize your variables. Having initialized your variables, you then return `self` from your initializer method.

In some cases, it may make sense to provide multiple initializers for your class. For example, if there are different ways to create an object and different parameters need to be passed to the initializer in these different states. In these cases, you can create multiple, different initializers that take different parameters. To avoid duplication in your code, however, it makes sense to call other initializers from within your initializer. Doing this allows you to keep specific initialization in one place and only one place.

In addition to the concept of an initializer, there is also the concept of the designated initializer. Typically it takes the fewest number of parameters of all your initializers, and it is the final initializer that all your other initializers will call to set up the initial state of your object.

An example of this is shown in Listing 3.6.

Listing 3.6

An example showing different initializers is calling the designated initializer

```
-(id)init
{
    if((self = [super init]))
    {
        memberVariable = [[NSMutableArray alloc] init];
    }
    return self;
}

-(id)initWithArray:(NSMutableArray *)inArray
{
    if((self = [self init]))
    {
        memberVariable = [inArray retain];
    }
    return self;
}
```

The second kind of special method that you need to be familiar with is the `dealloc` method. The `dealloc` method is the opposite of the `init` method. It enables you to free up resources that were allocated in your `commit` method or elsewhere in your object. You must be sure to call the superclass `dealloc` method before the method exits. Listing 3.7 shows an example of a `dealloc` method.

Listing 3.7

An example showing a different initializer calling the designated initializer

```
-(void)dealloc
{
    [memberVariable release]; memberVariable = nil;
    [super dealloc];
}
```

CAUTION

You should be sure not to call the super `dealloc` method before releasing your own variables. This can cause a crash.

I discuss initializer and `dealloc` methods in greater detail in Chapter 4. For now, it's important that you simply be familiar with the methods because you will be using these methods in the upcoming example code.

Writing class methods

In Objective-C, classes themselves also have many of the same capabilities as objects. For example, classes have the ability to have static methods declared upon them that can be called directly from the class itself. When using these kinds of methods, you don't need to have instantiated an instance of the class that you're working with. This can be convenient for methods that are used for creating instances of your class, such as factories and singletons. In fact, the Cocoa frameworks utilize class methods for many of the built-in classes for the purposes of creating instances of the class. In other languages, such as C++ or Java, class methods are often referred to as "static methods." If you are familiar with these languages, you may be familiar with this terminology.

NOTE

A factory method in Objective-C is a class method that is used as a convenience for constructing an object. It always returns an autoreleased object. Factory methods are covered more in Chapter 4.

CROSS-REFERENCE

Singletons are covered in Chapter 17.

Declaring a class method is very similar to declaring an object method; the only difference is that instead of using a hyphen in front of the method declaration, instead you use a plus sign. Listing 3.8 shows an example of a class method declaration.

Listing 3.8

A class method declaration

```
@interface Foo : NSObject
{
    NSMutableArray *memberVariable;
    NSString *anotherMemberVariable;
}
@property (nonatomic, retain) NSMutableArray * memberVariable;
@property (nonatomic, retain) NSString * anotherMemberVariable;

-(id)init;
-(id)initWithArray:(NSMutableArray *)inArray;

// a class method
+(id)fooWithArray:(NSMutableArray *)inArray;

@end
```

The implementation of a class method is identical to the implementation of an object method. However, class methods do not have access to any of the object's member variables. To understand why, remember that a class method is called directly off the class itself, not off an instance of that class. Therefore, there is no object that the data can be stored within in order to operate on that data. Listing 3.9 shows an example of a class method implementation.

Listing 3.9

A class method definition

```
@implementation Foo

+(id)fooWithArray:(NSMutableArray *)inArray
{
    return [[[self alloc] initWithArray:inArray] autorelease];
}

@end
```

The most common use of class methods is in the use of factories, like this method. Many classes in Cocoa and Cocoa Touch have factory methods defined on classes to make creation of objects easier. For example, the NSArray class includes the factory method [NSArray array] which returns a properly constructed NSArray object. (I discuss some special memory management rules in Chapter 4.) When creating class methods, you can use the self object to refer to the class itself, as in this case.

Declaring objects

I've now shown you how to declare classes, including their data, their methods, and so on, but all of this would be useless if you couldn't declare instances of your classes and use them. So now, let's take a look at how you declare an instance of your class in your code.

Listing 3.10 shows an example of code where I've taken the class that we created in the previous section and now I want to use that class in my code to do something useful.

Listing 3.10

Creating an instance of your class

```
{
    // plain old initializer
    Foo *object;
    object = [[Foo alloc] init];
    [object doSomethingWithParameter:arg];

    // all on one line
    Foo *object = [[Foo alloc] initWithArray:[NSMutablArray array]];
    [object doSomethingWithParameter:arg];

    // using a class method factory
    Foo *object = [Foo fooWithArray:[NSMutableArray array]];
    [object doSomethingWithParameter:arg];
}
```

As you can see, declaring an instance of your class is very straightforward. First, you use your class name, filed by the pointer operator (*). Then you place the name of the variable that will hold the instance of your class, in this case "object". You can, if you choose, initialize the object variable immediately, on the same line, as its declaration. To do this, you simply use the equal operator to assign the initialized value to your object variable. In the example code above, I've shown it both ways, first not initializing the variable, and then initializing the variable all on one line. I'm introducing an important new syntax in this code. You've seen it before in other sections of this book, and now I'm going to explain exactly what it's all about. The syntax I'm referring to here is the use of the square bracket operators ([]).

In Objective-C, methods are called on classes and objects by surrounding them in square brackets. You put the opening square bracket at the beginning of the object or class that the method relates to, and then you place the closing square bracket at the end of the method invocation. Thus, looking at the code above, you can see that in the initialization of our object variable, we actually have two method calls in both of the initialization code snippets. The first one is a call to `alloc`. This method is actually being called on the class. The second method call is for the method `init`. This method call is actually being called on the object that is returned from the `alloc` call. It's important to recognize when looking at this code that the `alloc` call is in fact returning an object and that the `init` method is being called on that object. This is not uncommon whatsoever in Objective-C code to see nested calls like this where calls are made on objects returned from prior method calls.

Initializing an Objective-C object is actually a two-step process. The first step is used to allocate the memory that will be used to store the data and the methods that make up the object. This is what the `alloc` call is for. This is why the init and method can be called on the object that is returned from `alloc`.

I cover this in more detail in the chapter on memory management, but it is important to note that any object that you allocate, using an `alloc` method, like shown here, must also be released. To release an object ,you simply call the method `release` on the object. `Release` is a method that is defined on `NSObject`.

Making calls on objects

After you have declared and created an instance of your class, you will, likely, want to make calls on that instance. You can call any of the methods that you have declared in your class as object methods, using the square bracket syntax I showed you in the previous section. However, only methods that are declared in the interface file of your class definition should be called from modules other than the class itself. Although it is technically possible to call methods that are not declared in the interface file, the compiler will issue a warning when you compile your code. Additionally, the compiler will be unable to determine the types of arguments and return values that the method requires, and thus it may not be able to catch errors that it would normally be able to catch.

In some cases, you may want to create methods in your class which are only for internal use to your class. Meaning, you don't want to expose their functionality to outside classes. In other languages such as C++ or Java, you might think of these methods as "private" methods. Objective-C has no syntax for declaring private methods, but if you do not expose the method in your interface file, then it is considered bad form by other classes to call those methods. Part of this is for the reasons that I mentioned in the previous paragraph, and part of it is because of social norms. You don't have to expose methods that you use strictly in your class to users of your class. You can declare methods in your implementation file alone, and they will be available for use in your implementation file. The only important thing to keep in mind when doing so is that the compiler still needs to know about your method signature before you use it. Therefore, methods that you use only in your implementation file, that you don't want to expose externally, should be placed above any methods that reference those methods. Listing 3.11 shows an example of what I mean.

Listing 3.11

"Private" methods in Objective-C

```
@interface Foo : NSObject
{

}

+(id)fooWithArray:(NSMutableArray *)inArray;
-(void)someOtherMethod;

@end

@implementation Foo

+(id)fooWithArray:(NSMutableArray *)inArray
{
    return [[[self alloc] initWithArray:inArray] autorelease];
}

-(void)somePrivateMethod;
{
    // do something private...
}

-(void)someOtherMethod;
{
    [self somePrivateMethod]; // this is OK.
    [self anotherPrivateMethod]; // this generates a warning
}

-(void)anotherPrivateMethod;
{
    // do something else private
}

@end
```

Notice that the first private method is physically above the method that calls it in the file and in the listing. The second private method is below the method that calls it. If you were to do this in your code, the second private method generates a compiler warning just like if you were calling a private method in another class.

NOTE

If this method of declaring "private" methods seems a bit sketchy to you because of the dependency on the location of the definition of the methods in the file, see Chapter 8 for another way of declaring private methods using categories.

Working with Properties

A recent addition to Objective-C is the concept of properties. Properties allow you to declaratively define accessor methods for the data members of your classes. They eliminate much of the boilerplate code that has been previously required for accessing those data members. They also enable you, the developer of a class, to define the contract for the state of your object. They are an important syntactical addition to Objective-C.

Understanding the differences between state and behavior

In previous sections, I talked about objects as a mechanism for encapsulating attributes and behavior. In this section, I approach this topic in a bit more depth in order to explain some concepts that can help you in your use of properties in Objective-C.

The purpose of properties in Objective-C is to assist you in exposing attributes of your object that represent your object's state. Internally, properties compile down to actual methods that can be used to get and set the data in your objects. These are called *accessors*. You can choose to use the compiler-generated accessors, or you can choose to override the compiler and generate your own.

NOTE

An accessor is a method which is defined specifically for the purpose of allowing users of your objects to set and get values in your object. They encapsulate the data members of your object and hide the implementation details of those objects from the outside. An accessor can allow direct access to a variable, or it can be nothing more than a calculation that is performed when accessed. Sometimes these methods are called setters and getters. Most people use properties instead of manually writing accessors, but in cases where you want to override the normal behavior of property accessors, you can easily override accessors and provide your own implementation. I show you how to do this shortly in the section on properties.

Objects are composed of state and behavior. State consists of the data that makes up your object. When thinking about object state, a good design rule that most developers follow states that though an object's state can be changed at any time, it is safe to consider that once an object's state has been set, it will maintain that state until otherwise acted upon by your application. It is also considered to be bad form to have side effects occur when simply modifying the state of an object. When you are tempted to have the act of changing the state of an object have an outside side effect, you should think carefully about the design decisions that have led you to that result.

Behavior, on the other hand, can be thought of as your object taking action. Behavior can be used to update other objects, and thus have side effects, or it can be used to change the internal data of your object or trigger other operations on your object.

Some schools of object-oriented design state that objects should only expose behavior to external entities. With the Objective-C 2.0 property notation, the designers of Objective-C decided that it is acceptable to expose the internal state of your objects as well. The property notation enables you to expose your object's state while still providing accessors through which the access to that state goes. Properties, similarly, should be used only for accessing and manipulating your object's state. To be clear, when writing properties, you should not create properties that have far-ranging external consequences. This is the kind of thing that should be limited to behaviors on your objects.

To give you an example, consider a class that represents an engine. This engine class might expose a property for specifying its throttle. Your property to specify the throttle setting should only set the throttle value. If you want to additionally expose behavior that causes the engine to change its behavior based on the throttle value, then you should additionally expose a method (a behavior) called something like `updateEngineSpeedFromThrottle`. This method would take no parameters, and it would return a Boolean value indicating whether or not it was able to successfully update the engine's speed based off of the throttle value.

By separating the state and behavior of your class, you are preventing potential side effects and dependencies between your behaviors and your object attributes.

Using properties to declare object state

For the purposes of this example, I'd like you to imagine that you're writing an HR application. This application will be used to track employee benefits, including salary, insurance, and so on. Therefore, you need to create an `Employee` class that will be used to encapsulate this data.

I'm sure that you can imagine the kinds of attributes and properties that an employee class would have to encapsulate. Typically, these would include things like the employee's first name, their last name, their Social Security number, their employee number, their salary, and perhaps a reference to another employee who is their manager. All these items can be represented as properties of the employee class.

Listing 3.12 shows an example of how you might create the employee class interface. It includes the listing of the data members that I just specified as well as properties for accessing each of those data members. As we explore each of these properties, it should help you to understand how properties work and which attributes properties can have.

Listing 3.12

The employee class interface

```
#import <Cocoa/Cocoa.h>

@interface Employee : NSObject
{
    NSString *firstName;
    NSString *lastName;
    NSDate *birthDate;
    NSDate *dateOfEmployment;
    Employee *manager;
    NSString *ssn;

    double salary;

}
@property (nonatomic, retain) NSString * firstName;
@property (nonatomic, retain) NSString * lastName;
@property (nonatomic, retain) NSDate * birthDate;
@property (nonatomic, retain) NSDate * dateOfEmployment;
@property (nonatomic, assign) Employee * manager;
@property (nonatomic, retain) NSString * ssn;
@property (nonatomic, readonly) NSTimeInterval age;
@property (nonatomic) double salary;

-(id)initWithFirstName:(NSString *)inFirstName
             lastName:(NSString *)inLastName
            birthDate:(NSDate *)inBirthDate ssn:(NSString *)inSsn;
-(id)init;
-(void)giveRaise:(double)percentage;
-(double)bonus;

@end
```

The first thing to note is that almost all the properties specified here have data members that they map to. A property declaration consists of the @property directive followed by attributes that affect the type of accessor that is created as part of this property. These attributes are specified inside the parentheses after the @property directive. The different attributes that can be specified for a given property are shown in Table 3.1.

Table 3.1 Property Attributes

Attribute	Purpose
getter=<name>, setter=<name>	Specifies the name of the accessor methods that will be used for this property.
readwrite or readonly	Specifies whether this property will be able to be written to. Default is readwrite.
assign, retain, or copy	Determines the type of setter generated for this property. Assign generates a setter with a plain assign to the variable. Retain generates a setter which retains the argument passed to it while assigning it to the variable. Copy generates an accessor which copies the passed in value to the member variable. The default is assign.
nonatomic	Specifies that the generated accessor will be nonatomic, and therefore not threadsafe. The default value is atomic, or threadsafe.

Following the property attributes, you must specify the datatype for the property. Properties do not always have to map directly to a data member variable, but when they do, that data member's datatype should match the data type of the property specified here. Finally, you have to specify the name of the property. It is possible to specify a property with a name that is different from the actual data member that the property represents. Most often, however, you won't need to do this. Therefore, this name should match the name of the data member that this property maps to.

As usual, things declared in your interface file also have a corresponding declaration in your implementation file. Properties are no different. To use the compiler-generated accessor methods, your properties must have a declaration inside of your implementation block in your implementation file. The possible types of property declarations in your implementation file can be either @synthesize declarations or @dynamic declarations. The @synthesize directive causes the compiler to completely generate all the necessary code to create the accessors for your property. Essentially, this directive is a "hands-off" method for using properties. If you use the @synthesize directive, no additional code needs to be written in your implementation file for your property.

On the other hand, if you want to create your accessors yourself, by hand, either in your unit or later, by dynamically loading code at runtime, you can do this by using the @dynamic directive. When using the @dynamic directive, the compiler will expect that you have created an appropriate pair of accessors for your property.

CAUTION

When you create your own accessors using the @dynamic directive, ensure that your accessors fulfill the contract that you have specified in the property's attributes. In other words, if you have specified a copy attribute, then you have to ensure that your accessor copies the value that's passed in when setting the property.

Listing 3.13 shows our employee class implementation. Note that there are different properties that are handled in different ways.

Listing 3.13

Employee class implementation

```
#import "Employee.h"


@implementation Employee
@synthesize firstName;
@synthesize lastName;
@synthesize birthDate;
@synthesize dateOfEmployment;
@synthesize manager;
@synthesize ssn;
@synthesize salary;
@dynamic age;

// parts removed to focus on properties...

-(NSTimeInterval)age;
{
    return [birthDate timeIntervalSinceNow];
}


@end
```

Most of the properties that are defined are using the @synthesize directive. This means that the compiler is completely in charge of creating accessors for those properties. There were a couple of properties of the employee class, however, which were purely calculated properties. For example, the employee's age can be calculated using the employee's birthdate. As you can see by looking at this code, in those particular cases, the properties have been specified to be "read-only" and "dynamic." What this means is that we've chosen to go ahead and create methods that dynamically calculate these attributes rather than storing them as data members. As you can see from looking at the code, to do this, we implemented methods that do the calculation for us.

Understanding synthesized property accessors

When specifying a property and allowing the compiler to generate synthesized accessories by using the apt @synthesize directive, the attributes of the property affect how the accessor behaves. The compiler itself will actually generate different code depending on those attributes.

Using the nonatomic attribute

One of the important attributes that you can specify as part of your property declaration is that of your property's accessor's atomicity. The atomicity of a property has to do with how it behaves in a multithreaded environment. An accessor that is atomic ensures that its value is completely set or retrieved in the thread that is accessing it. Therefore, an atomic accessor is considered to be thread safe. Essentially, the code generated by an atomic accessor look something like the code in Listing 3.14.

Listing 3.14

An atomic accessor

```
-(NSString *)firstName
{
    [threadLock lock];
    NSString *result = [[firstName retain] autorelease];
    [threadLock unlock];
    return result;
}
```

Accessors that are not atomic are not considered to be thread safe. A nonatomic accessor generated by the @synthesize directive might look like Listing 3.15.

Listing 3.15

A nonatomic accessor

```
-(NSString *)firstName
{
    return [[firstName retain] autorelease];
}
```

You may choose to use nonatomic accessors in applications in which you are certain there will only ever be one thread accessing your object.

Using nonatomic accessors can result in a slight performance boost because of the lack of necessity for the locking of the thread locks in atomic accessors.

Using the assign, retain, and copy Attributes

Among the property attributes are a set of important attributes used for specifying the semantics of the generated setter. These are the `assign`, `retain`, and `copy` attributes. These three attributes are mutually exclusive and define the behavior of the setter that is used in conjunction with this property.

The default value, `assign`, specifies that the value will simply be assigned to the data member. An example of this kind of the center is shown in Listing 3.16.

Listing 3.16

A simple assign style setter

```
-(void)setFirstName:(NSString *)inValue
{
    firstName = inValue;
}
```

This attribute is typically used for scalar properties, delegates, and other types of variables where it would be inappropriate retain them.

NOTE

Some of the language used in this section relates to Objective-C memory management, which is a topic that I cover in the next chapter. You may need to refer back to this section again after you have read that chapter.

The `retain` property attribute is used only when working with data members which are themselves objects. It specifies that the value that is passed to the setter will be assigned to the member variable and a retain message will be sent to it.

An example of a setter of this style is shown in Listing 3.17.

Listing 3.17

A retain style setter

```
-(void)setFirstName:(NSString *)inValue
{
    [firstName autorelease];
    firstName = [inValue retain];
}
```

Finally, the `copy` attribute specifies that the setter generated should copy the object to the member variable. Likely retain attribute, this is only used for member variables that are objects. An example of the generated accessor from a copy attribute style property is shown in Listing 3.18.

Listing 3.18

A copy style setter

```
-(void)setFirstName:(NSString *)inValue
{
    [firstName autorelease];
    firstName = [inValue copy];
}
```

Using properties with different data member names

Typically, the names of your properties will match the names of your member variables. There may be cases, for example, when you are dealing with legacy code, where this may not be desirable. In these cases, it is possible to specify that your property uses different accessor names. An example of this is shown in Listing 3.19.

Listing 3.19

Specifying accessor names for properties

```
@property (nonatomic, retain, getter=getFirstName) NSString *firstName;
```

NOTE

Objective-C accessors typically take the form of "`variableName`" for the getter and "`setVariableName`" for the setter. This is a standard in Objective-C and aides in making your objects Key-Value-Coding compliant. We discuss this more in Chapter 6.

Using dot notation

Internally, a property compiles to a method call, in the case of setting a value a setter, and in the case of getting a value a getter. When using Objective-C properties, you can either utilize these setters and getters directly using traditional method calls, for example `[object setFoo:bar]`, or you can use a special syntax, called dot notation. Listing 3.20 shows an example using both traditional accessors and dot notation.

Listing 3.20

Accessing properties using traditional accessors and dot notation

```
{
    // traditional method call...
    [employee setFirstName:@"John"];

    // new Objective-C dot notation
    employee.firstName = @"John";
}
```

CAUTION

Dot notation is ONLY available for values that have properties defined for them.

Some languages, such as C++, Python, and Ruby, utilize dot notation for making method calls to all their methods, not just properties. If you have a background in these languages, you may be tempted to use dot notation for accessing behaviors as opposed to state. This is considered to be extremely bad form.

Applying Objects

Now that I've shown you all the details of object-oriented programming, I'd like to walk you through creating a simple application that will demonstrate the use of object-oriented programming techniques.

The application that we're going to create is an application for managing human resources. It's a very simple application. The end result won't actually be a procedural application that you can use, but the process of creating it will demonstrate all the object-oriented programming techniques that I have shown you thus far.

To begin, create a new command line Foundation project.

Creating the employee class

The purpose of this application is simply to store a list of employees and their managers. Additionally, the employee class will enable you to give the employee bonuses and raises and to calculate the employee's age.

Additionally, there will be a special type of employee, a manager. The manager employees will have employees who report to the manager. Employees will have references to their manager so that you can access the employee's manager. Once you've created the application from the template, create a new class and name it `Employee`. Edit the interface of that class to match Listing 3.21.

Listing 3.21

The Employee class interface

```
//
//  Employee.h
//  HR
//
//  Created by Jiva DeVoe on 4/22/10.
//  Copyright 2010 __MyCompanyName__. All rights reserved.
//

#import <Cocoa/Cocoa.h>


@interface Employee : NSObject
{
    NSString *firstName;
    NSString *lastName;
    NSDate *birthDate;
    NSDate *dateOfEmployment;
    Employee *manager;
    NSString *ssn;

    double salary;

}
@property (nonatomic, retain) NSString * firstName;
@property (nonatomic, retain) NSString * lastName;
@property (nonatomic, retain) NSDate * birthDate;
```

continued

Listing 3.21 *(continued)*

```
@property (nonatomic, retain) NSDate * dateOfEmployment;
@property (nonatomic, assign) Employee * manager;
@property (nonatomic, retain) NSString * ssn;
@property (nonatomic, readonly) NSTimeInterval age;
@property (nonatomic) double salary;

-(id)initWithFirstName:(NSString *)inFirstName
              lastName:(NSString *)inLastName
             birthDate:(NSDate *)inBirthDate
                   ssn:(NSString *)inSsn;
-(void)giveRaise:(double)percentage;
-(double)bonus;

@end
```

Notice that the interface for this file has defined a variety of data members for all the attributes that an employee class might need to track. Additionally, we have defined properties to access those data members. Notice that some of the properties, for example the age property, do not directly map to data members but instead will wind up being calculated values.

Most of the properties utilize the `retain` attribute. The exceptions include the scalar value attributes, the calculated property (which is read-only), and the `manager` property. The `manager` property, in this case, is going to be a special case. The `manager` property will have a list of employees who report to him or her. Because the act of adding the employees to that list of reports will cause those employees to be retained by the manager, you wouldn't want the manager property on the employee to also be retained. I'll explain more about why this is the case in the next chapter on memory management. For now, simply understand that the manager property on an employee should be set to an `assign` attribute as opposed to a `retain` attribute.

After you've created the interface file, go ahead and edit the implementation file. Make it match the code in Listing 3.22.

Listing 3.22

The employee class implementation file

```
//
//  Employee.m
//  HR
```

```
//
//  Created by Jiva DeVoe on 4/22/10.
//  Copyright 2010 __MyCompanyName__. All rights reserved.
//

#import "Employee.h"


@implementation Employee
@synthesize firstName;
@synthesize lastName;
@synthesize birthDate;
@synthesize dateOfEmployment;
@synthesize manager;
@synthesize ssn;
@synthesize salary;
@dynamic age;

-(void)dealloc;
{
    [self setFirstName:nil];
    [self setLastName:nil];
    [self setBirthDate:nil];
    [self setDateOfEmployment:nil];
    [self setSsn:nil];
    [self setManager:nil];

    [super dealloc];
}

-(id)init;
{
    if(self = [super init])
    {

    }
    return self;

}

-(id)initWithFirstName:(NSString *)inFirstName
             lastName:(NSString *)inLastName
            birthDate:(NSDate *)inBirthDate
                  ssn:(NSString *)inSsn;
{
    if(self = [self init])
    {
```

continued

Listing 3.22 *(continued)*

```
        [self setFirstName:inFirstName];
        [self setLastName:inLastName];
        [self setBirthDate:inBirthDate];
        [self setSsn:inSsn];
    }
    return self;

}

-(NSTimeInterval)age;
{
    return [birthDate timeIntervalSinceNow];
}

-(void)giveRaise:(double)percentage;
{
    salary = salary + (salary * percentage);
}

-(double)bonus;
{
    return salary * .05;
}

@end
```

Important things to note here are that, first of all, there is an initializer that takes a variety of parameters which are used to initialize the member variables of the Employee class. By using this initializer, the object that you create will have all its basic attributes initialized and ready to use.

Another important thing to note in this code is the fact that we are creating a dynamic property for the purposes of calculating the employee's age. To do this, we utilize the @dynamic directive for the age property. We then create an age accessor method which calculates the age using the employee's birthdate. There are also two methods defined here, one for giving the employee a raise, and the other for giving the employee a bonus. Both of these methods will be overwritten in our manager class to give a different percentage of raise and bonus.

Creating the manager class

Now that you've created the Employee class, you need to create a subclass of the Employee class called Manager. This class has a list of employees who report to that employee, and it has different percentages for raises and bonuses.

To create the manager class, add a new class file to your project, name it Manager, and edit each interface file to match Listing 3.23.

Listing 3.23

The Manager class interface

```
#import <Cocoa/Cocoa.h>
#import "Employee.h"

@interface Manager : Employee
{
    NSMutableArray *reports;
}
@property (nonatomic, retain) NSMutableArray * reports;

-(void)addReport:(Employee *)inEmployee;

@end
```

Recall that in order to create a class that inherits from another class, you have to specify the parent class after the class name in the interface operation. As you can see from this code, you do exactly that. By doing this, remember that the Manager class will inherit all the attributes and behavior of its parent class, the Employee class.

When it comes to things that are different about the Manager class, you need to specify those items here. Specifically, you need to add the reports array for storing the employees that will report to this manager. Additionally, there is a method here for adding a report to the manager's report list. Switching over to the Manager implementation file, edit it to look like Listing 3.24.

Listing 3.24

Manager implementation file

```
#import "Manager.h"

@implementation Manager
@synthesize reports;

-(void)dealloc;
{
```

continued

Listing 3.24 *(continued)*

```
    for(Employee *employee in reports)
    {
        [employee setManager:nil];
    }

    [self setReports:nil];
    [super dealloc];
}

-(id)init;
{
    if(self = [super init])
    {
        [self setReports:[NSMutableArray array]];
    }
    return self;
}

-(void)addReport:(Employee *)inEmployee;
{
    [reports addObject:inEmployee];
    [inEmployee setManager:self];
}

-(double)bonus;
{
    return salary * .10;
}

@end
```

The important things to note about this code are that we have a designated initializer here which creates the `reports` array and initializes it. This designated initializer will be called from the `Employee` class when its initializer is called. If you refer to the `Employee` class implementation file, you'll see that there is a call to `[super init]` which calls this method. Notice that the `bonus` method is overridden in this class as well. This is so the amount of bonus awarded to the employee is given a different percentage than the amount of bonus for a standard employee.

One final item of note, in the `dealloc` method, the manager object iterates over its reports and removes itself as the manager of those reports when it is deallocated. Remember that the manager attribute on the employees is set with the assign attribute rather than the retain attribute. The result of this is, if the manager object is the allocated but the employees that report to that manager are not, the pointer that references the manager in the employee will become invalid. Therefore, it is important for the manager to set the manager property on its reports to nil when it deallocs itself. This is an important pattern to remember for future use when working with delegates.

Tying the classes together in the HR main

Now that you've seen the employee and manager class definitions, I'd like to show how you might create instances of these classes and tie them together.

If you edit your `main` procedure of your example application to look like Listing 3.25, then it will demonstrate some of the basic operations that we can do now that we have these classes.

Listing 3.25

```
#import <Foundation/Foundation.h>
#import "Employee.h"
#import "Manager.h"

int main (int argc, const char * argv[])
{
    NSAutoreleasePool * pool = [[NSAutoreleasePool alloc] init];

    Employee *joeBlow = [[Employee alloc]
                              initWithFirstName:@"Joe"
                                       lastName:@"Blow"
                                      birthDate:
                [NSDate dateWithNaturalLanguageString:@"12/01/1990"]
                                            ssn:@"555-12-1212"];

    Employee *janeDoe = [[Employee alloc]
                              initWithFirstName:@"Jane"
                                       lastName:@"Doe"
                                      birthDate:
                [NSDate dateWithNaturalLanguageString:@"11/01/1985"]
                                            ssn:@"555-12-1212"];

    Manager *johnAppleseed = [[Manager alloc]
                              initWithFirstName:@"John"
                                       lastName:@"Appleseed"
                                      birthDate:
                [NSDate dateWithNaturalLanguageString:@"11/01/1970"]
                                            ssn:@"555-12-1212"];
    [johnAppleseed addReport:joeBlow];
```

continued

Listing 3.25   *(continued)*

```
[johnAppleseed addReport:janeDoe];

joeBlow.salary = 50000;
janeDoe.salary = 75000;
johnAppleseed.salary = 100000;

NSMutableArray *allEmployees = [NSMutableArray array];
[allEmployees addObject:joeBlow];
[allEmployees addObject:janeDoe];
[allEmployees addObject:johnAppleseed];

for(Employee *employee in allEmployees)
{
    [employee giveRaise:.10];
    NSLog(@"Employee %@ %@'s salary is: %.2f with a bonus of: %.2f",
          employee.firstName, employee.lastName, employee.salary,
          employee.bonus);
}

[johnAppleseed release];
[janeDoe release];
[joeBlow release];

[pool drain];
return 0;
}
```

Essentially, this code creates three employees, Joe Blow, Jane Doe, and John Appleseed. John Appleseed is the manager of Joe Blow and Jane Doe. Each of these employees is created and added to an array that contains all the employees. Finally, the application iterates over the array of employees and gives them all a bonus and a raise.

SummaryIn this chapter, I've introduced you to the very basics of object-oriented programming and how you declare classes and work with them in Objective-C. I've shown you how to create classes, how to work with inheritance, how to work with polymorphism, and how to encapsulate your data in your classes using properties. Throughout the rest of the book, you work with objects a great deal.

Understanding Objective-C Memory Management

One of the biggest challenges you may face as a new Objective-C developer when coming to the platform from other languages, such as Java, Ruby, and Python, is that Objective-C requires that you think about memory management. Many other modern languages have built-in memory management systems (garbage collection, for example) which enable the programmer to ignore most memory management concerns. Objective-C has a garbage collected runtime version, but it is relatively new to the language and unavailable when working on some of the platforms that Objective-C runs on, such as iPhone and iPad. As a result, while it would be nice to say that a new Objective-C developer has no need to be concerned about memory management, doing so would be a disservice to you as a new student of Objective-C. It is entirely likely that even if you are not writing Objective-C code for platforms other than MacOS X, you will still run into MacOS X code, which does not have garbage collection and requires you to manage your memory manually.

Fortunately, however, if you become familiar with the Objective-C memory management rules, even managing your memory by hand can be a reasonably simple affair. By the time you finish this chapter, you should have all of the knowledge of all of the tools that you will require to work with both memory managed code as well as non-memory managed code.

Using Reference Counting

Before I begin reviewing the actual tools that you will use to manage your memory in Objective-C, I first want to introduce you to the mechanism that Objective-C uses under the hood to make manual memory management almost as easy as using a garbage-collected environment.

Every object that inherits from NSObject inherits certain memory management behaviors. Internal to these objects there exists a counter called the retain count. Using certain calls, this counter can

In This Chapter

be incremented or decremented. The Objective-C language runtime knows that when the retain count reaches zero, the object in question can be deallocated. When the object is deallocated, all of its memory resources are given back to the system to be reused.

The retain count can be incremented by using several standardized means. First and foremost, any time you create a new object using a method whose name contains the words alloc, or create, the object returned will have a retain count of one. Additionally, any time you acquire an object by using a method with a method name containing the word copy, that object will also have a retain count of one. You can manually increment the retain count by calling the method retain. Finally, you can decrement the retain count by calling the method release. Again, when the retain count reaches zero, the object, and its memory, are deallocated.

In the following listings, I go over a few scenarios to show how this works in practice. First, in Listing 4.1 I allocate an object using a standard alloc, and init.

Listing 4.1

A standard allocation of an object

```
Bar *foo = [[Bar alloc] init];
```

In this case, at the end of this method, the object foo has a retain count of one.

Now take a look at Listing 4.2

Listing 4.2

Retaining an object

```
Bar *foo = [[Bar alloc] init];
[foo retain];
```

In this case, in addition to allocating the object using an alloc call, I'm also incrementing the retain count by using the retain method. At the end of this code, the object has a retain count of two.

Now look at Listing 4.3

Listing 4.3

Allocating and releasing an object.

```
Bar *foo = [[Bar alloc] init];
[foo release];
[foo doSomething];
```

In this case, after calling the method `release`, the object has a retain count of zero, and would therefore be deallocated. The following line, because it's attempting to access a deallocated object, would result in a crash.

Obviously, that code is an error. Listing 4.4 shows another example of an error, in this case, a memory leak.

Listing 4.4

A memory leak

```
Bar *foo = [[Bar alloc] init];
[foo retain];
[foo release];
```

In this code, I've allocated an object, then retained that object, and then released it, but only once. If this were a member variable, and I was eventually sending it the second `release` to deallocate that object for good, that would be fine. In this case, however, we're only dealing with the code in this particular stack, and this would in fact be a memory leak.

Listing 4.5 shows another example of an error that can occur, can you tell what it is?

Listing 4.5

Failure to retain an object

```objc
@interface Foo : NSObject
{
    memberVariable
}

@end

@implementation Foo

-(void)someMethod;
{
    memberVariable = [someOtherObject getFoo];
}

@end
```

In this case, the code in question should be retaining the object that it received through the call that didn't have `alloc`, `copy`, or `create` in the method name. When the program exits this method, the object in question will be deallocated by the program's runtime releasing it. This will result in a crash the next time that object is accessed. Because the variable being used here is a member variable, it should be retained.

NOTE

Technically, the object will be deallocated at the end of the next run loop iteration assuming nothing else has retained it before then, but for the purposes of following the memory management rules, you can assume, if it goes out of scope and you haven't retained it, it's been deallocated.

Learning the memory management rules

Keeping track of retain counts may seem complicated, but memorizing them can make working with Objective-C much easier.

- Any object you create using a method call containing the word `alloc`, `copy`, or `create`, is an object, and thus memory, that you own. You are responsible for sending a `release` to that same object at some point in the future to free that resource. Anything that looks like `[[Foo alloc] init...]` is something you need to release. Anything that looks like `[foo copy]` you need to release. And anything that looks like `CreateFoo()` returns something you need to release.

- An object you acquire which is not received by calling a method with one of the aforementioned words in it, you don't own. These objects can be used as much as you want within the current execution stack, but after you leave your current stack you cannot expect that they will remain available for your use.

When you receive an object from some other method call, you're going to get back an object that has been "autoreleased." I discuss autoreleasing later in this chapter, but the important point is that an autoreleased object will be released the next time your application exits its run loop. This release will likely happen as soon as you leave your current method. Don't expect that object to live beyond the current method, for example, if you're assigning it to a member variable, then you need to retain it.

When you increment the retain count on an object, either by allocating it, copying it, or retaining it, you are taking ownership of that object, and staking a claim on it. You are stating that you require access to this object for some indefinite period of time, and when you are finished with it, you will give up ownership of that object, and allow it to be destroyed.

C A U T I O N

Although you are becoming the owner of an object by retaining it, ownership does not imply exclusivity. Others may own the object, as well. You are not the only person who could be accessing the object and changing its values.

Using autorelease

I've already mentioned `autorelease`. The `autorelease` concept is central to Objective-C memory management. It enables Objective-C to solve a critical problem that has faced other languages, such as C++ and C: defining a standard "handoff" mechanism for objects returned from other methods and how the memory associated with them is managed.

For example, if you think about a C++ method or function that returns an object, who is the owner of that object? Is it the method that was called? Or is it the calling method? How do you handle the transfer of that memory from one owner to another without somehow having it all spill out onto the floor somewhere in between? C++ and C have handled that through a variety of means. For the most part, it's been up to the individual developer to create and document whatever standard they want to follow. The end result is that when learning a new library, you also need to learn whatever memory management system it's using as well. Some libraries might prefer smart pointers, while others might prefer known contracts, for example.

When Objective-C was faced with this problem, the developers of Objective-C created the concept of `"autorelease"`. Autorelease is a method that you call on an object just like release. However, instead of immediately decrementing the retain count on the object, you can think of `autorelease` as a promise from the runtime that it will decrement the retain count the next time the application's run loop exits. Typically, this happens when your current method exits. When the retain count is decremented in this manner, the object will be released just like normal.

Any time you are returning an object that you have created from a method whose name does not contain Alloc, copy, or create, the object that you return should be autoreleased. The autorelease method actually returns the object that it is autoreleasing. Therefore, it is especially convenient, and somewhat of a standard, to use a pattern similar to that shown in Listing 4.6

Listing 4.6

Returning an autoreleased object

```
-(Foo *)getFoo
{
    Foo *foo = [[Foo alloc] init];
    // do something with foo here...
    return [foo autorelease];
}
```

Another common pattern where autorelease is used effectively is that of autoreleasing objects that you create instead of manually releasing them. By doing this, you are essentially giving up worrying about managing the memory for the object that you create, and instead allowing the "autorelease pool" to automatically clean out anything that you leave hanging when your method exits. An example of this is shown in Listing 4.7.

Listing 4.7

The alloc/autorelease pattern

```
-(void)someMethod
{
    Foo *foo = [[[Foo alloc] init] autorelease];

    // foo is still valid here,
    //it won't be released until the method exists
    [foo doSomething];
}
```

You may find a liberating simplicity in having the release coupled so closely to the allocation of the object. You are less likely to forget to do it later when using this pattern. Additionally, writing your code in this way enables you to think of Objective-C a bit more like a memory managed language, such as Python or Ruby. You can imagine that all of your variables that you are working with inside of this particular stack frame will always go out of scope and be deallocated. You only have to actually think about a particular object or variable when you want to keep it around outside of this particular stack frame.

The Cocoa and Cocoa Touch frameworks provide you with additional tools to help you follow this pattern, as well. Specifically, many of the foundation objects, such as NSString, NSArray, and NSDictionary, include factory methods that return autoreleased versions of the objects they create. By using these, instead of the alloc/init patterned constructors, you barely have to think about memory management at all.

Listing 4.8 shows an example of using these sorts of factory methods and compares them to the traditional pattern.

Listing 4.8

Using factory methods versus the traditional allocation pattern

```
-(void)usingFactories;
{
    NSMutableArray *array = [NSMutableArray array]; // nice, simple,
autoreleased.

    NSMutableArray *array2 = [[NSMutableArray alloc] init];
    // do stuff with array and array 2...

    // need to release this one.
    [array2 release];

    // [array release]; no need to release this,
    // it's already autoreleased
    // if you release it here, it will cause a crash
}
```

Because you are essentially leaving it up to the runtime to delete the objects that you create, you are giving up a certain amount of control over when those objects will be deleted. In an ideal scenario, they will be deleted the next time the runtime exits its run loop. In practice, of course it's not always quite that simple. Because of this, you want to avoid creating large amounts of objects using the `autorelease` pool. On platforms with especially strict memory limitations, it is even possible to exhaust your memory without having any memory leaks. Take, for example, the code shown in Listing 4.9.

Listing 4.9

Leaving many objects on the autorelease pool

```
-(void)inflateMemoryUsage
{
    for(NSUInteger n = 0; n < 100000; ++n)
    {
        // this object is autoreleased
            NSData *data = [self getBigBlobOfData];
        // do something with data...
        [self doStuff:data];
    }
    // all 100,000 data objects are still alive here.
}
```

In this case, the code seems simple enough. Notice, however, that I am executing a tight loop wherein objects are being allocated and being left on the `autorelease` pool to be released later. Because this code is looping, the execution flow is not exiting the current stack. The autorelease pool is never being drained. Thus, memory use continues to simply climb.

You can resolve this problem several different ways. The first, of course, is to simply release the objects instead of using autoreleased objects. For example, if you rewrote the code in Listing 4.9 to be like Listing 4.10, the problem would go away.

Listing 4.10

Releasing the objects inside the loop

```
-(void)inflateMemoryUsage
{
    for(NSUInteger n = 0; n < 100000; ++n)
```

```
    {

            // plain old retain count of 1
        NSData *data = [[NSData alloc] init];
        [self putBlobOfDataIntoData:data];
        // use the existing object you made
        // do something with data...
        [self doStuff:data];
        [data release]; // object is deallocated here.
    }
    // nothing left over.
}
```

However, there are times when you don't always have control over whether all of the objects inside of your loop can be released in this manner or not. Sometimes, due to libraries, for example, you may wind up with autoreleased objects in a loop like that in Listing 4.10. In these cases, the appropriate solution is to create your own autorelease pool inside your loop, and, when you are finished with the objects inside that code, drain your autorelease pool and dealloc it.

Exactly how you do all of this is the subject of the next section.

Understanding autorelease pools

You've already seen autorelease pools in the template code that is provided for you automatically when you create a new project. In case you missed it, here's an example from a typical Foundation command line application in Listing 4.11.

Listing 4.11

A typical main function

```
#import <Foundation/Foundation.h>

int main (int argc, const char * argv[])
{
    NSAutoreleasePool * pool = [[NSAutoreleasePool alloc] init];

    // insert code here...
    NSLog(@"Hello, World!");
    [pool drain];
    return 0;
}
```

As you can see, the first thing that this application does is create an NSAutoreleasePool to capture all of the objects that the application creates and which have received an auto release message. At the end of the main function, the autorelease pool is drained, before it is deallocated. The act of draining the autorelease pool is what actually causes the actual release messages to be sent to all of the objects that have been autoreleased.

All applications have at least one NSAutoreleasePool. If an application has multiple threads, each thread must have its own autorelease pool as well. Typically, most GUI applications have an autorelease pool that is drained each time the run loop executes. This causes your autoreleased objects to be released constantly while your application is running, unlike the code in Listing 4.11 that releases the objects only prior to the application exiting.

To create your own autorelease pool, you need to allocate a new NSAutoreleasePool object, and then perform the necessary operations you need to, including autoreleasing whatever objects you need to autorelease. When you are ready to actually deallocate the objects that you have autoreleased, you simply drain the pool using the drain method or deallocate it with a release. An example of this is shown in Listing 4.12.

Listing 4.12

Creating your own autorelease pool

```
-(void)inflateMemoryUsage
{
    for(NSUInteger n = 0; n < 100000; ++n)
    {
        NSAutoreleasePool *pool = [[NSAutoreleasePool alloc] init];
        // this object is autoreleased
        NSData *data = [self getBigBlobOfData];
        // do something with data...
        [self doStuff:data];
        [pool release]; // the autoreleased objects are deallocated here.
    }
    // nothing left over.
}
```

Autorelease pools work a bit like nested stacks, in that objects that are autoreleased are pushed onto the highest level autorelease pool that is available to them. Therefore, if you create multiple autorelease pools inside one another, objects autoreleased inside of the innermost autorelease pool will be deallocated when that autorelease pool is drained. Again, autorelease pools are a useful tool to aid in making manual memory management easier. They are not to be confused with automatic memory management.

In the next section, I explain how memory management looks from inside your objects and what you need to do to make sure that your object is managing its resources correctly.

Understanding memory from inside the object

You may be wondering what happens to your objects when you are allocating and releasing them." When someone instantiates one of your objects, they call your `init` method. When they release one of your objects, your `dealloc` method is called automatically by the runtime. When allocating and initializing a new object, your initializer should allocate and initialize all of the member variables of that object. Similarly, when releasing an object, your `dealloc` method should release all of the allocated memory both from your objects initializer as well as any dynamic memory that may have been allocated during execution of any of the methods on that object. Essentially, when initializing a new object, you allocate whatever resources that object will require, and when releasing the object you should deallocate those resources.

CAUTION

You should never call `dealloc` yourself.

You've already seen that when you create a new object, and assign it to a variable, you call `alloc` on the class which in turn, returns an allocated object, with no data members. You then use that object to call `init`, or another initializer that is appropriate for your class. The initializer is where you allocate the memory for your member variables in your object.

The `dealloc` method is never called directly by you. It is called indirectly, when you call the `release` method on your object. The `dealloc` method is also called automatically when your object is released by an autorelease pool.

How you allocate and deallocate memory inside of these methods is important. I go into to detail in the next section.

Writing initializers

When writing initializers, remember to call either the designated initializer for your class or call the superclass' designated initializer.

To call the designated initializer for your current class, you call it by using the special variable, self, like so: `[self init]`. To call the superclass's designated initializer, you use the special variable super, and call the superclass's designated initializer by calling `[super init]`. Both of these methods will return an initialized object, `self`, which represents the object that you are initializing, and which must be returned from your initializer as well. If an error occurs in the superclass, or designated initializer initialization, they will return `nil`.

One important, but unusual, step in writing a correct initializer is the assignment of the `self` returned from the superclass or designated initializer to the `self` variable inside of your initializer. This may look like an error, but it is an important aspect of Objective-C, and one which you should not bypass. The super class initializer may actually create a new object and return it as `self` instead of reusing the `self` object that you have allocated in your initializer. This is often done in cases where class clusters exist. *Class clusters* are the implementation of a given class by one of several subclasses. The initializer determines the correct subclass to instantiate, and returns it.

After calling the designated initializer, and assigning its results to `self`, you should verify that `self` is not `nil`. If an error occurs during initialization, you will receive `nil` from the parent initializer. If this occurs, you should not attempt to initialize your member variables, but should simply return `nil` as well.

The assignment and verification can occur on a single line, as shown in Listing 4.13.

Listing 4.13

A typical initializer

```
-(id)init
{
    if(self = [super init])
    {
        someMemberVariable = [[Foo alloc] init];
    }
    return self;

}
```

When the super class initialization has completed successfully, you can allocate and initialize your member variables. Doing this consists of simply calling standard Objective-C initializers for each of the member variables that you need. In some cases, you may want to delay allocating certain member variables until they are actually needed. If this occurs, adjust your code accordingly.

After allocating and initializing your member variables and other resources, you then return self from your initializer. Doing this fulfills the contract of the initializer, returning the now initialized object to the caller.

In some cases, special initializers are called by the Cocoa or Cocoa Touch frameworks under specific conditions. For example, when deserializing an object from a nib file, the special initializer `initWithCoder:` is called to decode the serialized class information from the file. These cases are rare, but important. Members of the Objective-C community currently debate about whether or not it is appropriate to use Objective-C 2.0 property accessors to initialize member variables in initializers and destructors because using these accessors triggers Key Value Observing events. (I discuss Key Value Observing and how it works in a future chapter) For now, I suggest initializing your member variables directly, and to not use the accessors in the initializer and destructor. That said, even if you choose to ignore this advice, you will probably not run into a problem. I use my accessors in initializers and destructors frequently, and I have never run into an issue. Nonetheless, the possibility exists that you can introduce an obscure bug by doing it this way.

This problem becomes slightly more complicated, because when using the 64-bit runtime, you can declare properties that do not have member variables associated with them. In this case, it is only possible to initialize or release your member variables by using your accessors. Therefore, Apple suggests that when using the 64-bit runtime, and using properties that do not have member variables associated with them, you should in fact use the accessors in the initializers and destructors of your objects and when using the older, 32-bit runtime, that you do not use accessors in your constructor or destructor.

Writing dealloc Methods

In order to free the memory that you allocated in your initializer, you also have to write a destructor as well. The method name for Objective-C destructor, is `dealloc`. As I mentioned before, `dealloc` is called indirectly when you call the method release on an object. It is also called automatically when an object is autoreleased, when the auto release pool is drained. An example `dealloc` method is shown in Listing 4.14.

Listing 4.14

A typical dealloc method

```
-(void)dealloc
{
    [someMemberVariable release];
    someMemberVariable = nil;
    [super dealloc];
}
```

Inside the `dealloc` method, you should free any resources that were allocated by your object, including any memory associated with any of its member variables. You do this by calling release on any member variables. After releasing a member variable, you should always make a point to assign the pointer which previously held the data for that member variable to `nil`.

Objective-C, unlike other languages, such as Java or C++, specifies that methods called on nil objects result in no operations at all (a "no-op" in comp-sci speak). Therefore, setting your pointers to nil after releasing them is always a good idea. When you release a member variable, though its memory may be freed, its pointer still points to the location in memory where that object once existed. Other data may immediately be written to that same location in memory. When this occurs, accessing that variable again may result in a crash or unexpected, undefined, behavior. If you fail to set the member variable to `nil`, access to that member variable will be accessing unknown values in memory. This is known as a "dangling pointer".

When working with objects that are using your object as a delegate, special care must be taken as well. When you assign your object as a delegate for another object, the delegating object, according to Cocoa standards, should not retain the assigned object (the delegate).

The reason is that if your object allocates an object for which it is a delegate, the result could be a circular retain cycle, wherein your object retains the sub object, which in turn retains your object as a delegate. In this case, deallocating either object will still result in both objects remaining allocated, because they contain references to each other. Because of this, the object with the delegate always has the delegate variable specified to be assigned rather than retained. Therefore, when deallocating an object that is the delegate for another object, always set the sub objects delegate property to `nil` in your `dealloc` method to prevent the sub object from trying to make calls on a delegate that has been deallocated.

Another common situation, similar to that of the delegates issue occurs when using the observer pattern, or the more Objective-C specific implementation of the observer pattern, the `NSNotificationCenter`. When using the `NSNotificationCenter` to have your object notified of certain events while your application is running, you should always be sure to remove yourself as an observer of the `NSNotificationCenter` when your object is deallocated. Failure to do so can result in a crash. The same also applies when having your object observe Key Value notifications for other objects. You should always remove yourself as a Key Value Observer from any objects for which you previously set yourself as an observer. I cover this topic in Chapter 6.

After you have deallocated your resources, and removed your object from any observing or delegation responsibilities that it may have had, then the last thing that you should always make sure to do is call the superclass `dealloc` method. This gives your superclasses an opportunity to free their resources.. If you fail to call your superclass `dealloc` method, your application will leak memory. The call to `[super dealloc]` should always be the last line of your `dealloc` method so that it comes after you've cleaned up your own memory allocations.

Using Garbage Collection

If the idea of manually managing your memory in your application sounds like a chore, then you will be glad to hear that recently Apple added garbage collection to Objective-C. If you are unfamiliar with the concept of garbage collection, garbage collection is a means by which an application's runtime dynamically determines objects that are no longer being used or referenced inside of your application, and automatically deallocates those objects. Applications that use garbage collection need not worry about releasing objects, retain cycles, or, for the most part, memory leaks. When used appropriately, garbage collection can help you avoid some of the most common pitfalls that beginning programmers run into.

Unfortunately, garbage collection does have a down side. Garbage collection is only available on MacOS X Version 10.5 or above. It is not available, currently, on iPhone, iPad, or any of the less common platforms, such as Linux or Windows. Because of this limitation, learning how to write proper Objective-C code for manual memory managed environments is important.

Also, although garbage collection solves a great many problems with regard to memory management, it also presents additional challenges that you must understand in order to use garbage collection effectively.

Understanding the Garbage Collector

If you're coming to Objective-C from another language, such as Java, Python, or Ruby, you are probably already familiar with the concept of garbage collection. Understanding how the Objective-C garbage collector works, however, can be useful in aiding you to write correct code for the specifics of the Objective-C environment.

Understanding the basics of how the Objective-C garbage collector functions is essential. For any application that has a run loop built into it, for example Cocoa or Cocoa Touch applications, when the main run loop executes, the garbage collector kicks in and searches for objects that have no active references to them. When the garbage collector finds some, it deallocates them.

How this works is that the garbage collector looks at a set of root objects within your application and searches all of the references that contain those root objects. Any object that cannot be reached from one of those root objects is considered to be "garbage" and will be collected. Root objects are defined to be global variables, stack variables, and external references.

So, for example, any object reference from the main application global instance, or any object referenced by any object referenced by the main application global instance would not be considered to be garbage references. However, if an object is allocated in a method assigned to a variable within that method and then never referred to again after that method has exited, the original variable that held it has gone out of scope. The object reference is now held in memory and has no reachable reference from a root object. That object can be collected.

When an object is collected, its memory is freed, but its `dealloc` method is not called. In a garbage collected environment `dealloc` methods are considered obsolete and are no longer used. Instead, a new object method has been introduced called `finalize`. The `finalize` method shares many similarities with the `dealloc` method, in that it is the last method that is called before your object is deleted, and it is, for the most part, considered to be the correct place to do whatever cleanup is necessary for your object. However, because of the way that garbage collection works, the `finalize` method has certain limitations that the dealloc method does not share. Having a `finalize` method for your object is entirely optional. In fact, arguably, you should actually strive not to have a `finalize` method at all.

Recall that the `dealloc` methods primary purpose is to manually release the memory allocated for your member variables. Because you do not need to do that in a garbage collected environment, this is not necessary in your `finalize` method. Therefore, the only reason to have a `finalize` method, is for freeing other finite resources. (Unfortunately, for reasons I explain later, `finalize` is actually a really poor place to free finite resources.)

Because the garbage collector is relatively nondeterministic in terms of when it will actually call your `finalize` method, ou can't determine when it will be called. Therefore, if the resources that you need to free are important, you probably want to put the code for freeing those resources in another method that can be called deterministically by your code rather than relying on the garbage collector and when it may get around to deallocating your object.

The order in which garbage objects are collected is also nondeterministic. Therefore, any case in which you might be calling other objects in your `finalize` method has potential for failure depending on whether your object or the objects you are calling are deallocated first.

Because of these reasons, avoid using a `finalize` method. If no other choice is available to you, I discuss the appropriate way to write a `finalize` method and how to manage your finite resources in that method later in this chapter.

Recall that any application containing a run loop, again, Cocoa or Cocoa Touch applications, automatically has a garbage collector (assuming that you have enabled garbage collection for your project). However, if you're writing a foundation-only application, such as the applications that you've written so far in this book, you must manually instantiate and launch the garbage collector as part of your application's main function.

For the most part, in the remainder of this book, I intend to use Cocoa GUI applications for the example projects. However, I wanted to show you how you launch the garbage collector in a Foundation application. To do so, you call the function `objc_startCollectorThread()` as shown in Listing 4.15.

Listing 4.15

Using the garbage collector in a foundation application

```
int main (int argc, const char * argv[])
{
    objc_startCollectorThread();

    // ...

    return 0;
}
```

Understanding reference types

To effectively understand how to use garbage collection in your applications, you need to understand two fundamental concepts that impact how garbage collection works within your application. These concepts are strong and weak references.

All object pointers in Objective-C are references, meaning that they refer to memory allocated for an object. A reference can be either strong or weak. By default, all references in Objective-C are strong references. A strong reference is the kind of reference that the garbage collector will follow to determine that an object is alive and should not be collected. Weak references, on the other hand, are references that are assignable and valid references to objects, but which are allowed to be garbage collected if the object that they refer to does not have an otherwise strong reference elsewhere.

This concept is useful when you want to have a reference to an object but if that object is marked to be deallocated, you don't want to hold onto it. For example, the NSNotification Center uses weak references for observers that are registered with it. Remember that in a reference counted environment, objects that are registered as an observer with the NSNotification Center must remove themselves as an observer in their dealloc methods. In a garbage collected environment this requirement is not necessary because when the object is deallocated, the weak reference to that object in the NSNotificationCenter becomes invalid and is set to nil. Therefore, the NSNotificationCenter no longer attempts to send notifications to that object.

Now, you may be reading this, and thinking that this would be an appropriate pattern to use when creating a delegate. Remember that in a reference counted environment, when an object has a delegate, it uses the assign property attribute to effectively create a "weak" reference to the delegate. The reason this is done in that environment is to prevent retain cycles. In a garbage collected environment, however, the garbage collector is able to detect and prevent retain cycles, and as a result, using a weak reference for delegates is unnecessary.

As I said before, the default for all references in Objective-C is to be strong. To define a reference as weak, you use the __weak keyword. An example of this is shown in Listing 4.16.

Listing 4.16

Defining a weak reference

```
@interface Foo : NSObject
{
    __weak NSString *memberVariable;
}

@end
```

In addition to being able to manually specify a given reference as being weak, there are also specialized container classes that can be used to store lists of weak references. You might use these classes in place of such classes as NSArray or NSDictionary in cases where you want to store weak references instead of strong references.

These classes are NSMapTable, NSHashTable and NSPointerArray. When you use these classes, if an element of these arrays is deallocated, the reference to that element is simply removed from the array. Normally, if you use an NSAray, or similar, the strong reference within the array keeps the objects alive.

Configuring your project for garbage collection

Configuring a project for garbage collection is relatively straightforward. All that's really necessary is to configure your build settings, and change the setting for Objective-C garbage collection. As shown in Figure 4.1, if you search for this setting in your build settings you can pull down a drop-down list of possible values. These include the following:

- Unsupported: Use the retain-count memory management system.
- Supported: Specifies that your project supports garbage collection but does not require it.
- Required: Garbage Collection is required for this application and all frameworks it uses.

Figure 4.1

Garbage Collection Build Settings

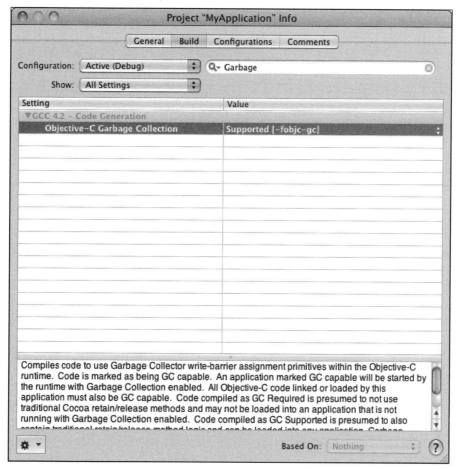

The first setting, of course, is no garbage collection at all. You can enable this by choosing the Unsupported option. The second option is the Supported option. This option adds the flag -fobjc-gc, which specifies that your project supports garbage collection but does not require it. When using this setting, you can link your project with applications that have not been compiled for garbage collection. This setting is normally only used for libraries. When using this setting, your code is expected to implement both dealloc methods as well as final-ize methods, so that it can be used regardless of whether the application that it is being linked with is compiled for garbage collection or not.

The final setting, Required adds the compiler flag -fobjc-gc-only to your compile settings, and specifies that your code does not use retain/release methods and thus cannot be loaded into an application that does not support garbage collection.

If you are converting an existing application from a non-garbage collected environment to a garbage collected environment, you should know that all of the methods specific to the non-garbage collected memory management model will no longer apply. Your initializer will still be called, but your `dealloc` method will not. You should thus re-factor your dealloc method, either removing any sort of resource deallocation you may have had before or moving it into a `finalize` method.

Using Frameworks in a Garbage Collected Project

When using garbage collection for your application, you must also ensure that any libraries or frameworks that you link to are compiled to support garbage collection. As I showed you before, when compiling a framework or library for garbage collection, you can choose to enable it exclusively, inclusively (allowing your framework to be used both in a garbage collected application and a non-garbage collected application), or to disallow garbage collection altogether. In the latter case, the library or framework will not be able to be linked with your application.

Fortunately, all of the Cocoa frameworks fully support garbage collection. The only cases where you may run into situations where libraries or frameworks do not support garbage collection are in the cases of third-party libraries. Garbage collection has been around in Objective-C on MacOS X for quite some time now, so libraries that don't support it are few and far between.

Exploring Key Garbage Collector Patterns

There are a few design patterns that you will inevitably run into when working on a garbage-collected application. Recognizing these patterns and understanding the ways that you should deal with the problems that they solve can be helpful.

Managing finite resources

One often-used design pattern in object oriented programming languages is the practice of writing an object wrapper for a finite resource. Using object wrappers is a common practice when working with files, sockets, and so on. The advantage of this pattern is that the resource can be allocated in the initializer of the object and deallocated in the dealloc method for the object. This provides a nice mental model for ensuring that the resource that has been allocated gets deallocated.

There are several problems with this design pattern in a garbage collected environment. The first, of course, is that the dealloc method is no longer called. Therefore, if you make no changes to your application other than enabling garbage collection, the finite resource that you are attempting to wrap and ensure is deallocated will never be deallocated. This can become especially problematic if, for example, the item in question is an operating system resource, such as a socket. It might seem tempting to simply move the deallocation from your dealloc method to a finalize method. (I've already discussed how your goal should be to have no `finalize` method at all.) Remember that in a garbage collected environment, your object may be deallocated at an arbitrary point in the future. In other words, you can't count on your `finalize` method to be called at any particular point in time in the execution of your application. Therefore, it is possible that the resource that you are expecting to be deallocated in your `finalize` method is not going to be deallocated until much later in your program's execution than you previously expected.

These two problems combined, result in a situation that requires you to rethink this design pattern and to do a little bit of extra work, both in the object itself, and objects that use that object to ensure that resources allocated by that object are closed properly before allowing the object to be garbage collected.

The easiest way to demonstrate this concept is probably to show you some code. Listing 4.17 shows a typical file wrapper class, which is allocating a resource, a file handle, its initializer, and then deallocating that resource in `dealloc` method.

Listing 4.17

A typical file wrapper class

```
@interface Foo : NSObject
{
    int fileHandle;
}

@end

@implementation Foo

-(id)init
{
    if(self = [super init])
    {
        fileHandle = open(...);
    }
    return self;

}
```

continued

Listing 4.17 *(continued)*

```objc
// methods here...

-(void)dealloc
{
    close(fileHandle);
    [super dealloc];
}

@end
```

To convert this class to an appropriate garbage collectible class, you need to take the deallo-cation of the file handle out of the dealloc method, and put it in another method that can be called manually by users of your object. For example, a close method.

Listing 4.18 shows the same class updated and able to be used in a garbage collected environment.

Listing 4.18

A garbage collectible file wrapper

```objc
@interface Foo : NSObject
{
    int fileHandle;
}

@end

@implementation Foo

-(id)init
{
    if(self = [super init])
    {
        fileHandle = open(...);
    }
    return self;
```

```
}

-(void)close;
{
    if(fileHandle != -1)
        close(fileHandle);
    fileHandle = -1;
}

-(void)finalize;
{
    [self close];
    [super finalize];
}
@end
```

Writing foundation applications with garbage collection

I touched on the subject of Foundation command line applications written with garbage collection briefly before. You already know that to create a commandline Foundation application that uses garbage collection, you must manually start the garbage collector at the beginning of your main function, before you allocate any objects. However, another detail is important for you to understand.

The way that the Objective-C garbage collector works is that it searches for pointers that refer to objects in both the global scope and the current local stack. When it does this, it looks at all of the currently active variables in the local stack. When doing so, it doesn't take into account whether the local stack variable has been initialized or not. Remember that a variable, before it is initialized, is pointing to memory locations which previously may have contained initialized data for objects or variables that have been previously deleted. In other words, an uninitialized variable in your current stack may be pointing to an object that you allocated in a previous function call but subsequently is no longer referenced. Therefore, the garbage collector may mistakenly think that your local variable may be referencing an object which should be garbage collected.

To prevent this problem from happening, you need to clear the local stack on a regular basis. The low-level Objective-C runtime method you use to do this is `objc_clear_stack(OBJC_CLEAR_RESIDENT_STACK)`. Typically, in a command line Foundation application, one without a run loop provided by the frameworks, you would be providing your own run loop for your own application events to be processed. The top of this run loop is considered to be an ideal location to clear the local stack and prevent this problem from occurring.

Taking these two things into consideration, a typical command line Foundation application main function should probably look something like Listing 4.19.

Listing 4.19

Commandline Foundation application main function

```
int main (int argc, const char * argv[])
{
    objc_startCollectorThread();

    // ...

    while(running)
    {
        objc_clear_stack(OBJC_CLEAR_RESIDENT_STACK);

        for(RunnableItem *item in runnableItems)
        {
            [item run]; // ..
        }
    }

    return 0;
}
```

Working with objects in nib files

An uncommon but difficult to debug problem can occur when working with objects in nib files that have no reference from an instantiated object in your application. Again, the garbage collector searches for any objects which have no references from global objects or objects on the current stack. In some rare cases, you may create a nib file, which contains objects that don't have references to them, for example, view controllers with no external reference. Under normal conditions, these objects are garbage collected. The solution to this problem is to create an IBOutlet in the object that owns your nib, and connect this outlet to the object in question. This provides a strong reference to the object and prevents it from being garbage collected.

 NOTE

Nib files, or "NeXT Interface Builder" files are used in defining interfaces on iOS and Mac OS. I don't discuss them in this book other than here since it's specific to Cocoa and Cocoa Touch. For more information, see the Wiley books Cocoa Developer Reference or Cocoa Touch for iPhone OS 3 Developer Reference.

Forcing garbage collection

In some cases, you may want to force the garbage collector to collect whatever may be available for collection at a particular point of execution in your application. For example, if you have just recently allocated and then deallocated a large collection of objects, it may be appropriate for you to tell the garbage collector to start collecting so that those objects can be completely deallocated as quickly as possible.

To do this, you can use the low-level method `objc_collect()`. This method forces the garbage collector to begin a collection cycle. I detail this method later in this chapter.

NOTE

When working with converting non-garbage collected code to garbage collection or code which has to function in both environments, the presence of an autorelease pool will act as a hint to the collector that it should attempt a collection as well. This is an undocumented but somewhat well-known feature of the garbage collector.

Working with void pointers and garbage collection

Another common Objective-C pattern that can cause difficulty in garbage-collected applications is using a `void*` data type for passing application-specific data between callbacks. The advantage of this approach is that the data passed between methods can be any type of data the developer desires. It could be an object, or it could be just a blob of bytes. The receiving method typecasts the `void*` parameter to whatever type of data it expects to receive.

The problem in a garbage-collected environment arises because the void pointer is opaque, and so may be mistaken for an object without a reference, and thus garbage collected. This can occur between the initiating method and the callback method such that the pointer received by the callback method winds up pointing to a deallocated object.

The solution to this problem is to use the Core Foundation methods CFRetain and CFRelease to force a strong reference to be maintained in the global Core Foundation framework. An example of how this works is shown in Listing 4.20.

Listing 4.20

Retaining opaque pointers for use with a callback

```
@implementation Baz

-(void)callbackMethodForObject:(id)object withUserInfo:(void *)inData
{
```

continued

Listing 4.20 *(continued)*

```
    Bar *bar = (Bar *)inData;

    // do stuff with bar...

    CFRelease(bar);
}


-(void)startLongOperation
{
    Bar *bar = [[Bar alloc] init];
    CFRetain(bar);
    foo = [[Foo alloc] init];
    [foo startLongOperationWithDelegate:self callbackMethod:
     @selector(callbackMethodForObject:withUserInfo:)
                                 userInfo:bar];
}

@end
```

Essentially, before passing your user data pointer to the object which is going to call your call-back, you manually call a CFRetain, passing your user data pointer as its parameter. At this point, a strong reference is established for the object in question.

Subsequently, when your callback is called, and passed the user data pointer, you should call the CFRelease, again, passing the pointer as its parameter. This removes the strong reference to the pointer and makes it so that the next time the garbage collector executes, assuming you don't establish another strong reference to this object, it will be collected.

Using the object oriented interface to the garbage collector

In addition to the functional interface of the garbage collector, which is appropriate to use in low-level code, Apple also provides a higher-level abstraction for working with the garbage collector the NSGarbageCollector class.

The NSGarbageCollector class is a singleton that allows you to interact with the garbage collector through an Objective-C interface. You can access the current thread's garbage collector by calling the defaultCollector method. After you have the singleton instance of the garbage collector, you can use it to disable or enable collection for specific pointers, or even for the entire thread. Additionally, you can use it to force a collection by using the methods collectExhaustively or collectIfNeeded.

A list of the methods available on the NSGarbageCollector class are shown in Table 4.1

Table 4.1 Commonly Used NSGarbageCollector Methods	
Method	*Purpose*
+defaultCollector	Returns the NSGarbageCollector singleton for the current thread.
-disable/-enable	Disables or enables garbage collection temporarily.
-isEnabled	Returns YES if garbage collection is currently enabled, otherwise NO.
-collectExhaustively	Triggers an exhaustive collection of garbage objects.
-collectIfNeeded	Triggers a collection, but only if memory consumption has grown beyond thresholds since the last collection.
-disableCollectionForPointer:	Causes the given pointer to become a root object, and thus ineligible for collection.
-enableCollectionForPointer:	Removes the given pointer from the list of root objects, making it eligible for collection.

Understanding What Memory Management Model to Use for Your Projects

Perhaps the most important thing to understand about garbage collection is when it's appropriate to be used and when it's not appropriate to be used. For certain, in many cases garbage collection is not a good choice for your application. As I've mentioned before, it's only available on MacOS X Versions 10.5, and later. If your code needs to run on any other platform, including iPhone or iPad, garbage collection isn't even an option for you. In addition to this, however, if you have an application that does not use garbage collection, and which has a large existing code base that is using reference counted memory management, it probably doesn't make sense to convert it to garbage collection. The effort required to do so may be prohibitive.

Finally, because the garbage collector is slightly less efficient with regard to how many objects are actively alive in the application at any given time, the deallocated objects aren't truly deallocated until the collector finds them. Additionally, the garbage collector itself must utilize CPU cycles in order to do its work. If either of these are a consideration for you, then using garbage collection in your application may not be an appropriate choice.

However, using garbage collection in your application can also have significant advantages. For example, generally speaking, applications using garbage collection are easier to make thread safe. This is because accessors can become simple assignment operations that no longer require thread locks to be thread-safe.

Garbage collected applications typically are also easier to code. The lack of necessity for maintaining weak references to delegates, and so on results in simpler code that is easier to maintain.

Finally, and most obviously, the ability to practically ignore the typical boilerplate code required for reference counted memory management is a huge win. They say that the best code, and the most bug free code, is code that you don't have to write at all. Certainly, garbage collection helps to reduce the opportunities for bugs in your code by reducing the amount of code you have to write.

Remember that you should use the highest level of abstraction that will achieve your goals while working within the performance parameters that you require. Meaning, if you can use garbage collection, and it will perform adequately for your problem domain, then you should. If garbage collection results in subpar performance for your particular problem domain, then don't use it. One of the greatest advantages that Objective-C provides developers is the ability to easily move up and down the framework stack and use the level of abstraction that most easily solves the problems that need solving.

Summary

This chapter may be one of the most important chapters in this book. An understanding of memory management technologies and proper use of both reference counting and garbage collection is a vital skill for all Objective-C programmers. In this chapter, I introduced you first to the traditional memory management model of Objective-C, reference counting. I've shown you how to allocate memory in your objects, and how to free that memory when you're no longer using it. I also show you how to use the new technology available on MacOS X, garbage collection. Garbage collection can make your code simpler and less bug-prone than traditional reference counted memory management. You must decide for yourself which memory management technology is appropriate for your project. However, I hope that I have given you sufficient tools to be able to make that decision effectively.

Exploring Deeper Features

In This Part

Working with Blocks

One of the newest and most powerful additions to Objective-C is the inclusion of a capability known as blocks. Using them, you can specify arbitrary portions of code which can be passed around to methods and functions like objects. In this chapter, I show you how to use them.

Understanding Blocks

If you are coming to Objective-C from another language, such as Ruby or lisp, you may already be familiar with the concept of *blocks*, also known as *closures*. Listing 5.1 shows an example of a block in Ruby.

Listing 5.1

An example block in Ruby

```
items.each { |item| puts item }
```

Essentially, a block enables you to define a function object in-line in your code. These function objects can be referenced by using traditional variables, including being passed to other functions. What this means, is that you can define reusable chunks of code that function and can be passed around just like objects enabling that code to be executed inside other objects, dynamically. This may sound confusing, but I think as we work through the upcoming examples, the concept will become clearer.

In the case of the above block, this code is actually iterating over each item in the items array, and then executing the code inside the curly braces, passing the current item into the block.

In This Chapter

Using blocks to encapsulate algorithms

Using the block directive

Creating map and filter functions using blocks

Running blocks in parallel using threads and Grand Central Dispatch

Declaring code blocks

In this section, I introduce you to what block looks like in Objective-C. Listing 5.2 shows an example of a simple block.

Listing 5.2

A simple block in Objective-C

```
int main (int argc, const char * argv[])
{
    NSAutoreleasePool * pool = [[NSAutoreleasePool alloc] init];

    void (^myBlock)(NSString *x);

    myBlock = ^(NSString *x)
    {
        NSLog(@"%@", x);
    };

    [pool drain];
    return 0;
}
```

A block, at its heart, is a variable like any other variable. What makes blocks different is that the data stored inside the block is the body of a function. When using a block, you can call the function just like any standard function, passing it arguments and receiving a return value from it.

In the case of this code, the variable that holds the block is called `"myBlock"`. First, you declare the variable with the line `void (^myBlock)(NSString *)`. Normal variables, when declared, are relatively simplistic. Normal variables do not need to have arguments passed to them, nor do they return values. A block, on the other hand, is stored in a variable and does have to have its arguments and return type declared. Therefore, its declaration is more complex than that of a traditional variable.

A block declaration consists of its return type (in this case, `void`). The return type of the block is placed at the location where you normally expect to see the type definition of the variable you are declaring. In a block declaration, however, you are declaring the value type that will be returned from the block when it is executed.

Following the return type definition, there is a special operator that is used to tell the compiler that you are defining a block instead of another type of variable. This operator is the ^ character.

You may find it easier to think of this like declaring a pointer variable. Just like when declaring a pointer variable the *character is used to indicate that the variable in question is a pointer. In the case of a block, however, the ^ character is used.

Following the ^ character, the variable name that stores the block (myBlock) is given. This variable name is enclosed within parentheses to separate it from its arguments afterwards.

The variable name follows the same conventions of variable names in the rest of the language; it must contain only alphanumeric characters, and cannot begin with a number.

Following the closing parenthesis of the block variable name, the arguments that need to be passed to the block when it is used are listed separated by commas and enclosed in an additional set of parentheses (here, this is (NSString *x)). When listing these arguments, you do not need to provide the variable names for the arguments themselves. Doing so is up to you, but it's not required. A good way to think about this is that you are not actually declaring the body of the function at this time. Therefore, providing the variable names for the arguments serves no purpose, because they would not be used at this time. Instead, you simply have to tell the compiler what types of arguments to expect. You simply provide the types of the arguments separated by commas. A lot of block documentation omits this argument name in declarations. I choose not to, because I think that it makes the code confusing, particularly for new developers.

As always, you terminate the statement with a semicolon. At this point, you have declared a variable, which can store a block that returns the value type that you specified, and takes the arguments that you specified. The name of that variable is, in our example above, myBlock.

Just declaring the variable, as we know, is not sufficient. You also have to store the block in order to use it. Initializing your new variable with a block is done simply by using the assignment operator, and then, again, a special syntax indicates that you are creating the actual block that you will store into the variable.

The definition of the block again uses the ^ character to tell the compiler that what follows is a block definition. You can omit the return type in the definition, because the compiler can determine the return type by looking at the variable that the block is being stored within. You must, however, provide the argument specification for the block, again, inside parentheses. In this case, you must also provide the variable names for the arguments that are being passed. This makes sense, because you are declaring the variable names for the arguments as they will be used within the body of your block.

After the closing parenthesis of your argument list, you then provide the actual body of the block. This body of code takes a form that is nearly identical to declaring a normal function. You enclose the block code within curly braces, execute whatever operations you choose, utilize your arguments as needed, and return whatever value is appropriate after you finish. Just like when defining a standard function, the code inside a block can be spread over multiple lines, though normal white space rules do apply.

Listing 5.3 shows some additional examples of typical block definitions.

Listing 5.3

Different kinds of block definitions

```
void (^myBlock)(NSString *x) = ^(NSString *x)
{
    NSLog(@"%@", x);
};

void (^anotherBlock)(NSString *x) = ^(NSString *x) { NSLog(@"%@", x); };

void (^aVoidBlock)() = ^{ NSLog(@"blah"); };

doIt(^(NSString *x){ NSLog(@"%@", x); });
```

NOTE

When defining blocks that take no arguments, it is syntactically acceptable to not provide the enclosing parentheses for the arguments, which are not there. You must still provide the parentheses for the definition, however.

As shown here, you can perform the declaration of a block variable as well as its initialization, all within the same expression. Again, this is just like working with regular variables. You can declare the variable and then initialize it separately, or you can do it all in one shot.

In the last line of listing so-and-so, you can see it's also possible to simply define your block inline in place of whatever parameter requires it in the same way you can pass a hard-coded value in place of a variable as an argument to a function. This is perfectly legal.

Using code blocks

The main reason that you declare blocks is so that they can be used elsewhere. Therefore, understanding how blocks are passed to other functions and methods, and how you use a block object when you have received one is important.

To declare that a function or method takes a block as a parameter, you declare the parameter just like declaring a block variable in your code. For example, Listing 5.4 shows a function that takes a block as a parameter. The block in question, takes an argument of an NSString and returns an NSComparisonResult.

Listing 5.4

Declaring a function which takes a block parameter

```
void useCodeBlock(NSComparisonResult (^theBlock)(NSString *value));
```

Inside the body of the function that utilizes a block, you call the block by treating its variable just like a normal function name. In other words, you simply use the variable just as if it were a function, passing the parameters that the block requires inside parentheses, and storing the return result however, you need to use the assignment operator.

Listing 5.5 shows the same function that we declared earlier, but shows how it might use the block that was passed to it.

Listing 5.5

A function which uses a block

```
void useCodeBlock(NSComparisonResult (^theBlock)(NSString *value))
{
    if(NSOrderedSame == theBlock(@"foo"))
        doSomethingIfSame();
    else
        doSomethingElse();
}
```

When passing a block parameter as an argument to an object or class method (versus an argument to a function) the syntax is slightly different. Listing 5.6 shows an example of how you do that.

Listing 5.6

Passing a block to an object method

```
-(NSMutableArray *)filterArray:(NSArray *)inArray
                withBlock:(BOOL (^)(NSInteger))block
{
    NSMutableArray *result = [NSMutableArray array];
```

continued

Listing 5.6 *(continued)*

```
    for(NSNumber *number in inArray)
    {
        if(block([number integerValue]))
            [result addObject:number];
    }
    return result;
}
```

Notice that you pass the block parameter's name (the name the variable, which will hold the block has within the method body) after the definition of the block. Because of this, the area where block definition normally provides the block variable name is passed as just (^).

What's great is that the Objective-C new feature is tremendously powerful. You can create code that is much more flexible and reusable than what could previously be done.

First, however, there are a few details that you should be aware of when using this powerful language feature.

Understanding Important Block Scoping

If blocks were limited to only utilizing the parameters that were passed to them, and only returning the value that they defined , then it would be a powerful feature in its own right. However, blocks have more tools under the surface that make them even more powerful.

When you define a block inside of another section of code, the block that you define, that is the instructions inside your block, have access not just to all of the normal global variables that all the rest of your code has access to, they also automatically receive read-only copies of all of the stack variables that are within scope in the stack in which the block is defined. This means, that your block has access (read-only) to the entire state of your program as it is running when the block was defined.

To give you an idea of what I mean by this, take a look at Listing 5.7.

Listing 5.7

A block which accesses variables from the stack within which it is defined

```
int main (int argc, const char * argv[])
{
    NSAutoreleasePool * pool = [[NSAutoreleasePool alloc] init];
```

```
NSString *formatStr = @"%s";

void (^myBlock)(char *x) = ^(char *x){ NSLog(formatStr, x); };

doIt(myBlock);

[pool drain];
return 0;
}
```

As you can see, the block accesses a variable (formatStr) that is not passed to it, but which comes from the environment from within which the block is created.

Again, these variables are read-only inside the block. However, you can explicitly make a variable read-write inside of any referencing blocks by using the special language directive __block when declaring the variable.

Because of the ability for blocks to "take a snapshot" of your application state, and make it available to other parts of your application in this way, it provides an incredibly powerful mechanism for encapsulating and manipulating your data.

I will show you momentarily some other cool uses for blocks, but before I do that, there is a small amount of housekeeping that needs to be addressed.

Managing code block memory

In Objective-C, blocks are objects, just like anything else. The data that makes up a block is allocated on the stack just like normal variables. Therefore, if you pass a block to another function or object, and that object needs to store that block for later use, the receiving object must retain the block, as though it were receiving an object passed to it.

Listing 5.8 shows an example of how this works.

Listing 5.8

An object which stores a block in a member variable

```
@interface Foo : NSObject
{
    void (^myBlock)(NSString *);
```

continued

Listing 5.8 *(continued)*

```
}
-(void)doSomethingWithBlock;
-(void)setMyBlock:(void (^)(NSString *))inBlock;
@end;

@implementation Foo

-(void)dealloc;
{
    [myBlock release];
    [super dealloc];
}

-(void)setMyBlock:(void (^)(NSString *))inBlock
{
    myBlock = [inBlock copy];
}

-(void)doSomethingWithBlock
{
    myBlock(@"foo");
    // ....
}
@end
```

As you can see, all of the standard Objective-C reference counting memory management methods work with blocks just like any other Objective-C object. Although you should use `-copy` instead of `-retain` for the block object that is passed in since it's allocated on the stack and you'll want to be sure to get a copy on the heap if you want to keep it around.

The way this works is that the runtime will make a const copy of any external variables that the block uses and the self object to the heap. This way you have access to those variables and all of the member variables of the object within which the block is created. Any variables marked with the __block directive are bit-copied to the heap, and the block is responsible for any additional memory management involved in working with those variables.

All this said, if your application uses garbage collection, instead of reference counted memory management, copying, retaining, and releasing are all done for you.

Making blocks easier to read with typedef

It can sometimes make your code easier to read if you `typedef` your block definition. This enables you to reuse the definition without having to retype all the arguments and return types of the block. Listing 5.9 shows the class from the last section, but this time, it's using a typedef for its block arguments. As you can see, this makes the code much clearer and more readable.

Listing 5.9

Same code using a `typedef`

```
typedef void (^BlockWithCharArg)(char *);

@interface Foo : NSObject
{
    BlockWithCharArg myBlock;
}
-(void)doSomethingWithBlock;
-(void)setMyBlock:(BlockWithCharArg)inBlock;
@end;

@implementation Foo

-(void)dealloc;
{
    [myBlock release];
    [super dealloc];
}

-(void)setMyBlock:(BlockWithCharArg)inBlock
{
    myBlock = [inBlock copy];
}

-(void)doSomethingWithBlock
{
    myBlock("foo");
    // ....
}
@end
```

Using Blocks with Threads

I'm sure that you can think of many different uses for blocks in your code. I'm going to touch on a couple of them in the next few sections.

If you think about the way that blocks enable you to encapsulate functionality in your application in a nice neat package, functionality that can be easily reused, then it makes sense that one of the most commonly used design patterns for blocks in Objective-C is to provide code that can be run in parallel. In other words, threads.

Indeed, one of the first use cases that Apple demonstrated when it introduced blocks in Objective-C was the ability to use them in its (at the time) brand-new parallelization framework, Grand Central Dispatch.

Working with Grand Central Dispatch

Grand Central Dispatch is a framework that ships with Mac OS X version 10.6. It provides an easy-to-use abstraction layer that enables developers to take advantage of multiprocessor and multicore architectures without having to deal with lower-level thread management.

Using GCD, developers need only provide blocks of code, which encapsulate functionality that can safely run in parallel. They hand these blocks off to GCD queues, which then handle all of the low-level details surrounding things such as the creation of threads, the management of those threads, even how many threads should be created to run the tasks provided on a given system. GCD knows how many cores a machine has and will only allocate enough threads to maximize performance over those cores. It completely handles queuing up the tasks provided to it and distributing those tasks to the threads that it creates.

Tasks can be provided to Grand Central Dispatch as either functions or blocks. Obviously, given the topic of this chapter, we are going to focus on using blocks with Grand Central Dispatch.

Using GCD functions to dispatch code blocks in threads

The core of the GCD API centers around the concept of queues. By using GCD, you can either select one of the pre-existing system queues, such as the global queue. You access it by using the method `dispatch_get_global_queue()`, which returns the global concurrent queue associated with your application, or you can create your own private serial queue by using the function `dispatch_queue_create`.

Queues themselves can be either concurrent or serial, indicating that the objects placed within them can be run in parallel, relative to each other, in the case of a concurrent queue or sequentially, relative to each other in the case of a serial queue.

NOTE

Serial queues are often used when you require exclusive access to a given resource for a series of operations. Typically, you might utilize a thread lock to ensure the exclusive access to these resources. Using GCD, you can simply cue the different operations up into a serial queue. Each item can only run after the previous item has completed.

Dispatching blocks into queues is simple. Listing 5.10 shows an example, using a block which performs some lengthy operation. In this case, we are dispatching this block onto the global concurrent queue. As you can see, we can dispatch multiples of these processes onto the queue. Grand Central Dispatch can handle scheduling and management of these tasks automatically for us with no intervention from us whatsoever.

Listing 5.10

Dispatching a block onto the global concurrent queue

```
dispatch_async(dispatch_get_global_queue(0, 0), ^{ doSomethingSlow(); });
```

You get the global queue with the method `dispatch_get_global_queue`, then you `dispatch` your block (`^{ doSomethingSlow(); }`) onto that queue. Here, if you wanted, you could use any of the previous block patterns I already showed you. Of course, normal thread safety requirements apply.

Working with Common Block Design Patterns

I showed you how you can use blocks with GCD to dispatch units of work to threads. Now take a look at some other common block patterns. In these cases, there are examples of where you might use blocks with standard framework APIs to do things a bit more efficiently or cleanly than you would be able to do them without blocks.

Using code blocks for maps

A common operation that is used to demonstrate the power of blocks in other languages is in implementing a map algorithm.

A map, if you're not aware, is a function that applies a given function to each element of an array, and returns a list of results. Implementing a map using blocks in Objective-C is trivially easy. First, you need to create your `map` function. The `map` function takes a block and your array of items as arguments. It's shown in Listing 5.11.

Listing 5.11

A map function using blocks

```
NSArray *map(NSArray *items, id (^block)(id item))
{
    NSMutableArray *result = [NSMutableArray array];

    for(id item in items)
    {
        [result addObject:block(item)];
    }

    return result;
}
```

To use this map function, you simply construct your block object and your array and pass them to the map function. This is shown in Listing 5.12.

Listing 5.12

Calling the map function

```
NSArray *mappedResults = map(items, ^(id item){ return transformItem(item); });
```

Using Blocks in the Standard API

Constructing your own map function is great, but the real power of blocks comes when you combine it with some of the standard Cocoa framework APIs that now take blocks as parameters.

Some classes in Cocoa take blocks as parameters for performing operations, typically on elements of collections that they manage. Notable classes that do this include `NSArray`, `NSDictionary`, `NSIndexSet` and `NSSet`. Additionally, `NSString` and `NSAttributed String` provide methods for enumerating over lines and attributes using blocks, as well.

A collection of the most commonly used methods in Cocoa that use blocks is shown in Table 5.1.

Table 5.1

Class	Method	Purpose
NSNotificationCenter	addObserverForName:object:queue:usingBlock:	Executes the given block when the notification is sent.
NSIndexSet	enumerateIndexesInRange:options:usingBlock:, enumerateIndexesUsingBlock:, enumerateIndexes WithOptions:usingBlock:	Enumerates over the indices of the set, executing the given block, and passing the index to the block.
NSDictionary	enumerateKeysAndObjectsUsingBlock:,enumerate KeysAndObjectsWithOptions:usingBlock:	Enumerates over the keys and objects of the dictionary, executing the given block, with the keys and objects passed to it as parameters.
NSString	enumerateLinesUsingBlock:,enumerateSubstrings InRange:options:usingBlock:	Enumerates the lines of a string, calling the given block with the line as a parameter.
NSArray	enumerateObjectsAtIndexes:options:usingBlock:,e numerateObjectsUsingBlock:,enumerateObjects WithOptions:usingBlock:	Enumerates the elements of the array, passing each item to the given block.
NSSet	enumerateObjectsUsingBlock:,enumerateObjects WithOptions:usingBlock:	Enumerates the elements of the set, passing each item to the given block.
NSOperationQueue	addOperationWithBlock:	Adds the given block to the queue.
NSBlockOperation	+blockOperationWithBlock:	Creates a new NSOperation using the given block.

Of particular interest are the methods on `NSOperationQueue` and `NSBlockOperation`, which enable you to utilize `NSOperation` objects with blocks. This is a higher level API than the GCD functions I showed you earlier in the section entitled "Using GCD to Dispatch Blocks in Threads." I show you how to use these APIs in Chapter 16.

Applying Blocks to an Embarrassingly Parallel Task

Now that I've shown you everything you need to know about how to use blocks in your code, you can apply this knowledge. Though blocks are certainly not limited to their uses in parallelization and threading, they are uniquely good at these tasks.

In programming circles, they are known as *embarrassingly parallel problems,* — problems that are uniquely well suited to parallelization.

An example of this kind of problem is that of calculating prime numbers. Although you can use other ways to calculate prime numbers that are faster than brute force, for the purposes of the following example, I show how you can improve the performance of a brute force solution. Therefore, I'm going to have you write a simple program to calculate all of the prime numbers between 2 and 150,000. Then you will rewrite the application two different ways. The first way uses a block and an `NSArray`, to demonstrate encapsulating the determination of the primeness of a given number. The second form takes advantage of Grand Central Dispatch to parallelize the calculation. The sample code has the ability to print out the prime numbers it finds. Feel free to uncomment this code if you want to see it working. The important thing for you, however, is to note how long it takes to calculate each of these. The program will print out the time it takes for each program. You should see that the naive, plain approach and the array filtering approach should take about the same amount of time, whereas, the parallel version should be much faster.

Creating the project

The first thing you need to do is create the project. (You've already done this several times, so I won't belabor it here.) Make sure to create a new command line Foundation project. Although it's not really necessary, I'm going to have you create a class for actually doing prime number calculations. The vast majority of programming you do using Objective-C uses objects and classes. Therefore, becoming familiar with them and using them in your day-to-day work even now is a good idea.

After you've created the new project, modify the main source file so that it looks like Listing 5.13.

Listing 5.13

The main source file for the prime number calculator

```
#import <Foundation/Foundation.h>
#import "PrimeFinder.h"
```

```
int main (int argc, const char * argv[])
{
    NSAutoreleasePool * pool = [[NSAutoreleasePool alloc] init];

    PrimeFinder *finder = [[PrimeFinder alloc] initWithMaxNumber:150000];
    [finder start];

// uncomment if you want to print out all the primes.
//    for(NSNumber *number in [finder primes])
//    {
//        NSLog(@"Found prime: %@", number);
//    }

    NSLog(@"Found all the primes in %fs", [finder elapsedTime]);

    [finder release];
    [pool drain];
    return 0;
}
```

This source file stays the same for all three versions of the example application. After you've modified the main source file, you can create a class that does the prime number calculations. Go ahead and choose to add a new class to your project. Name the class "PrimeFinder". For the first version of this application, you are not going to use blocks at all so that you can see what this program would look like if you were just doing things the old-fashioned way.

The interface and implementation for PrimeFinder is shown in Listings 5.14 and 5.15.

Listing 5.14

Interface file for PrimeFinder

```
#import <Cocoa/Cocoa.h>


@interface PrimeFinder : NSObject
{
    NSInteger maxNumber;
    NSDate *startedDate;
    NSDate *endedDate;
    NSMutableArray *primes;
}
```

continued

Listing 5.14 *(continued)*

```
@property (retain, nonatomic) NSMutableArray * primes;
@property (retain, nonatomic) NSDate * startedDate;
@property (retain, nonatomic) NSDate * endedDate;
@property (readonly) NSTimeInterval elapsedTime;
-(id)initWithMaxNumber:(NSInteger)inMaxNumber;
-(void)start;


@end
```

Listing 5.15

Implementation file for PrimeFinder

```
#import "PrimeFinder.h"


@implementation PrimeFinder
@synthesize startedDate;
@synthesize endedDate;
@synthesize primes;
@dynamic elapsedTime;

-(void)dealloc;
{
    [primes release];
    [startedDate release];
    [endedDate release];
    [super dealloc];
}

-(id)initWithMaxNumber:(NSInteger)inMaxNumber
{
    if(self = [super init])
    {
        maxNumber = inMaxNumber;
        primes = [[NSMutableArray alloc] init];
    }
    return self;

}
```

```
-(BOOL)isPrime:(NSInteger)number
{
    for(NSInteger n = 2; n < number; ++n)
        if((number % n) == 0)
            return NO;
    return YES;
}


-(void)start
{
    [self setStartedDate:[NSDate date]];

    for(NSInteger n = 2; n <= maxNumber; ++n)
    {
        if([self isPrime:n])
            [primes addObject:[NSNumber numberWithInteger:n]];
    }

    [self setEndedDate:[NSDate date]];
}

-(NSTimeInterval)elapsedTime
{
    return [endedDate timeIntervalSinceDate:startedDate];
}

@end
```

In Listing 5.15, the code is pretty straightforward. Essentially, we have a tight for loop which counts from 2 all the way to 150,000, our maximum number that we have passed. It then takes each one of those numbers in turn and calls the method isPrime:. If that method returns true, then it adds that number to the list of primes for our result set. The isPrime: function takes whatever number is given to it, and tries to divide that number by every number below that number. If it divides cleanly, — if there is no remainder — then that number is not a prime. If, however, it gets to the end of all of the numbers less than the number itself, then it is a prime number and it returns true.

If you compile and run this program, it should print out the amount of time that it takes for your computer to calculate all of those primes. On my computer, it takes about 15 seconds. If your computer is significantly faster than mine is, and yours is done much faster than that, you might want to increase the maximum number of prime candidates by increasing the 150,000 to some higher number. It's important, for the purposes of this example, that your computer spend at least some time chugging away on this problem. Don't go too high though. Computing primes is a pretty intense task for your CPU and if you go too high, it may take a long time to complete.

Using blocks with an array to filter for primes

The first example that shows the use of block won't actually give us any kind of improvement in performance. I'm showing you this because it's a useful design pattern that you can use for solving other kinds of problems.

Essentially, what you're going to do is modify the `PrimeFinder` class so that it takes all of the possible prime numbers in our sequence of candidate prime numbers and places them in an array. You will then write a method that filters the array by using a block that you pass to the filter method. The filter method then returns a new array containing only the numbers from the candidate array that are prime. This kind of pattern might be used in cases where you want to filter an array for elements of the array that matches certain criteria. The nice thing about using blocks in this case, is that you can change the criteria dynamically at any time, simply by passing a different block to the filter function.

NOTE

Another way to do this might be to create an NSPredicate using the NSPredicate class method +predicateWithBlock: and then use it with the NSArray method filteredArrayUsingPredicate:. Again, my purpose here is to explain the underlying concepts, so we're doing it the hard way.

Listing 5.16 shows the changes necessary to the interface file for this version of the program. The important items are the addition of the candidates array.

Listing 5.16

Interface file for the filtered version of the `PrimeFinder`

```
#import <Cocoa/Cocoa.h>


@interface PrimeFinder : NSObject
{
    NSInteger maxNumber;
    NSDate *startedDate;
    NSDate *endedDate;
    NSMutableArray *primes;
    NSMutableArray *candidates;
}
@property (retain, nonatomic) NSMutableArray * candidates;
@property (retain, nonatomic) NSMutableArray * primes;
```

```
@property (retain, nonatomic) NSDate * startedDate;
@property (retain, nonatomic) NSDate * endedDate;
@property (readonly) NSTimeInterval elapsedTime;
-(id)initWithMaxNumber:(NSInteger)inMaxNumber;
-(void)start;


@end
```

The important changes are in the implementation file, which is shown in Listing 5.17.

Listing 5.17

Implementation file for filter version of PrimeFinder

```
#import "PrimeFinder.h"


@implementation PrimeFinder
@synthesize startedDate;
@synthesize endedDate;
@synthesize primes;
@synthesize candidates;
@dynamic elapsedTime;

-(void)dealloc;
{
    [self setCandidates:nil];
    [self setPrimes:nil];
    [self setStartedDate:nil];
    [self setEndedDate:nil];
    [super dealloc];
}

-(id)initWithMaxNumber:(NSInteger)inMaxNumber
{
    if(self = [super init])
    {
        maxNumber = inMaxNumber;
        candidates = [NSMutableArray new];
        for(NSInteger n = 2; n <= inMaxNumber; ++n)
        {
```

continued

Listing 5.17 *(continued)*

```
            [candidates addObject:[NSNumber numberWithInteger:n]];
        }
    }
    return self;

}

-(NSMutableArray *)filterArray:(NSArray *)inArray
                    withBlock:(BOOL (^)(id))block
{
    NSMutableArray *result = [NSMutableArray array];
    for(id item in inArray)
    {
        if(block(item))
            [result addObject:item];
    }
    return result;
}

-(void)start
{
    [self setStartedDate:[NSDate date]];

    BOOL (^isPrime)(id) = ^(id number)
    {
        NSInteger value = [number integerValue];
        for(NSInteger n = 2; n < value; n++)
            if((value % n) == 0)
                return NO;
        return YES;
    };

    [self setPrimes:[self filterArray:candidates withBlock:isPrime]];

    [self setEndedDate:[NSDate date]];
}

-(NSTimeInterval)elapsedTime
{
    return [endedDate timeIntervalSinceDate:startedDate];
}

@end
```

First, you create your candidates array in your initializer.

After your candidate array is created, you have to modify the start method. In this version, you take your `isPrime:` method, and instead of creating it as an object method on your `PrimeFinder` class, you actually create it as a block.

You also have to create the filter method which will be called with your candidate array and your block and which will return your filtered array containing only numbers for which the block returns true. In the code listing above, this method is called `-filterArray:withBlock:`.

The cool part of this particular code, is that you can pass any kind of block to this filter function that you want. It will iterate over the members of the array, and simply call the block for each one of those elements, passing the element as the parameter to the block. The block can do anything it wants. All it needs to do is return true if the element in question should be in the result array and return false if it should not. The ability to decouple this logic from the iteration of the array is very powerful and can be very useful in certain circumstances.

Using Grand Central Dispatch

The final version of our PrimeFinder class utilizes GCD to actually run the prime number calculations in parallel. Again, I discuss GCD in much greater depth later. For now, simply understand that we are going to dispatch instances of our block on to the GCD global queue for each number that we want to test for primeness.

In order to do this, we have to do a little bit of jockeying to make sure that our access to any variables that are shared among the different threads is safe. There are a couple of things that this impacts. First, you are going to store all of your results, that is, the prime numbers, into an array, called `result`. Because that array is going to be shared among all of your blocks, you're going to declare it inside the scope of the start method itself. Recall that when the block is declared, it receives all of the scoped variables and state from the stack within which it is created. However, recall also that those variables are all read-only, that includes our `result` array. We don't have to use the `__block` directive however, because though the result variable itself is read-only, the contents of `result`, through it's pointer reference, are not. This is a subtle but important nuance to note.

In addition to making the result array writable, we also have to ensure that no two blocks attempt to write to that array at the same time. We do this by using a simple thread safety mechanism built into Objective-C, the `@synchronized` key word.

Finally, in order to actually dispatch your blocks onto GCD, you need to create a dispatch group, which allows you to put your blocks into a global queue that will be completely managed by Grand Central Dispatch. It will automatically spawn an appropriate number of threads for the number of cores and processors on the machine that you run it on, and then remove blocks from the queue one by one, sending them out onto these threads to do their work.

Listing 5.18 shows how you need to modify your `PrimeFinder` implementation to do all this. Go ahead and modify your class to match it.

NOTE
Be sure to remove the candidates array from your interface, if you are working off the project from the previous example.

Listing 5.18

Implementation file for the GCD version of `PrimeFinder`

```
#import "PrimeFinder.h"


@implementation PrimeFinder
@synthesize startedDate;
@synthesize endedDate;
@synthesize primes;
@dynamic elapsedTime;

-(void)dealloc;
{
    [self setPrimes:nil];
    [self setStartedDate:nil];
    [self setEndedDate:nil];
    [super dealloc];
}

-(id)initWithMaxNumber:(NSInteger)inMaxNumber
{
    if(self = [super init])
    {
        maxNumber = inMaxNumber;
    }
    return self;

}

-(void)start
{
    [self setStartedDate:[NSDate date]];

    NSMutableArray *result = [NSMutableArray array];


    dispatch_queue_t globalQueue = dispatch_get_global_queue(0, 0);
    dispatch_group_t group = dispatch_group_create();
    for(NSInteger number = 2; number <= maxNumber; ++number)
```

```
    {
        dispatch_block_t isPrime = ^
        {
            for(NSInteger n = 2; n < number; ++n)
                if((number % n) == 0)
                    return;

            @synchronized(result)
            {
                [result addObject:[NSNumber numberWithInteger:number]];
            }
        };

        dispatch_group_async(group, globalQueue, isPrime);
    }

    dispatch_group_wait(group, DISPATCH_TIME_FOREVER);

    [self setEndedDate:[NSDate date]];
    [self setPrimes:result];
}

-(NSTimeInterval)elapsedTime
{
    return [endedDate timeIntervalSinceDate:startedDate];
}

@end
```

In this code, the block in question is being specified to be of type `dispatch_block_t`, which is a special typedef provided by the Grand Central Dispatch functions for use in defining blocks to be passed to the GCD queues. The important thing to understand is that these are normal blocks just like you've been working with previously. The actual definition of the `dispatch_block_t` is shown in Listing 5.19 for your reference.

Listing 5.19

The definition of `dispatch_block_t`

```
typedef void (^dispatch_block_t)(void);
```

If you run this version of the program, you should see a substantial improvement in performance. On my computer, it shaves about 45 to 50 percent off the runtime involved in calculating the prime numbers. Your mileage will vary, of course.

Summary

In this chapter, I introduced you to a powerful new tool in the Objective-C toolbox. Code blocks are incredibly useful in that they give you the ability to encapsulate small anonymous chunks of code and pass those chunks of code around as if they were objects. This gives you the ability to create generic methods that can be retooled with different functionality by simply passing new types of blocks to them as arguments. Additionally, blocks make working with Grand Central Dispatch incredibly simple because they provide you with the ability to express chunks of functionality and then send that functionality into a queue to be executed.

Using Key Value Coding and Key Value Observing

The Objective-C runtime provides you with a variety of advanced tools for not just interacting with the operating system frameworks, but also for interacting with the attributes of your code. One tool available to you is the concept I cover in this chapter called Key Value Coding. Key Value Coding, or KVC as it is often referred to in Objective-C circles.

Accessing Object Properties Using Key Value Coding

Key value coding gives you the ability to access attributes of your classes using a set of standardized accessor methods in addition to your normal setters and getters. You can use these accessor methods to get and set properties of your classes by specifying string identifiers that represent the names of the attributes you want to access. In addition to enabling you to access these attributes using these string identifiers, you can also access object relationships and sub objects by using a standardized syntax.

To give you an example of what I'm talking about, take a look at Listing 6.1

In This Chapter

Learning about key value coding

Writing KVD compliant accessors

Using KVC to simplify complex tasks

Observing changes to other objects using key value observing

Implementing manual and automatic KVO notifications

Listing 6.1

```
Some example classes.

@interface Bar : NSObject
{
    NSArray *array;
    NSString *stringOnBar;
}
```

continued

Listing 6.1 *(continued)*

```objc
@property (retain, nonatomic) NSArray * array;
@property (retain, nonatomic) NSString * stringOnBar;
@end

@interface Foo : NSObject
{
    Bar *bar;
    NSString *stringOnFoo;
}
@property (retain, nonatomic) Bar * bar;
@property (retain, nonatomic) NSString * stringOnFoo;
@end
```

Given the two classes shown, as you can see, we have a class called `Foo`. This class has a string attribute, as well as another attribute defining a relationship between `Foo` and the class `Bar`. This relationship is defined by virtue of the bar property on Foo.

I've already shown you how by defining properties for the attributes of a given class, Objective-C gives you setters and getters for each of those properties. In addition to those standard setters and getters, it also provides you a set of Key Value Coding accessors as well.

The most commonly used of these key value coding accessors are the ones that enable you to access the attributes of a given class directly. These are the calls -`valueForKey:`, which allows you to read an attribute by specifying a parameter representing the name of the attribute you wish to access as a string, set -`setValueForKey:`, which allows you to set the value of a given attribute, also by specifying the name of the attribute as a string.

When working with more complicated relationships, where you want to access an attribute of an attribute, you can specify a more complex key path using dot notation. So, for example, if you have an object with an attribute of type `Bar` called bar, which additionally has an attribute called `stringOnBar`, you can use the method -`valueForKeyPath:`, specifying the dot notation path to the attribute, "`bar.stringOnBar`". Additionally, there's the -`setValue:forKeyPath:` method as well.

Again, looking at code may be the easiest way to describe what I'm talking about. The Objective-C runtime automatically generates for you code that enables you to read and write to the attributes of those classes by using the calls that I just talked about, as shown in Listing 6.2

Listing 6.2

Accessing the attributes of our classes using KVC accessors

```
Foo *foo = [[Foo alloc] init];
[foo setValue:@"blah blah" forKey:@"stringOnFoo"];
NSString *string = [foo valueForKey:@"stringOnFoo"];
[foo setValue:@"The quick brown fox." forKeyPath:@"bar.stringOnBar"];
NSString *string2 = [foo valueForKeyPath:@"bar.stringOnBar"];
```

So, as you can see, literally speaking, you can specify the name of the attribute that you want to access using a string, and you can read its value or you can write its value. You can even, as shown in the case where you are accessing the attributes of the Bar class, traverse a relationship between two objects and access the attributes of child objects of the primary object that you are accessing.

This may seem a bit confusing at first, and you may wonder why you need to know this. For most of your day-to-day coding, using Key Value Coding methods to set and access your properties probably will wind up being more typing, and more error-prone than simply accessing the setters and getters on your class directly. However, a small number of edge cases where being able to access these attributes dynamically, using values that can change at runtime rather than at compile time, can be incredibly powerful.

Listing 6.3 shows an example of a class that needs to serialize a pen object into a database table. In the first example shown, the serialization routine iterates over each of the fields of the table. As it iterates it needs a complex if statement to determine what accessor to call on the object that it is attempting to serialize so it can get the value to be serialized into the given field.

Listing 6.3

Serializing a table without KVC.

```
-(BOOL)serializeToTable:(Table *)inTable
{
    Row *row = [inTable addRow];
    for(Column *column in row)
    {
        if([[column name] isEqualToString:@"firstName"])
            [column setValue:[self firstName]];
```

continued

Listing 6.3 *(continued)*

```
        else if([[column name] isEqualToString:@"lastName"])
            [column setValue:[self lastName]];
        else if([[column name] isEqualToString:@"age"])
            [column setValue:[self lastName]];
        else if([[column name] isEqualToString:@"birthDate"])
            [column setValue:[self lastName]];
        ...
    }
    [row save];
}
```

This code is going to get hairy pretty quickly. Now take a look at the same code using the key value coding method. Listing 6.4 shows the updated code.

Listing 6.4

Serialize method using KVC

```
-(BOOL)serializeToTable:(Table *)inTable
{
    Row *row = [inTable addRow];
    for(Column *column in row)
    {
        [column setValue:[self valueForKey:[column name]]];
    }
    [row save];
}
```

As you can see, the new version isn't just smaller in terms of lines of code, but it's also more resilient and flexible. As you add new columns to the table, you need only additionally add attributes to this object to store the values for those fields. This serialize method automatically extracts those values from the attributes and stores them for us without any changes to this method whatsoever. Again, the serialize method isn't something that you're going to use everywhere in your code. I want to stress that. Using KVC accessors instead of normal accessors is usually more code than you need. But in these kinds of conditions it enables you to write code that is more dynamic and also enables you to reduce the number of places in your code where you have to represent the information about the attributes of your objects. When you can query an object about its attributes, you don't have to commit that information to as many places in code. That's always a good thing — the most bug-free code is code that isn't written.

Working with key paths

In order to use key value coding, you must first figure out which key paths you can construct and what you can access with those keep paths.

You can think of working with KVC accessors like using a dictionary. The keys to the dictionary are strings. The strings themselves are the names of the attributes on the object on which you are operating. Because of this requirement, a certain number of rules have to be followed in terms of your key and thus attribute naming. First, your keys must use ASCII encoding. This means that you cannot have keys that use unusual characters that would not normally be usable in an attribute name. Secondly, your keys must begin with a lowercase letter. Underscores are also allowed for this first letter, but no numbers, and no uppercase. Finally, your key cannot contain any whitespace.

Thankfully, because the attribute that you're accessing has to be a valid symbol name anyway, most of these rules are rules that you are probably already following in the first place.

Listing 6.5 shows some examples of valid key paths and invalid key paths.

Listing 6.5

Valid and invalid key paths.

```
// valid
[foo valueForKeyPath:@"someMember"];
[foo valueForKeyPath:@"someMember.someAttributeOnMember"];
[foo valueForKeyPath:@"someOtherMember"];

// invalid
[foo valueForKeyPath:@"4fun"];
[foo valueForKeyPath:@"kermit the frog"];
[foo valueForKeyPath:@"SomethingWickedThisWayComes"];
[foo valueForKeyPath:@"THISWONTWORK"];
[foo valueForKeyPath:@"thisAlsoWon'tWork"];
```

As I discuss earlier, you can traverse relationships between objects and access attributes on sub objects by using a key path. A key path is the key in which the relationships between different objects are spanned by using dots, as in the example above @"someMember.someAttributeOnMember". The key path accesses the someMember attribute on the foo object, finds the someAttributeOnMember attribute on whatever class someMember is, and it returns the value stored there. A variety of syntactical sugar has been provided in the specification of these key paths. In addition to being able to traverse these relationships, you can even access functions that operate on collections of objects, such as their count, and so on. For example, Listing 6.6 shows some of the built-in functions that you can use as part of these key paths.

Listing 6.6

Using functions inside key paths.

```
[anArrayOfProducts valueForKeyPath:@"@avg.price"];
[anArrayOfProducts valueForKeyPath:@"@sum.cost"];
[store valueForKeyPath:@"products.@count"];
```

Functions operate only on arrays and sets of objects. In the example, the first two lines are accessing product objects. Those products have attributes, such as price and cost. The functions given take the values specified for the attributes on each object in the array and then perform the specified function on those values. In other words, the first item iterates over each of the items in the array of products, collects the price from each of those products, and then averages them.

The syntax for using these functions consists of prefixing the name of the function with the @ sign, then the name of the function, a "." and then the attribute on which to operate. The one exception to the requirement for the attribute on which to operate is the "@count" function, which simply returns the count of items in the collection.

Table 6.1 shows a list of these functions.

Table 6.1

Function	Purpose
@avg	Returns the average of all elements of the array or set.
@count	Returns the count of elements in the array or set.
@max	Returns the max value of all of the elements in the array or set.
@min	Returns the minute value of all of the elements in the array or set.
@sum	Returns a sum of all of the values of all of the elements in the array or set.

Function	Purpose
@unionOfArrays/@ distinctUnionOfArrays	Given a collection of arrays returns an array containing all of the arrays in the collection. In the case of the distinct aversion, it returns only unique arrays.
@unionOfSets/@ distinctUnionOfSets	Given a collection of sets returns a set containing all of the sets together. In the case of the distinct version, it returns only unique sets.
@unionOfObjects/@ distinctUnionOfObjects	Given a collection of sets or arrays, returns all of the elements of all of the collections as a single array. The distinct aversion returns only unique elements.

Writing KVC compliant accessors

The Objective-C runtime accomplishes all of this magic partially through capabilities of the underlying frameworks and partially thanks to coding style conventions. Although the Objective-C runtime does the heavy lifting as far as the functionality of KVC, it relies upon you, the developer, to write accessors for your properties that follow specific conventions so that it can retrieve and set values by using KVC.

The KVC standard for setters and getters is to use setters that follow a pattern of `set<Value>:` and getters that follow the pattern of simply `<value>`. In both of these cases, the `<value>` part of the pattern should be replaced with the name of the property that you are accessing. This property should be a member variable whose name is specified using camel case.

 N O T E

The term *camel case* refers to a standard for variable naming in which the words in a variable are packed together into one long string. In this string, the first letter of each word, with the exception of the first word, is capitalized. For example, to write a variable name called "some variable name," you would write it as someVariableName. Notice, when looking at the variable name, that the capital letters in the inner part of the variable name resemble the hump on a camel. This is where it derives its name.

So, given a class definition as shown in Listing 6.7, you might write accessors as shown in Listing 6.7.

Listing 6.7

Class definition with member variables.

```
@interface MyClass : NSObject
{
    float x;
    float y;
    NSString *something;continued
```

continued

Listing 6.7 *(continued)*

```
}
-(void)setX:(float)inX;
-(void)setY:(float)inY;
-(void)setSomething:(NSString *)inSomething;
-(float)x;
-(float)y;
-(NSString *)something;
@end
Listing so-and-so

KVC compliant accessors.

@implementation MyClass
-(void)setX:(float)inX;
{
    x = inX;
}

-(void)setY:(float)inY;
{
    y = inY;
}

-(void)setSomething:(NSString *)inSomething;
{
    NSString *oldValue = something;
    something = [inSomething retain];
    [oldValue release];
}

-(float)x;
{
    return x;
}

-(float)y;
{
    return y;
}

-(NSString *)something;
{
    return something;
}

@end
```

If you use properties to encapsulate your objects attributes, then it automatically generates accessors that are KVC compliant. In other words, if you're using properties, you don't have to do anything else. You're done. That said, the normal caveats apply. If you use properties and you choose to override the standard property accessor naming conventions, then your accessors will not be KVC compliant, and they won't work with KVC.

Using KVC with arrays

When talking about object-oriented design, thinking about the relationships between your objects is helpful. When one class has a member variable which is of another class type, this relationship can be said to be a one-to-one relationship. Listing 6.8 shows an example of a class interface of this type.

Listing 6.8

The class Foo which has a one-to-one relationship with the class Bar

```
@interface Foo : NSObject
{
    Bar *bar;
}
@property (retain) Bar * bar;
@end;
```

For example, if a given class contains a member variable that is actually a collection of other objects, this relationship is said to be one-to-many. A one-to-many relationship is typically implemented through the use of an `NSArray` or `NSSet` member variable containing elements that are instances of whatever the other class is.

Listing 6.9 shows an example of this type of relationship. Note, however, that the array contains instances of the class `Bar`, but it is not specified here.

Listing 6.9

A one to many relationship from the class Foo to many instances of class Bar

```
@interface Foo : NSObject
{
    NSArray *bars;
}
@property (retain) NSArray * bars;
@end;
```

In these cases, when accessing these values through KVC, you may not necessarily want to simply access the array member variable, but instead access the elements of the array directly. In some cases, this can be more efficient, but at the very least, it more directly represents the actual relationship that exists between these two objects.

KVC provides a special set of accessors specifically for these types of operations. They are used specifically to access the properties of one-to-many relationships as well as the individual elements involved in those relationships.

These accessors fall into two broad categories. The first is that of indexed accessors. These accessors are used when you want to access an individual element in a one-to-many relationship represented as an array. An `NSArray` is an ordered collection and typically, this is the sort of container class that is used in this case. The second type of access for a one-to-many relationship is one that is used in the case when you're relationship member variable is in an unordered collection, such as an NSSet. In this case, the accessors that are used to access the elements in this type of one-to-many relationship are known as unordered accessors. Both of these types of accessors have both mutable and immutable variations.

NOTE

Though typically these relationships are modeled using NSArray and NSSet, technically, they can be modeled using any sort of collection that you choose. The key issue is that your accessors that you create must obey the contract specified for each of the types of access.

Using indexed accessors

When working with indexed accessors for a one-to-many relationship, there is one method that you must implement for retrieving the count of elements, `-countOf<VariableName>`, and then several other methods which you must choose amongst to implement for retrieving the elements of the relationship. The methods for retrieving the elements in the indexed collection, are either `-object<VariableName>AtIndex:` or `-<variableName>AtIndexes:`. These methods are designed to enable users of your class to access a given element at the given index or indexes and should return the appropriate object accordingly. Examples of implementations of these accessors include the one-to-many relationship of `Foo` to `Bar` in Listing 6.10.

Listing 6.10

Implementation of immutable one-to-many indexed accessors

```
@implementation Foo

-(NSUInteger)countOfBars
{
```

```
    return [bars count];
}

-(id)objectInBarsAtIndex:(NSUInteger)inIndex;
{
    return [bars objectAtIndex:inIndex];
}

// OR...

-(NSArray *)barsAtIndexes:(NSIndexSet *)inIndexes;
{
    return [bars objectsAtIndexes:inIndexes];
}

// OR ...

-(void)getBars:(Bar **)outBuffer range:(NSRange)inRange;
{
    [bars getObjects:outBuffer range:inRange];
}

@end
```

In addition to these accessors, you can also implement the optional method `-get<Variable Name>:range:`, which can provide some performance gains by limiting the search to a specified range within the array as shown in the previous listing. The result is stored in the `"outBuffer"` variable.

If you can imagine our previous `Foo` and `Bar` relationship, implemented, instead with an `NSMutableArray`, the relationship becomes a mutable one-to-many relationship. When you need to implement a mutable one-to-many relationship, where you can add, remove, or change elements in the indexed collection, you must also implement either `-insertObject: in<VariableName>AtIndex:` or `-insert<VariableName>:atIndexes:` for inserting items, `-removeObjectFrom<VariableName>AtIndex:` or `-remove<Variable Name>AtIndexes:` for removing items, or, for high performance replacement of objects, `-replaceObjectIn<VariableName>AtIndex:withObject:` or `-replace<Variab leName>AtIndexes:with<VariableName>:`. Replacing objects is considered to be an optional operation that you only really need to implement in cases where it is indicated by performance measurement. Often, simply replacing an object at a given index, without removing the original object and then reinserting a new one can be faster than the alternative. Implement these methods at your discretion.

The additional code required for the `Foo` and `Bar` implementation with mutable access to the objects in the relationship is shown in Listing 6.11.

Listing 6.11

Implementing a mutable one-to-many relationship with an indexed collection

```
-(void)insertObject:(Bar *)inBar inBarsAtIndex:(NSUInteger)inIndex;
{
    [bars insertObject:inBar atIndex:inIndexes];
}

-(void)insertBars:(NSArray *)inBars atIndexes:(NSIndexSet *)inIndexSet;
{
    [bars insertObjects:inBars atIndexes:inIndexSet];
}

-(void)removeObjectFromBarsAtIndex:(NSUInteger)inIndex;
{
    [bars removeObject:inIndex];
}

-(void)removeBarsAtIndexes:(NSIndexSet *)inIndexSet;
{
    [bars removeObjectsAtIndexes:inIndexSet];
}

-(void)replaceObjectInBarsAtIndex:(NSUInteger)inIndex
                       withObject:(id)inBar;
{
    [bars replaceObjectAtIndex:inIndex withObject:inBar];
}

-(void)replaceBarsAtIndexes:(NSIndexSet *)inIndexSet
                   withBars:(NSArray *)inBars;
{
    [bars replaceObjectsAtIndexes:inIndexSet withObjects:inBars];
}
```

Using Unordered Accessors

When working with a one-to-many relationship in which the collection of objects is an unordered collection, there are a different set of KVC-compliant accessors that you can implement.

Just like when working with the indexed accessors, there are immutable accessors that enable you simply to read values from the collection, and mutable accessors that enable you to change values in the collection.

For the immutable accessors, just like with the indexed collection, you must implement the -countOf<VariableName> method to return the number of elements in the set. Additionally, you must also implement the methods -enumeratorOf<VariableName>, and -memberOf<VariableName>:. In the case of the method -enumeratorOf <VariableName>, this should return an NSEnumerator initialized to be used for the purposes of iterating over the collection. In the case of -memberOf<VariableName>:, this method takes an instance of an object as a parameter, and should return any object inside the set which isEqual: to that object. If no object can be found within the set for which isEqual: returns true, it should return nil.

Listing 6.12 shows examples of implementations of these methods for a one-to-many relationship using an NSSet.

Listing 6.12

Accessors for an immutable unordered collection.

```
@implementation Foo

-(NSUInteger)countOfBars
{
    return [bars count];
}

-(NSEnumerator *)enumeratorOfBars
{
    return [bars objectEnumerator];
}

-(Bar *)memberOfBars:(Bar *)inBar;
{
    return [bars member:inBar];
}

@end
```

When it comes to mutating an unordered one-to-many relationship, you must implement either the methods -add<VariableName>Object: or -add<VariableName>: for inserting new objects, either -remove<VariableName>Object: or

-remove<VariableName>: for removing objects, and -intersect<VariableName>: for removing a group of objects from the set.

Listing 6.13 shows an example implementation of these methods using an NSSet to actually implement the relationship.

Listing 6.13

Implementing mutable accessors for an unordered one-to-many relationship

```
// adding...

-(void)addBarsObject:(Bar *)inBar;
{
    [bars addObject:inBar];
}

// OR...

-(void)addBars:(NSSet *)inBars;
{
    [bars unionSet:inBars];
}

// removing

-(void)removeBarsObject:(Bar *)inBar;
{
    [bars removeObject:inBar];
}

// OR...

-(void)removeBars:(NSSet *)inBars;
{
    [bars minusSet:inBars];
}

// intersect

-(void)intersectBars:(NSSet *)inBars;
{
    return [bars intersectSet:inBars];
}
```

Using KVC with structures and scalars

An important limitation when working with KVC is that all of the methods, `-valueForKey:`, `-setValueForKey:`, and so on, all take id as the type for both parameters and return values. For most attributes, this isn't a problem, because, for the most part, you work with objects when defining these attributes, and they can be manipulated by using the id datatype. However, when you have attributes that are structures or scalar types, variables like ints, floats, and so on, this presents a bit of a problem.

Specifically, the Objective-C runtime can't actually use these types of variables directly when using Key Value Coding. It actually has to convert these values from their native types into types that are full-fledged Objective-C objects.

Thankfully, Objective-C, for the most part, handles this for you. When accessing KVC attributes that are not objects, the Objective-C runtime automatically and transparently looks at the type of the variable being accessed, and will create an `NSNumber` or `NSValue` to wrap the value so that it can be used with KVC.

I discuss `NSNumbers` and `NSValues` in Part III of this book, however, for now, simply understand that these are special classes that enable you to wrap scalars and structures within them and treat them as Objective-C objects. This enables you to do things like storing them in arrays, storing them in dictionaries, and using them in KVC.

Again, Objective-C handles this for you automatically, but there is one edge condition that you need to be aware of. In the case where you use a KVC accessor to set a scalar value, but you pass nil as the value, there isn't a generic way that this can be handled in all cases automatically. As a result, in this specific case, the Objective-C runtime will instead call the method `-setNil ValueForKey:`. This method, by default, throws an exception. If needed, however, you can override this method in your class to do whatever may be appropriate. For example, you might define that passing a nil value for a particular variable on your class means that the value should be -1.0. In this case, you would simply override the `-setNilValueForKey:` method, check to see what the key is that's being passed in, if it matches the variable that you have defined should be -1.0 in the case of a nil, you can then simply create your own `NSNumber` instance and set the value yourself manually by using the `-setValue:forKey:` method.

Again, this is simply an edge condition. For the most part, the wrapping and unwrapping of scalars and structures to `NSNumbers` and `NSValues` is totally transparent. Even your own structures are handled automatically by using NSValue's `-getValue:` capabilty.

Searching objects for attributes

When accessing your KVC-compliant attributes, the runtime follows a specific set of rules to attempt to find the correct accessor for a given key path. Those rules are as follows.

When setting a value for a particular key, the runtime first searches the class for any accessor that matches the standard accessor pattern I've mentioned before, that is, `-set<ValueName>:`. If no accessor is found, your class can also implement the optional method `-access InstanceVariablesDirectly`, and return `YES`. In this example, the runtime then searches the class for any instance variables that follow the naming pattern of `_<valueName>`, `_is<valueName>`, `<valueName>`, or `is<valueName>`, in that order. If none of these apply, the method `-setValue:forUndefinedKey:` will be called. The default behavior for this method is to raise an exception.

When getting a value by using Key Value Coding, the runtime follows a similar procedure in finding the variable that a given key represents. Specifically, first it searches your class for an accessor whose name matches the pattern `-get<ValueName>`, `-<valueName>`, or `-is<ValueName>`, in that order. If it finds such an accessor, then it retrieves the value using it. If no accessor following these specifications can be found, it next attempts to determine if the value that you are trying to access is instead an array. To do this, it checks for methods which match the pattern `-countOf<ValueName>` and `-objectIn<ValueName>AtIndex:` and `-<valueName>AtIndexes:`. The existence of these array KVC accessors, indicates that the value being accessed is an array stored in a member variable. If these accessors are found, the runtime returns a proxy `NSArray` object containing proxy methods correlating to all of the above `accessors` it found. Accessing any of these methods on the `NSArray` object causes the corresponding accessor on the original object to be called instead.

Next, the runtime tries to determine if the value that you are trying to access is accessible as a set. To do this, it checks for the methods `-countOf<ValueName>`, `-enumeratorOf<ValueName>`, and `-memberOf<ValueName>:`. If all three of these methods are found, a proxy NSSet object is returned. When accessing this proxy object, if any of the aforementioned methods are called on the proxy object, they are automatically forwarded to the corresponding method on the original object.

Again, just like when setting values, if the class method `-accessInstanceVariables Directly` is implemented and returns `YES`, the runtime will search for member variables following the standard naming convention of `-_<valueName>`, `-_is<ValueName>`, `-<valueName>`, or `-is<ValueName>`. Also, just like setters, if it finds any of these member variables, it will access them directly.

Finally, if none of this works, the runtime will call the method `-valueForUndefinedKey:` just like when setting a value.

Observing Changes to KVC-Compliant Values

One of the neat Objective-C technologies that builds on Key Value Coding is Key Value Observing. Key Value Observing allows you to register as an observer of a given object and receive notification when specific properties on that object are changed. It's an incredibly powerful capability, and it is built into Objective-C at its very core.

Writing KVC accessors may seem like a lot of effort (though if you use properties, it's really not), but the great part is that if you create KVC compliant accessors for all of your class attributes, you get Key Value Observing totally for free.

Using KVO

Key Value Observing enables you to automatically observe changes on other objects. So, for example, you can use it to be notified when an object changes its state, such as when the user changes a setting by using the settings panel in your application. Using Key Value Observing, the Windows and objects that utilize the setting that the user just changed can automatically be notified that the user changed that value. You don't have to manually tell your other objects to update themselves. They automatically receive the new value and can take whatever action is appropriate. This is incredibly powerful. Settings are one of the most powerful uses of this technology, but additionally, things like core data and other technologies in the Cocoa frameworks take advantage of Key Value Observing to do a lot of the magical things that they do.

To use Key Value Observing, first, the object being observed must be using KVC-compliant accessors for the attributes that you want to observe. Second, the object that wishes to observe the changes, the Observer, must implement a special method to receive the notification of the change. That method is `-observeValue:forKeyPath:ofObject:change:context:`. This method is called when the value changes and can be configured to receive both the old value and the new value as well as other information defined by you.

Finally, the Observer asked to register with the observed object by calling the method `-add Observer:forKeyPath:options:context:`. Calling this method tells the object what KVC keypath it wishes to observe changes to, what changes it wants to see, and also provide a context object which it will receive back when it receives a notification of changes to that object.

After the observer has done this, any changes to the property specified by the keypath will automatically call the observer's callback method. When the observer is finished observing the observed object, it must also remove itself as an observer of that object. If you fail to do this and then allow the observer to be deallocated, then future notifications to the observer may cause your application to crash.

Registering as an observer

Registering as an observer is easy. Simply call the method `-addObserver:forKeyPath: options:context:` on the object that you want to observe. This is shown in Listing 6.14.

Listing 6.14

Adding an observer

```
[obj addObserver:self
     forKeyPath:@"memberVariable"
        options:(NSKeyValueObservingOptionNew |
                 NSKeyValueObservingOptionOld)
        context:NULL];
```

The Observer parameter is usually self, and is the object that receives the notification when the observed value changes. The key path parameter specifies the key path to the attribute for which you want to observe changes. The options parameter specifies a set of flags that tell KVO how you want the changes to be sent to you. These values are or'd together using the '|' operator. The possible values that can be passed here are shown in Table 6.2.

Table 6.2

Value	Purpose
NSKeyValueObservingOptionNew	Send the new value as part of the change information.
NSKeyValueObservingOptionOld	Send the old value as part of the change information.
NSKeyValueObservingOptionInitial	Send an initial update as soon as the observer is registered.
NSKeyValueObservingOptionPrior	Send separate updates before and after the change is made rather than only one update after the value has changed.

The context parameter is a `void *` parameter is passed unchanged through the KVO system and back to your object when the change notification occurs. Essentially, as far as KVO is concerned, this parameter is an opaque blob of data that is entirely implementation dependent. Whatever you want to pass in here is passed through unchanged.

NOTE

Remember when working with void * context parameters that there are special rules that apply for garbage collection and that is up to you to make sure that whatever data that void * is pointing to is still allocated and valid when you later need to access it. In other words, don't pass things that are stored on the stack into this parameter. That will cause a crash.

After you register as an observer, if you passed the flag `NSKeyValueObservingOption Initial`, you can get an initial notification of the initial value for the attribute that you're observing. Additionally, as the value changes over time, you receive notifications of those changes.

In order to receive those notifications, you have to implement the callback method shown in the next section.

Defining callbacks for KVO

The next step in using KVO is in writing the callback method for the Observer. Listing 6.15 shows an example implementation of the method `-observeValue:forKeyPath:of Object:change:context:`.

Listing 6.15

An example implementation of the KVO callback method.

```
-(void)observeValueForKeyPath:(NSString *)inKeyPath
                     ofObject:(id)inObject
                       change:(NSDictionary *)inChange
                      context:(void *)inCtx;
{
    if([inKeyPath isEqualToString:@"memberVariable"])
    {
        NSString *newValue = [inChange
              objectForKey:NSKeyValueChangeNewKey];
        // do something with the new value...
    }
    else if([inKeyPath isEqualToString:@"..."]) // etc...
    {

    }
    [super observeValueForKeyPath:inKeyPath
                         ofObject:inObject
                           change:inChange
                          context:inCtx];

}
```

As you can see in this method, the first thing that you have to do is to find out what attribute of the observed object is changed. The method is automatically passed an object parameter, which tells you what object is sending you the notification. By using the `-isEquals` method with the passed in value for the key path, you can determine exactly what attribute it was on the object that changed. The key parameter is nothing but a string, just like when you are using it with KVC. Therefore, you can use the `NSString` method `-isEqualToString:` to determine which key path this notification is for.

When you have determined what attribute on the object has changed, you can then take whatever appropriate action is necessary. The actual change is passed to you by the `change` parameter. This parameter is an `NSDictionary`, containing keys and values associated with whatever change information you requested when you registered as an observer. Those keys and values are shown in Table 6.3.

Table 6.3

Key	Value
NSKeyValueChangeKindKey	An NSNumber specifying the type of change.
NSKeyValueChangeNewKey	The new value.
NSKeyValueChangeOldKey	The old value.
NSKeyValueChangeIndexesKey	When NSKeyValueChangeKindKey is one of NSKeyValueChangeInsertion, NSKeyValueChangeRemoval, or NSKeyValueChangeReplacement, this value contains the indexes of the values changed.
NSKeyValueChangeNotificationIsPriorKey	Used in conjunction with the NSKeyValueChangeOptionPrior to indicate the "prior" notification.

As you can see, if you chose to receive both the old value and the new value, they are both provided to you inside the change parameter, accessible using the appropriate key. After you have retrieved the value from the change dictionary, you can use it in your object to do whatever is necessary.

Remember that KVC has to use objects for sending values — it cannot use scalars and structures directly. Therefore, if the value that you are observing is a scalar or a structure, the value that you will receive here will be an `NSNumber` or an `NSValue`, respectively. Therefore, you must use that value and extract the actual scale or value or structure value that you require, as needed. The example code shown above demonstrates this.

The NSKeyValueChangeKindKey specifies the kind of change you are receiving. The possible values are shown in Table 6.4.

Table 6.4

Value	Purpose
NSKeyValueChangeSetting	Specifies that the value is being set.
NSKeyValueChangeInsertion	Specifies that values are being inserted, as in a collection or one-to-many relationship.
NSKeyValueChangeRemoval	Specifies that values are being removed from a one-to-many relationship.
NSKeyValueChangeReplacement	Specifies that values are being replaced in a one-to-many relationship.

Removing an observer

Remember that after you are done observing changes to an object, you have to remember to remove yourself as an observer. If you don't, your application may crash.

NOTE

In a garbage-collected environment, crashes are not an issue if you forget to remove yourself as an observer. However, they can still be a good practice to do so anyway so that you get in the habit of it when you're not working in a garbage-collected environment.

To remove yourself as an observer, you simply call the method -removeObserver:forKeyPath:, passing the Observer as the first parameter, and the key path that you are observing as the second parameter. Listing 6.16 shows an example doing this in the dealloc method of the observer.

Listing 6.16

Removing an observer.

```
-(void)dealloc;
{
    [obj removeObserver:self forKeyPath:@"memberVariable"];
    [super dealloc];
}
```

Implementing manual notifications

All of these notifications happen automatically. All you need to do is use KVC compliant accessors for your properties and everything will work fine. Sometimes, you don't necessarily want to take advantage of the automatic notifications. Where you want to instead manually send notifications that you've just changed a value or set of values. For example, if you are about to make many changes at once, you may want to group up the notification and only send one notification. In these cases, you want to use manual notifications.

To use manual notifications, you must first override the class method `+automatically NotifiesObserversForKey:` to tell Objective-C that you do not want it to automatically notify observers of changes. You do this by returning NO for any keys for which you want to implement manual notification. An example of this is shown in Listing 6.17.

Listing 6.17

Overriding +automaticallyNotifiesObserversForKey:

```
+(BOOL)automaticallyNotifiesObserversForKey:(NSString *)inKey;
{
    if([inKey isEqualToString:@"memberVariable"])
        return NO;
    return YES;
}
```

When you actually want to perform a manual notification for change, you must call the method `-willChangeValueForKey:` prior to the change and then `-didChangeValueForKey:` after. An example of this is shown in Listing 6.18.

Listing 6.18

Implementing manual notifications

```
-(void)setMemberVariable:(CGFloat)inValue;
{
    [self willChangeValueForKey:@"memberVariable"];
    memberVariable = inValue;
    [self didChangeValueForKey:@"memberVariable"];
}
```

These calls can be nested when needed, in cases where you need to modify multiple variables in one call. There are corresponding calls for one to many relationships. These are -will Change:valuesAtIndexes:forKey: and -didChange:valuesForIndexes: forKey:.

Understanding risks with KVO

Using KVO is not without problems. Any time you let the computer just "do things" on its own, there's always the possibility that you might wind up with some unusual combination of factors that, once in a blue moon, may cause problems. KVO is not immune to this.

More specifically, the biggest risk factor that you have in using KVO is that, if observers are watching your every move, those observers can sometimes have side effects, and because you don't control those observers, you can't control those side effects either.

For the most part, this isn't an issue, but in one case this can cause problems. This case is when you use your accessors to free your member variables in your initializer or your dealloc method, as shown in Listing 6.19.

Listing 6.19

Using accessors to release member variables in your dealloc

```
-(void)dealloc
{
    [self setFoo:nil];
    [self setBar:nil];
    [super dealloc];
}
```

Writing your dealloc method like this is great! You can simultaneously release your member variable and set it to nil, all in one shot.

The problem is, when you're calling those accessors, the KVO observers will be receiving notifications of those changes. If they are not expecting to receive nil, or if they are expecting to be able to manipulate the object itself when the notification is received, bad things can happen.

Furthermore, if you can imagine an observer that when receiving a notification for a change to the bar variable, expects to be able to access the foo variable obviously, in this case, it would have a problem because the foo variable has already been deallocated and set to nil.

Apple's current recommendation is that you do not use accessors for initializing or deallocating member variables in your initializer or dealloc method. This is further complicated by the fact that under the 64-bit runtime is possible to declare properties that do not have member variables associated with them. In these cases, the only way to initialize and deallocate as member variables is by using their accessors.

In my code, I use accessors for initializing and deallocating member variables unless I know that doing so in a given circumstance will cause a problem. Also, when I implement a key value observer I ensure that the observer can properly handle nil values and I try to minimize any side effects.

If you feel that this is a risk worth taking, then feel free to write your initializers and dealloc method by using your accessors. Just be aware of the potential hazards involved, so that if and when you do encounter a problem, you know immediately where to look.

On the other hand, if you don't feel that you can ensure this with your observers, follow Apple's advice and do not use accessors in initializers and destructors unless you must.

Applying Key Value Observing

Now that you understand all the details of Key Value Coding and Key Value Observing, take a look at a small example application with a few classes. One of those classes will observe the other classes, and as it receives notifications of changes to the attributes on the observed classes, it will print out those changes to the console.

Listing 6.20 shows the first class in this application. This simple point class has a couple of properties, x, and y. Just put the interface into the interface file, and the implementation in an implementation file.

Listing 6.20

Interface and implementation of the MyPoint class.

```
// Interface - goes in MyPoint.h
#import <Cocoa/Cocoa.h>

@interface MyPoint : NSObject
{
    CGFloat x;
    CGFloat y;
}
@property CGFloat x;
@property CGFloat y;

@end
```

```
// implementation - goes in MyPoint.m
#import "MyPoint.h"

@implementation MyPoint
@synthesize x;
@synthesize y;

@end
```

Listing 6.21 shows the `Observer` class. This class will simply take a `MyPoint` and add itself as an observer. Nothing to it.

Listing 6.21

The Observer class

```
// Interface - goes in Observer.h
#import <Cocoa/Cocoa.h>
#import "MyPoint.h"

@interface Observer : NSObject
{
    MyPoint *point;
}
@property (retain) MyPoint *point;
-(id)initWithPoint:(MyPoint *)inPoint;
@end

// Implementation - goes in Observer.m
#import "Observer.h"

@implementation Observer
@synthesize point;

-(void)dealloc;
{
    [point removeObserver:self forKeyPath:@"x"];
    [point removeObserver:self forKeyPath:@"y"];
    [point release];
```

continued

Listing 6.21   *(continued)*

```
    point = nil;
    [super dealloc];
}

-(id)initWithPoint:(MyPoint *)inPoint;
{
    if(self = [super init])
    {
        point = [inPoint retain];
        [point addObserver:self forKeyPath:@"x"
                    options:(NSKeyValueObservingOptionNew|
                             NSKeyValueObservingOptionOld)
                    context:nil];
        [point addObserver:self forKeyPath:@"y"
                    options:(NSKeyValueObservingOptionNew|
                             NSKeyValueObservingOptionOld)
                    context:nil];
    }
    return self;
}

-(void)observeValueForKeyPath:(NSString *)keyPath
                     ofObject:(id)object
                       change:(NSDictionary *)change
                      context:(void *)context;
{
    NSNumber *oldValue = [change objectForKey:NSKeyValueChangeOldKey];
    NSNumber *newValue = [change objectForKey:NSKeyValueChangeNewKey];


    if(keyPath == @"x")
        NSLog(@"Value for X changed from: %f to %f",
              [oldValue floatValue],
              [newValue floatValue]);
    if(keyPath == @"y")
        NSLog(@"Value for Y changed from: %f to %f",
              [oldValue floatValue],
              [newValue floatValue]);
}

@end
```

Finally, the `main` function. Listing 6.22 shows this code.

Listing 6.22

The main function.

```
#import <Foundation/Foundation.h>
#import "Observer.h"
#import "MyPoint.h"

int main (int argc, const char * argv[])
{
    NSAutoreleasePool * pool = [[NSAutoreleasePool alloc] init];

    MyPoint *point = [[MyPoint alloc] init];
    Observer *observer = [[Observer alloc] initWithPoint:point];

    point.x = 42.0;
    point.y = 55.1;

    point.x = 4200.0;
    point.y = 5500.1;

    [observer release];
    [point release];

    [pool drain];
    return 0;
}
```

All it does is create the point, then creates the observer, passing it the point. Then it changes the values. All of the output happens inside the Observer class, and it's all automatic.

Go ahead and compile and run this application and see what I mean.

Summary

In this chapter, I've introduced you to Key Value Coding and Key Value Observing, two core technologies that Objective-C and the Cocoa and Cocoa Touch frameworks provide you. By using these capabilities, you can build application designs that are more flexible by not coupling disparate parts of the application too tightly. Loose coupling means more flexible designs, and KVO and KVC provide you with the tools needed to keep your application components loosely coupled.

Working with Protocols

Objective-C does not feature multiple inheritance, which has advantages as well as disadvantages. It is advantageous because multiple inheritance results in complicated issues that can be difficult to resolve. However, it is also a disadvantage because there are times when you want to have a class, which implements a specific interface without necessarily inheriting from the class that specifies that interface. Thankfully, the designers of Objective-C included a feature to address exactly this situation, protocols.

Essentially, a protocol defines an interface that can be implemented by multiple other classes without the use of inheritance. This enables you to mix and match functionality on a given class so that the class can be adapted to different uses.

Favoring Composition Over Inheritance

An object oriented design axiom known as "favor composition over inheritance" means that rather than always turning to inheritance as a tool for extending functionality of a given class, you should instead first try to solve the problem by using other classes compositionally within your class. For example, if you needed to implement a class that provided an interface between a network service and your application, instead of inheriting from a socket class (a class that gives you access to network resources), you should include another object in your class, which provides that network connectivity. You should "compose" your design from other reusable components. Building your designs in this way results in more flexibility, because those bits and pieces that you are composing together to solve a given problem can later be swapped out and changed to solve another problem. This is an incredibly powerful design philosophy and one which you should strive for in your code.

It is certainly possible to follow this design philosophy simply by using standard object oriented techniques. However, designing components for reuse causes complications.

In This Chapter

Solving object-oriented design problems with protocols

Implementing protocols for your classes

Adopting protocols

Working with optional methods

Understanding formal versus informal protocols

Figure 7.1 shows a class diagram describing the relationships between a class, which holds business logic and a class provided for network connectivity. This is a classic "compositional" design.

The idea here is that the NetworkConnector class provides all the interaction with the network server. It connects, disconnects, and sends and receives data. The BusinessLogic class takes the data that the NetworkConnector receives, and it decides where in the application that data needs to go.

Figure 7.1

Tightly coupled BusinessLogic and NetworkConnector.

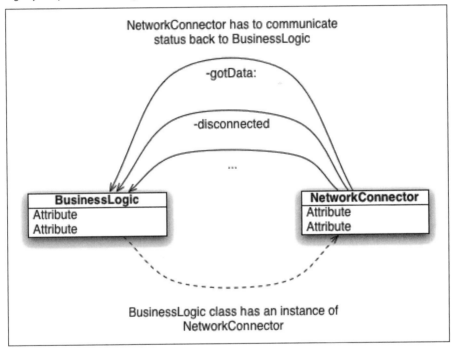

The problem arises when you have to talk from the NetworkConnector class back to the BusinessLogic class, for example when receiving data. Network connectivity is an incredibly generic concept. Something you could definitely reuse in other applications, or even in the same application in different locations. If you want to design the network class in a completely generic way so that the network class can be reused over and over again, you have to design it so that it is not in any way tightly coupled to its client classes, in other words the BusinessLogic class.

You can't have the NetworkConnector requiring the BusinessLogic class as a dependency because you can't always count on the existence of the BusinessLogic class being the class that's using your NetworkConnector.

One way to solve this using inheritance is to force the `BusinessLogic` class to inherit from some parent class which the `NetworkConnector` class can rely upon. This is shown in Figure 7.2.

Figure 7.2

`BusinessLogic` class inheriting from generic `NetworkClient` class.

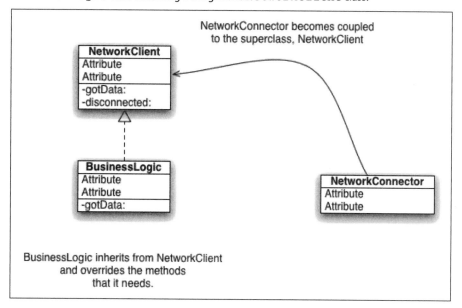

In this situation, you are limiting the developer of the client class by forcing them to inherit from a particular parent. If that parent class doesn't smoothly fit into that developer's object hierarchy, then this can present significant design problems. For example, imagine that the `BusinessLogic` class needed to both communicate with the network, as well as communicate with a disk I/O system that had a similar callback mechanism. Using straight inheritance such as this simply won't work in that situation.

Understanding why you don't need (or want) multiple inheritance

Some languages, such as C++, solve this kind of problem through multiple inheritance. Figure 7.3 shows an example of how you might solve the network communication problem in C++.

The problem with multiple inheritance is typically referred to as the "diamond problem" and is illustrated in Figure 7.4.

Figure 7.3

Using multiple inheritance.

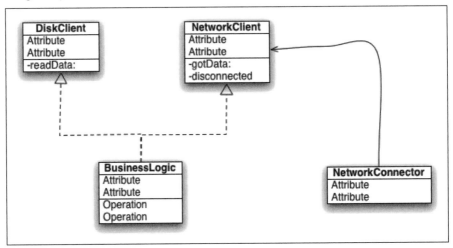

As you can see in the class diagram, the main problem with multiple inheritance arises from the fact that it is possible to inherit from two different classes (above, class D inheriting from classes B and C), which both inherit from a common superclass (class A). In this situation, an ambiguity can occur wherein a method on the class A is called on an instance of class D. In this situation, if class D has not overridden that method and provided its own implementation, which superclass method should be called, B or C?

Because of this problem, multiple inheritance is simply not something that Objective-C provides. If you only have single inheritance, then you don't have to worry about the diamond problem.

Understanding how protocols solve the problem

Protocols solve the problem by enabling you to declare an interface, which a class implements without providing any default implementation of that interface. Protocols do not provide a mechanism for specifying the implementation of the methods within them. They only provide a mechanism for declaring the interface for those methods. Rather than making a reusable component depend on a specific class implementation, you can instead make that component depend on the existence of the interface in the form of a protocol. Classes that implement a given protocol are expected to provide their own implementations of the methods specified in the protocol declaration. By implementing protocols in this manner, you enable classes to be written so that they depend only on an interface existence while at the same time removing the ambiguity question because any class that declares that it implements a given interface must also implement the methods in question. There is no "diamond problem" because any protocol that you declare and support has to have an implementation in your class.

Figure 7.4

The diamond problem.

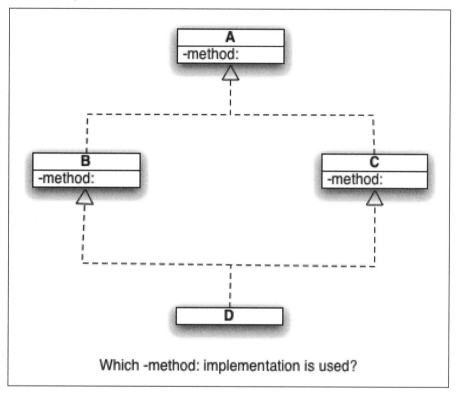

Which -method: implementation is used?

From an object-oriented design point of view, the class diagram for this solution looks nearly identical to that of multiple-inheritance, but it doesn't allow for the problems that multiple inheritance invariably brings with it.

This solution is not unique to Objective-C. Java, which in a lot of ways was based on Objective-C, also implements a similar concept using its version of protocols called interfaces. If you are coming to Objective-C from a Java background, the concept of protocols and interfaces is very similar, and you should feel right at home.

Documenting an expected interface for others to implement

Another way to think about protocols is to imagine that you are documenting an expected interface for others to implement. In the NetworkConnector example, we are documenting all of the different conditions for which the network class might need assistance from the developer in terms of determining what to do in these situations.

For example, if the `NetworkConnector` receives data from the network, it is reasonable to assume that the application itself contains whatever knowledge (the business logic) is necessary to determine what to do with that data. In other words, there is no generic way to say "when I receive data, here's what I'm going to do with it." You really have to ask the rest of the application "I just got some data, what do you want me to do with it?" It is these kinds of situations where protocols are perfectly and uniquely suited. You can declare a protocol for all of the different unresolved questions ("I got data, what do I do with it?" - "I got disconnected should I reconnect?!") that your generic component needs to be able to delegate to a higher authority.

By declaring these different "questions," you are establishing a clear and precise contract that users of your class can then fulfill. When they fulfill this contract by implementing the protocol, they will know all of the different situations that they will need to be prepared to handle. This system is much more flexible than any system involving return codes, exceptions, and so on. It's even more powerful than simply generic callbacks, because of the uniquely verbose nature of Objective-C method declarations and how the act of declaring a clear and obvious protocol becomes a self-documenting callback API for your reusable components. If you think about it in this way, the term "protocol" actually makes more sense than "interface" because a "protocol" can be thought of as an agreed upon code of procedure or behavior, as in diplomacy and etiquette.

So, enough theory, now you can get your hands dirty with some code.

Implementing Protocols in Your Objects

Using protocols is very straightforward, and follows many of the same syntax conventions that you've already seen when working with classes.

Essentially, you first have to create the protocol declaration. You can do this in an existing interface file, in the case where you are declaring a protocol for use with an already existing object, like in our previous discussion with the `NetworkClient`, or in its own separate interface file in cases where you might be using this protocol for many different purposes. The protocol itself only declares an interface and does not provide an implementation whatsoever. Because of this, if you are creating a separate .h file for your protocol declaration, you do not need to provide any .m file at all. The interface in the .h file is sufficient.

After you have declared your protocol, for any classes which implement that protocol, they should also declare that they implement it. This is so that the compiler can verify that the class in question is implementing all of the methods required for the program.

N O T E

It is not actually absolutely necessary to declare that your class implements a protocol that it supports. As we discuss shortly, some types of protocols do not need to be declared at all. Additionally, your class can choose simply to implement the protocol methods rather than declaring its support. In these cases, the compiler will not be able to determine if your class supports the protocol at compile time, so you will have to do extra work at runtime to ensure that any objects upon which you are calling the protocol methods actually implements them. This can, however, result in a compiler warning if another class declares that it expects your class to implement the protocol.

When you reference objects in your code, which are expected to implement a given protocol, there is a special syntax that you can use in the type declaration of that object to show that, although you may not know what the actual class of the object is, you expect it to implement a given protocol. If the protocol is a formal protocol, any object that is stored in that variable is checked at compile time to determine if it implements all of the required methods for that protocol. If it does not, a warning is raised.

Protocols can have both required and optional methods. In cases where you have optional methods, an object that implements the protocol may not necessarily implement one of its optional methods. In this situation, you are expected to check to verify that the object in question is implementing the optional method before you attempt to call it. If you attempt to call an optional method and the object does not implement that method, then you will get an exception.

Declaring a protocol

Declaring the protocol follows many of the same syntactical standards that you've already come to recognize. Superficially, it most resembles declaring a class. You begin a protocol declaration by using the keyword `@protocol`, followed by the name of the protocol you are declaring. Protocols do not by default inherit from each other or from classes, but if you want to inherit from another protocol you can, optionally, by providing the name of protocols that you inherit from enclosed in angle brackets <> after the name of the protocol you are declaring. When you do this, classes implementing your protocol must implement not only the protocol methods that you declare but also the protocol methods of any protocols that you inherit from. After the `@protocol` declaration, you then declare any methods that are required for your protocol. Declare these just as if you were declaring methods on a class.

Inside the protocol definition itself, where you are declaring your protocol methods, two key words can be used. The first is the `@required` key word. This keyword dictates that all of the following methods are required methods for implementations of this protocol. This is the default behavior of a formal protocol, so if you do not specify the `@required` key word, then all methods declared in the protocol default to required status.

The second keyword that is usable within the `@protocol` declaration is the `@optional` keyword. This is used to indicate methods that are optional for the implementing classes to implement. Classes that implement this protocol can choose not to implement any methods declared after the `@optional` keyword.

At the end of the protocol declaration, just like with the class, you end the protocol declaration with the `@end` keyword. An example protocol declaration for our `NetworkClient` class that we discussed previously is shown in Listing 7.1

Listing 7.1

Example protocol declaration

```
@protocol NetworkClient
-(void)networkConnector:(NetworkConnector *)inNetConnector
            gotData:(NSData *)inData;
@optional
-(void)networkConnectorDisconnected:(NetworkConnector *)inNetConnector;
@end
```

NOTE

This protocol shows the delegate pattern at work, which is why the first parameter is the object sending the message. I go over more about that in Chapter 17.

Again, if you wanted to derive your protocol from another preexisting protocol, for example, to extend that preexisting protocol, you can do that by having your protocol extend or inherit from that preexisting protocol, as shown in Listing 7.2.

Listing 7.2

NetworkClient extending the IOClient protocol

```
@protocol NetworkClient <IOClient>
-(void)networkConnector:(NetworkConnector *)inNetConnector
            gotData:(NSData *)inData;
@optional
-(void)networkConnectorDisconnected:(NetworkConnector *)inNetConnector;
@end
```

Protocols are incapable of having member variables. Therefore, there is no place in the protocol declaration to declare member variables. Do not confuse this with the idea that a protocol can't access member variables, it certainly can, but that's a detail that is specific to the implementation of the protocol and not part of declaring the protocol itself. When you implement the methods of the protocol on whatever class has adopted it, you can certainly use any member variables declared in the header of that particular class.

Declaring that a class implements a protocol

To declare that a class implements a specific protocol you simply place the protocol name inside angle brackets after the superclass in the class declaration. For example, Listing 7.3 shows an example class implementing the protocol from the previous section.

Listing 7.3

A class implementing the NetworkClient protocol

```
@class BusinessLogic : NSObject <NetworkClient>
{
    // member variables
    NSString *someMemberVariable;
}
-(id)init;
@end
```

Classes can implement more than one protocol simultaneously. When doing this, you simply list the different protocols inside the angle brackets separated by commas, as shown in Listing 7.4.

Listing 7.4

A class implementing multiple protocols

```
@class BusinessLogic : NSObject <NetworkClient, DiskClient>
{
    // member variables
    NSString *someMemberVariable;
}
-(id)init;
@end
```

In this case, the `BusinessLogic` is being said to implement both the `NetworkClient` and `DiskClient` protocols.

Though you must import the header file for the protocol declaration, you do not need to declare the protocol methods in your interface as well. Simply declaring that you implement the protocol is enough information to tell the compiler what methods to expect to find in your implementation.

NOTE

Categories, which are described in Chapter 8, can also declare that they implement a protocol, just like classes.

Declaring an object that must implement a protocol

When declaring an instance variable that is expected to implement a given protocol, typically you use the `id` datatype so that any object can be stored in the variable. If you want to have the compiler verify that the required protocol methods are in fact implemented on whatever object you are actually storing in the variable, then you must also tell this to the compiler by specifying the protocol type information along with the datatype. To do this, in addition to the `id` datatype, you also specify the protocol you expect the object to adhere to after the id keyword, in angle brackets, as shown in Listing 7.5.

Listing 7.5

Declaring a variable which implements a specific protocol

```
id<NetworkClient> *delegate;
```

In this case, the delegate object is being defined as adopting the `NetworkClient` protocol, and thus will be expected, by the compiler, to implement the appropriate required methods from that protocol.

Anywhere you are expected to declare a variable datatype, you can use this syntax. This includes method declarations, variable declarations, return types, and so on.

NOTE

In those rare cases where you have not declared that your variable must implement a specific protocol, but you do require it, you can force the compiler to assume that a given object does implement a given protocol by typecasting it. To typecast a given variable to a given protocol, you actually typecast it to (`id<SomeProtocol>`). This isn't required if you specify your protocols as part of your variable declarations, as is generally recommended.

Exploring formal and informal protocols

I've mentioned it briefly before, but it bears further discussion here before we deal with how you handle optional methods.

There are, in fact, two different kinds of protocols, formal and informal. Informal protocols are the older style of protocols that are still used in part of cocoa and Objective-C. Informal protocols do not require a formal protocol declaration as I've shown you so far in this chapter. Informal protocols are typically declared as categories on the `NSObject` class. I discuss categories in the next chapter, so I won't go into a great amount of detail here.

Because of the greater type safety that formal protocols provide and because of the fact that formal protocols have the `@optional` keyword that enables you to selectively mark individual methods as optional, generally speaking, formal protocols are the preferred way to create new protocols in your code.

Typically, the only place that you are likely to run into informal protocols today is when you are working with older frameworks, such as portions of the Cocoa frameworks themselves.

You can recognize these circumstances, because rather than the documentation pointing you to a formal document declaring and documenting the interface that you are expected to implement, typically you will see these protocol methods documented as part of the class that you are actually using. For example, the Cocoa class NSURLConnection uses an informal protocol for its delegate methods. If you look at the documentation for that class, you'll see that the delegate methods themselves are actually documented in the documentation on the NSURLConnection class itself. They are marked "delegate." Contrast this with the Cocoa Touch class, SKPayment Queue, which was recently added for in-app purchase support on iPhone. It separates its delegate methods into a formal protocol by using the SKPaymentTransactionObserver protocol.

When needing to implement an informal protocol in one of your classes, you do not need to declare that your class implements the protocol in its declaration as you would normally with a formal protocol. Instead, you simply implement the methods that you choose to implement, and if they are available, classes that need to use your object will call them.

When working with informal protocols, all the methods in the protocol are optional, so you need to verify that the object in question implements them before you call them. I explain how to do this in the next section.

Determining if an object implements optional methods

Within your code, you can determine if a given class implements a specific protocol by using the object method -conformsToProtocol:. The method, which is called using the object in question, takes one parameter, which is expected to be a protocol object. To get the protocol object for a specific protocol, you use the built-in Objective-C directive @protocol(). This is different from the @protocol directive that you used in declaring your protocol, in that it takes a parameter inside parentheses, which is the name of the protocol that you want to get the object for.

So, for example, to determine if a given object adheres to our NetworkClient protocol, you would do something like Listing 7.6.

Listing 7.6

Determining if an object adheres to the NetworkClient protocol at runtime.

```
-(void)receivedData:(NSData *)inData;
{
    if([delegate conformsToProtocol:@protocol(NetworkClient)])
        [delegate networkConnector:self gotData:inData];
    // else do something else...
}
```

Typically, you would only need to do this in cases where you did not specify the type of the protocol as part of the datatype for the variable in question. If you had specified the protocol is part of the datatype for the variable then the compiler would have flagged this variable for you if it did not implement the protocol required.

NOTE

The `-conformsToProtocol:` method shown in Listing 7.6 only works with formal protocols. If you're using an informal protocol, use the `NSObject` method `-respondsToSelector:` as shown in Listing 7.7 instead.

Even when you are certain that a given object implements a given protocol, there is still the possibility that the object may not implement any of the optional methods of the protocol.

Remember, if an object does not implement an optional method and you call that method on that object, then your application will crash. Therefore, you need a way to determine if that object actually implements an optional method before you attempt to call it.

Fortunately, `NSObject`, which all objects inherit from, has a method which does exactly this. This method is `-respondsToSelector:` and it takes as a parameter a selector object.

Just like with the protocol object, a special directive can be used to convert a method signature into a selector object. That directive is the `@selector()` directive. Its use, along with the `-respondsToSelector:` method, is shown in Listing 7.7.

Listing 7.7

Testing to determine if an object implements an optional method

```
-(void)disconnected;
{
    if([delegate respondsToSelector:@selector(networkConnectorDisconnected:)])
    [delegate networkConnectorDisconnected:self];

    // else implement some default behavior...
}
```

In this example, you first check to see if the object which implements the protocol in fact implements one of the optional methods using the call `-respondsToSelector:`. If it does, then it goes ahead and calls that method. If it does not, you can choose to either do nothing, or to implement some kind of default behavior instead.

Avoiding Circular Protocol Dependencies

Protocols can refer to other protocols within their own declarations. For example, imagine a protocol which requires another protocol for use as a parameter to one of its methods, as shown in Listing 7.8.

Listing 7.8

A protocol requiring another protocol

```
@protocol Foo
-(void)someMethodRequiringBar:(id<Bar>)inBar;
@end
```

If the required protocol (`Bar`) also requires the original protocol (`Foo`), as shown in Listing 7.9, then a circular dependency is created between the two protocols. This generates a compiler error.

Listing 7.9

The Bar protocol, which requires the Foo protocol

```
@protocol Bar
-(void)someMethodRequiringFoo:(id<Foo>)inFoo;
@end
```

To resolve this problem, you can give a forward declaration of the required protocol which enables you to not include the file for the protocol that is required. For example, to prevent this circular dependency, you can add to the `Bar.h` interface file, the directive `@protocol Foo;` instead of importing the `Foo.h` file. This is shown in Listing 7.10.

Listing 7.10

A corrected version of the Bar protocol.

```
@protocol Foo;
@protocol Bar
-(void)someMethodRequiringFoo:(id<Foo>)inFoo;
@end
```

This occurrence is rare, but it's important to know that you have this tool available to you if needed. By adding the `@protocol Foo` directive above the Bar protocol declaration, you are telling the compiler "Trust me, `Foo` is a protocol, and I'll include it in my compilation, but I'm not importing the `Foo.h` here."

Exploring examples of protocol use

Protocols are used throughout Objective-C when working with application frameworks, such as Cocoa and Cocoa Touch. The biggest area of use is in delegation and datasource objects. Often, these are cases where the delegating object requires information at runtime that can't be determined in a generic way, such as what columns to display in a given table view. Alternatively, they're also used in cases where some process needs to happen in the background. You might call a method like `-start`, which returns immediately, and then receive a callback on a delegate protocol method telling you that the process has completed.

Just to give you an example of this in action, take a look at Listing 7.11. In this code, the application is creating an `NSURLConnection`, and firing it off. Later, as the data comes back from the URL request, it receives notice of that data via the protocol method `-connection:didReceiveData:`.

Listing 7.11

A class using an `NSURLConnection` **and implementing the** `NSURLConnection` **delegate protocol methods**

```
@implementation NetworkConnector
-(id)init
{
    if(self = [super init])
    {
     NSURL *url = [NSURL URLWithString:@"http://www.google.com"];
     NSURLRequest *req = [NSURLRequest requestWithURL:url];

     connection = [[NSURLConnection alloc] initWithRequest:req

    delegate:self startImmediately:YES];
    }
    return self;
}
// protocol methods
(void)connection:(NSURLConnection *)connection
     didReceiveData:(NSData *)inData
    {
```

```
    [data appendData:inData];
}
- (void)connectionDidFinishLoading:(NSURLConnection *)connection
{
    // do something with all that data!
}
@end
```

Summary

In this chapter, you learned about a powerful decoupling mechanism in Objective-C, protocols. Protocols enable you to write code that is more reusable by allowing you to keep your components decoupled from specific implementations. Using protocols, you can simply say "I don't care what type of object you are, as long as you implement this interface, I'll talk to you." Protocols are really one of the key technologies in Objective-C that make it different, and better, than most other languages.

Extending Existing Class Capabilities

No matter how well designed a class or framework is, inevitably, there will always be circumstances that you will encounter that the framework designer did not anticipate. Some developers go so far as to say that you should not plan for reusability in your code because at the end of the day, it is so difficult to achieve true universal reusability. I disagree with this notion, and I think that Objective-C provides some of the best tools for fostering reusability of any language available today.

In this chapter, I'm going to delve into some of the most powerful of those tools. While not completely unique to Objective-C, they are certainly examples of how the dynamism of Objective-C enables more flexibility and reuse than almost any other compiled language.

The technologies that I explain in this chapter center on the ability to extend the functionality of existing classes.

Working with Third-Party Frameworks and Classes

If you've worked with any kind of programming frameworks at all in the past, you've probably run into a situation in which existing classes that are provided by the standard library of the language give you about 90 percent of the functionality that you're looking for, but not the final 10 percent of the functionality that you really need. For example, you might have a string class, which doesn't provide a regular expression search.

Because these frameworks are built by a third-party, usually you don't have access to the source code of those frameworks. Because of this, changing the existing framework itself to add that additional 10 percent of functionality is not an option. Even in cases in which you do have access to the source code, it would be an extremely bad practice to have to distribute a modified, custom version of a standard library with your application.

In This Chapter

Extending existing classes with categories

Exposing private APIs using anonymous categories

Adding variables to classes using associative references

Another option that you might consider, would be to inherit from the existing class, creating your own custom version of whatever class is that you need to change. By doing this, you could add whatever functionality you wanted to in your custom version of that class.

On the surface, this seems like it might be a good idea, and indeed, many new object oriented developers would jump on this opportunity as being the logical way to solve this problem. However, in practice, this actually leads to other problems. Specifically, other readers of your code may have difficulty grasping your intent. They might ask themselves why you created a custom string class. If you are only adding a few methods, creating a custom subclass is probably overkill.

The amount of confusion caused by your custom string class probably outweighs the benefit. Additionally, merging disparate subclasses from different code bases can be complicated and fraught with error. Imagine two different code bases with two slightly different subclasses of NSString. Imagine now that you want to use part of the functionality from the first code base and part of the functionality from the second code base. Aside from just the difficulty of merging the two NSString subclasses, if the two classes have different names then one or the other of the two code bases will have to be extensively edited in order to use the new, combined NSString class.

Metaphorically speaking, using subclasses in order to extend existing classes, in some cases, is akin to requiring that someone have a completely custom-built automobile delivered directly from the factory whenever the customer simply requires a different type of hubcaps.

I'm not trying to say that subclassing is inappropriate in all cases. In certain cases, subclassing is absolutely the right solution to a reusability problem. However, revisiting the object oriented development axiom that I mentioned in the last chapter, "favor composition over inheritance," it's easy to see that classes, when designed like automobiles, with reusable and replaceable parts, results in greater flexibility and greater customizability for anyone who has to reuse that class.

So, all that being said, let me introduce you to some parts of Objective-C that enable you to bolt on functionality from outside the classes without having access to source code and without subclassing.

Working with Categories

The first technology that I want to talk about is called categories. Categories enable you to extend the functionality of existing classes by declaring and implementing methods on those classes, which then become usable throughout your application anywhere the original class is used.

This may sound cool, just on the surface, but what makes it even cooler is that when declaring a category, you do not need to have access to the original source code of the class that you are extending. Furthermore, a category is not a subclass. Meaning, the methods that you are adding are actually being added to the implementation of the class that you are directly manipulating. Any users of that class in your application will have access to those methods on instances of that class simply by virtue of you declaring a category on it.

Although it is considered poor form to do so, you can use categories to override existing methods. When doing this, even third-party libraries will call your modified method when referencing the class in question instead of the original.

If you're coming to Objective-C from another dynamic language such as Ruby or Smalltalk, you may be familiar with the concept of mixins. Mixins and categories share a lot in common, and you could even say that categories are the Objective-C version of a mixin.

Declaring categories

Categories are declared similarly to how you declare class interfaces. Meaning, you declare a category by first typing @interface and then the class name that you wish to modify. After the class name, instead of the superclass, as in the case of declaring a class, you put the name of the category that you are declaring inside parentheses. Listing 8.1 shows an example category declared on the NSMutableString class.

Listing 8.1

An example category on NSMutableString adding the ability to insert a GUID into the string

```
#import <Foundation/Foundation.h>

@interface NSMutableString (GUID)

-(void)appendGuid;

@end
```

In this particular code, I'm adding a category to the NSMutableString class that will generate a globally unique identifier (GUID). For now, this category simply appends the GUID onto the end of whatever string is there.

Implementing category methods

Unlike protocols, simply declaring the interface of the category is not enough, because you are actually adding the implementation of the method to the class that you are modifying. This means that in addition to declaring the interface of your category, you must also add the implementation for the methods in question. Listing 8.2 shows the implementation for the methods that I just declared for the NSMutableString class in the previous section. Notice that the @ implementation line, just like when declaring a class, tells the class name that you are creating an implementation for, in this case, NSMutableString, again followed by the category name in parentheses.

Listing 8.2

Implementation for the GUID category on NSMutableString

```
#import "NSMutableString+GUID.h"


@implementation NSMutableString (GUID)

-(void)appendGuid
{
    CFUUIDRef uuid = CFUUIDCreate(kCFAllocatorDefault);
    NSString *str =
        (NSString *)CFUUIDCreateString(kCFAllocatorDefault, uuid);
    [self appendString:str];
    CFRelease(uuid);
}

@end
```

Just like defining methods on a class implementation, you define methods in a category inside the implementation block. These methods have access to all member variables in the class, can call other methods on the class using self, and can even call methods on the superclass using the super keyword.

The only limitation is that you cannot declare new member variables as part of your category. There is a way to add variables to existing classes, which I will show you later in this chapter, but categories are not able to do so.

Declaring categories in header files

Categories are typically declared in .h and .m files just like classes. In some cases, it can be convenient to group similar functionality for different extended classes in one file. For example, if you have multiple classes that you need to extend with similar functionality. By grouping them together in a single .h/.m unit, you are conceptually segregating that functionality together. If, in the future, you need to change that functionality, all of the similar methods, albeit for different classes, are located in a single file.

Using a category

Simply declaring and defining a category makes the methods of that category available anywhere that the extended class is used. However, the compiler still needs to be told that the methods of the category exist to avoid it generating a warning at compile time.

To do this, you simply include your .h file containing the category declaration in whatever .m file uses the methods of the category.

In other words, in order to use the GUID category I have to include its .h file in any compilation unit that I use it in, for example, the main.m file shown in Listing 8.3.

Listing 8.3

Using the GUID **category**

```
#import <Foundation/Foundation.h>
#import "NSMutableString+GUID.h"

int main (int argc, const char * argv[])
{
    NSAutoreleasePool * pool = [[NSAutoreleasePool alloc] init];

    NSMutableString *aString = [NSMutableString string];

    [aString appendGuid];

    NSLog(@"The guid: %@", aString);

    [pool drain];
    return 0;
}
```

Once I've included the header file, I can simply use the methods just like if they were actually declared on the original class.

Breaking up functionality using categories

Another convenience that categories provide you is the ability to extract components of functionality from classes that have grown too large. In these cases, you might have a class containing a lot of code. Large class files can quickly become unwieldy when you need to modify them. Searching through lots of source code to find the method that you need to change can be made easier by extracting discrete parts of the functionality of the class into categories. In this way, when you go to make a change to a given class that impacts just a portion of its functionality, you can have all of the methods relating to that functionality in one category file, making it easier to make your changes.

Obviously, you should try to keep your classes as simple as possible. You shouldn't use a category as excuse for adding excessive extra features to a given class. However, classes do have a tendency to grow orthogonally, and it's nice to know that you have this tool available to you when the time comes for refactoring.

Extending class methods

Categories are not limited to object methods. You can also use them to add class methods. For example, if you wanted to add a factory method to NSMutableString for the GUID category, you could simply add the factory method as shown in Listing 8.4.

Listing 8.4

Adding a factory method to NSMutableString

```
#import <Foundation/Foundation.h>

@interface NSMutableString (GUID)

-(void)appendGuid;
+(id)stringWithGuid;

@end


@implementation NSMutableString (GUID)

-(void)appendGuid
{
```

```
    CFUUIDRef uuid = CFUUIDCreate(kCFAllocatorDefault);
    NSString *str = (NSString *)CFUUIDCreateString(kCFAllocatorDefault, uuid);
    [self appendString:str];
    CFRelease(uuid);
}

+(id)stringWithGuid;
{
    NSMutableString *ret = [self string];
    [ret appendGuid];
    return ret;
}

@end
```

Again, all of the same rules apply here in terms of referencing the class versus the object, the keyword self in a class method refers to the class object, whereas self refers to the instance object when working inside an object method. As before, you can use the class method as though it were declared on the original class, as shown in the updated main file in Listing 8.5.

Listing 8.5

The updated main function

```
#import <Foundation/Foundation.h>
#import "NSMutableString+GUID.h"

int main (int argc, const char * argv[])
{
    NSAutoreleasePool * pool = [[NSAutoreleasePool alloc] init];

    NSMutableString *aString = [NSMutableString stringWithGuid];

    NSLog(@"The guid: %@", aString);

    [pool drain];
    return 0;
}
@end


@implementation NSMutableString (GUID)
```

continued

Listing 8.5   *(continued)*

```
-(void)appendGuid
{
    CFUUIDRef uuid = CFUUIDCreate(kCFAllocatorDefault);
    NSString *str =
        (NSString *)CFUUIDCreateString(kCFAllocatorDefault, uuid);
    [self appendString:str];
    CFRelease(uuid);
}

+(id)stringWithGuid;
{
    NSMutableString *ret = [self string];
    [ret appendGuid];
    return ret;
}

@end
```

Exploring category limitations

Categories do have certain limitations associated with them. Categories cannot add any member variables to the extended class. They can absolutely declare and use local variables within the scope of the category methods, and they can certainly use global variables, or any variables passed into them as parameters, but they cannot add any member variables to the class.

Categories can call superclass methods by using the super keyword. However, there is no mechanism in place to allow a category to call the original implementation of a method that the category itself is overriding. In other words, if you override an existing object method by using a category, there is no way for you to call the original existing object method.

Recall that when I talked about the dangers of multiple inheritance when I described how to create protocols, that the problem was that if two superclasses defined implementations of the same method, the compiler would have difficulty in determining which implementation to call in a given circumstance. This problem does not affect protocols, because the protocol is simply a declaration of an interface and not an implementation. Categories on the other hand are not so lucky.

Just like in the case of multiple inheritance, if two categories define the same method on the same class, which method actually gets called at runtime is undefined. As a result, you should always avoid this. You may even want to consider adopting a unique method naming prefix system to avoid conflicting with other categories, such as prefixing your method names with your initials. For example, I might use `-jdAppendGuid:` instead of just `-appendGuid:`.

You also need to be careful with naming your methods when you're extending a system framework. Remember that Apple is constantly enhancing their own frameworks, and they might add a method named the same as yours. The other methods in the framework might rely on the implementation Apple provides, so your method might cause Apple's code to break. So when possible, you should also use prefixes for your category method names to avoid this kind of problem.

Implementing protocols with categories

I introduce protocols in Chapter 7. In that chapter, I touch on the concept of informal protocols. An informal protocol is a protocol that is actually implemented as a category defined on `NSObject`. When doing so, the given protocol declaration does not actually require a corresponding implementation. In other words, you can simply declare the protocol interface as a category on `NSObject`, but you need not actually provide the implementation of the methods for that category. Adopters of the informal protocol must provide the actual implementation of the given methods.

Because of its unique place in the object hierarchy, `NSObject` is usually the class upon which these protocols are defined. Your implementing class always inherits from `NSObject`, so any categories declared upon it are available as part of your interface to be implemented at your option.

Understanding the dangers of creating categories on NSObject

Unfortunately, there are also risks associated with declaring categories on `NSObject` in particular. You must be aware that any category method you declare on `NSObject` becomes part of the interface and, if implemented, the implementation of every class in the runtime. In some cases, this can actually affect behavior of the system by virtue of the fact that some classes change their behavior based on the existence of specific methods. Therefore, if you create a category which implements a method that falls under this umbrella, you could inadvertently affect behavior in parts of the system that you did not expect. Remember, when you declare a category on the class, that category becomes available throughout your application even to the foundation frameworks.

Another risk to be aware of when declaring a category on `NSObject` is the fact that `NSObject` has no superclass. Therefore, if you call super, it may compile, but it will certainly result in a runtime error.

NSObject is a "special class" in that it provides certain functionality to the runtime that other classes do not. The end result of this is that the NSObject class, speaking about the class object itself and not the class definition, is capable of calling object methods. It is the only class in Objective-C that is able to do this. In order to do this, NSObject does some unusual voodoo with the self object. Therefore, self, when used within the context of a category defined on NSObject, they refer to the class or the object.

Because of these hazards, generally speaking, you should only declare categories on NSObject in the form of interfaces alone and did not provide implementations. The category implementations should probably be limited to subclasses. Although the capability exists to provide implementations for NSObject categories, for the most part, expect that categories on NSObject will only be used for the purposes of declaring informal protocols.

Extending Classes using Anonymous Categories

Although Objective-C does not have a mechanism for declaring private methods baked into the class declaration syntax, there is a way of defining a private API, which you exposed only to privileged users of your class and not to others using categories.

The tool that you use to do this is called an anonymous category. Essentially, an anonymous category is a category declared on a given class without a name. That is, when you declare the category, rather than placing the name of the category inside parentheses after the category name, the parentheses are there, but they are left empty. When working with anonymous categories, you declare only the interface, but not the implementation as part of the category itself. Typically, you place this category declaration in another header file that can be imported by users of your class that have access to the private API. The implementation is done inside the implementation of the original class. You are simply creating a mechanism for accessing that implementation externally.

What this gives you is the ability to have a method which is declared as part of the private API in the anonymous category but which is not part of your public API in your public class declaration. When the anonymous category interface is imported, the compiler will then expect that the methods declared in the anonymous category interface will be implemented by the extended class. Therefore, this also provides a method for you to have a declared, compilation time checked API, which is private and invisible to users of your class unless they know to include the private API category header.

Listing 8.6 shows an example of an anonymous category declaration.

Listing 8.6

An anonymous category declaration, this would go in Foo+PrivateMethods.h

```
#import <Foundation/Foundation.h>

@interface Foo ()

-(void)somePrivateMethod;

@end
```

Listing 8.7 shows the implementation of the `Foo` class itself. Note that the interface does not declare the private method, but the implementation does provide the definition for it.

Listing 8.7

The `Foo` class implementation

```
@interface Foo : NSObject
{

}

@end

@implementation Foo

-(void)somePrivateMethod
{
    // secret things go here. ;)
}

@end
```

Just so it's clear what's happening here. The anonymous `Foo` category is declaring the private methods that are implemented in the actual `Foo` class.

At the risk of having my object oriented design certification revoked (as if one existed in the first place), I think that private methods are overrated, and I can't really think of a case where you would want to use this for the purposes of actually hiding private methods from users of your class. Considering the fact that I just demonstrated to you that using categories, if a developer were sufficiently motivated, he or she could easily crack open your class and access any private methods they so desired, I think any attempt to prevent such access is kind of futile.

However, I can think of cases where you may want to expose particular methods to particular users of your classes and simply not include it as part of your documented public API. For example, if you are a proponent of unit testing, you may want to be able to test "non-public" methods without having to expose them in the public class declaration. Non-public methods might be methods that simply have no place in the public API, or no use outside of the class. In this case, anonymous categories may be an excellent solution for you.

Associating Variables with Existing Classes

Categories are incapable of adding new member variables to the class that they are extending. While this may seem like a limitation in categories, in practice it's not so bad. In cases where you really need to add member variables to a class that you're extending, you can easily subclass class and do it that way. However, there are cases where you really don't want to subclass but you really do need to add some additional variables to the class that you are extending. Fortunately, as of MacOS X version 10.6 and iOS 3.2, there is a low-level capability built into the Objective-C runtime for doing exactly this. It is a capability which is leveraged by the runtime itself, and one which you can use in extreme cases when you need to associate a variable with an existing object without subclassing and without changing the class declaration of that object. This technique is called associative references. It is available regardless of whether it's through a category or not. I will show you how to use it, and then show you how to implement a category for cached sorted keys on the `NSMutableDictionary` class using it.

Before I get too deeply into this, I want to clear up any confusion that may occur. When working with associative references, you will not actually be adding a member variable to the class itself. It will not have a property associated with it. It will not have an accessor associated with it. At its heart, associative references are simply storage associated with a specific instance of your class. Notice that I didn't say that its storage associated with the class. If you do not explicitly associate a reference with a given instance of your class it will not have it.

To add an associative reference to an instance of your class you simply use the Objective-C runtime function `objc_setAssociatedObject`. This function takes four arguments, the object you wish to associate the data with, a key so that you can retrieve the data later, the value you want to store the reference, and finally an association policy, which defines how the stored values memory is managed.

After an association is created, you can access the value stored in the Association by using the Objective-C runtime function `objc_getAssociatedObject`. This function takes two parameters, the first is the object with which the data is associated, and the second is the key that you specified when associating the data in the first place.

Finally, when you are no longer using an associated object, you can remove the association by again calling the Objective-C function `objc_setAssociatedObject`, but in this case passing nil as the value to be associated.

In all cases, the key associated with the value must be unique to that value. The actual data type of the key is a `void *`. Typically, you want to use a variable which has been declared to be static for this key. By doing so, you are ensured that the pointer associated with the key will always point to a singular instance of that pointer and be unique.

The association policy can be one of the following values, as shown in Table 8.1

Table 8.1

Value	Purpose
OBJC_ASSOCIATION_ASSIGN	Specifies the value will simply be assigned. No retain or release will be used.
OBJC_ASSOCIATION_RETAIN_NONATOMIC	Specifies the value will be assigned and retained in a non-threadsafe way.
OBJC_ASSOCIATION_COPY_NONATOMIC	Specifies the value will be copied in a non-threadsafe way.
OBJC_ASSOCIATION_RETAIN	Specifies the value will be assigned and retained in a threadsafe way.
OBJC_ASSOCIATION_COPY	Specifies the value will be copied in a threadsafe way.

As you can see, these values closely resemble the property attributes that can be specified when declaring properties for objects. It uses much the similar mechanism for associative references.

As an example of how an associative reference actually works in code, Listing 8.8 shows a category declared on `NSMutableDictionary`, which will maintain a cached, sorted list of the dictionaries keys. There are several methods defined here for housekeeping purposes. If you were actually implementing this category, there might be better ways to do it. The purpose here is simply to illustrate the lifecycle of the associative reference which will be used to store the sorted keys.

Listing 8.8

A sorted keys category

```
@interface NSMutableDictionary (SortedKeys)

-(void)generateSortedKeys;
-(NSArray *)sortedKeys;
-(void)dropSortedKeys;
```

continued

Listing 8.8 *(continued)*

```
@end

@implementation NSMutableDictionary (SortedKeys)

-(void)generateSortedKeys;
{
    NSMutableArray *keys = [NSMutableArray arrayWithArray:[self allKeys]];
    [keys sortUsingSelector:@selector(compare:)];
    objc_setAssociatedObject(self, @"KEYS", keys, OBJC_ASSOCIATION_RETAIN);
}

-(NSArray *)sortedKeys;
{
    return objc_getAssociatedObject(self, @"KEYS");
}

-(void)dropSortedKeys;
{
    objc_setAssociatedObject(self, @"KEYS", nil, OBJC_ASSOCIATION_RETAIN);
}

@end
```

As you can see, when the sorted keys array is created, it's stored as an associative reference on self, or that is, the dictionary upon which we are operating, this is shown in `-generate SortedKeys`. When finished with the sorted keys, the associative reference can be removed using the `-dropSortedKeys` method.

Because you're not subclassing, you do need to make sure you explicitly call the `-dropSorted Keys` (or whatever your cleanup method is) in order to release the memory associated with the object before deallocating it.

NOTE
If you use the newer LLVM 1.5 compiler and the modern runtime, they include the ability to declare instance variables in class extensions, so you can avoid most of this rigmarole. To do so, you simply declare them as part of your extension interface, just like if you were declaring them in a class. See the LLVM documentation for the flags required to enable this behavior.

NOTE
You can use `NSString` constants (as I have used here) for keys, because they are defined by the language to be static references to each other when defined inline like I have done here.

Summary

In this chapter I have introduced you to some of the unique and powerful tools that Objective-C provides you for building object-oriented designs from small reusable components. The approaches shown may seem unusual, or even magical, if you are coming to the language from a language that is less dynamic, such as C++ or Java. But the power of Objective-C comes from the fact that these kinds of meta-programming tools are available as part of the language itself and fully supported in the language frameworks. Working with a language that is so expressive, so powerful, and so dynamic is a wonderful experience.

Writing Macros

The topic of this chapter is macros. Macros are a special feature of the Objective-C preprocessor that enable you to execute special commands or replace particular values in your code at compilation time. Macros are unique in that the commands are actually executed as part of the compilation process. The results of those commands are usually insertions of values or files, and so on. The term "macro" comes from the idea that something small can expand into something larger, and in a lot of ways, this is exactly what preprocessor macros do.

Reviewing the Compilation Process

I've discussed the compilation process before, but here I want to focus on the earliest stage of compilation called the preprocessor. The preprocessor, as its name implies, is a stage of compilation which happens prior to the actual processing of the bulk of the source code. Its job is primarily to take raw source files and prepare them for the compilation process itself.

To do this, it first strips out any comments in the source code, replacing them with spaces; then it performs any line transformations required. Finally, it expands any preprocessor directives, also known as macros.

A preprocessor directive is any line that begins with a # symbol, directly followed by the directive itself, and any parameters to that directive. So in other words, all the items in Listing 9.1 are preprocessor directives.

In This Chapter

Revisiting the Compilation Process

Creating constants using preprocessor Defines

Conditionally compiling portions of code based on compiler settings

Writing preprocessor macros to manipulate your code at compile time

Listing 9.1

Some preprocessor directives or macros

```
#define FOO 1
#ifdef BAR
#endif
#define BAZ(X, Y) NSLog(@"%s - %s", (X), (Y));
#import <Foundation/Foundation.h>
```

Each of these items is a preprocessor directive. The #define is defining a constant called FOO with a value of 1. The #ifdef and #endif are defining a conditional block of code that will only be compiled if BAR has been defined. #define BAZ(X, Y) NSLog(@"%s - %s", (X), (Y)); is a preprocessor function, which takes parameters and logs them. Finally, the #import directive, which you have seen before, loads the given header file and puts its source code inline into this source file.

These directives are expanded during the compilation process, not at runtime. Therefore, the things they do impact the source code before it's actually compiled. In some ways, you can think of preprocessor macros as a means for writing programs that manipulate your source code when it's compiling.

Understanding how macros work

This idea of manipulating your source code while it's being compiled is an interesting concept. Take a look at Listing 9.2. In this code, there is a particular string constant, @"MY_IMPORTANT_ DATA", which is used over and over again to access items from NSUserDefaults.

Listing 9.2

Code that uses a string to access an item from NSUserDefaults

```
#import <Foundation/Foundation.h>

int main (int argc, const char * argv[])
{
    NSAutoreleasePool * pool = [[NSAutoreleasePool alloc] init];
```

```
    NSString *someValue = @"foobar";
    [[NSUserDefaults standardUserDefaults] setObject:someValue
                            forKey:@"MY_IMPORTANT_DATA"];

    // do stuff...

    NSString *theValue = [[NSUserDefaults standardUserDefaults]
                        stringForKey:@"MY_IMPORTANT_DATA"];



    [pool drain];
    return 0;
}
```

The biggest problem with this code is that I'm using a constant string for the key in this code, you open yourself up to syntax errors that won't be caught by the compiler. If you make a mistake in typing the string, the compiler will not be able to tell that it was a mistake and instead will allow it to go all the way to win your application is running. This makes for bugs that are difficult to track down.

It would be nice if you could create some kind of macro that the compiler will expand to your string but which it can check for syntax errors when it goes to compile. This is exactly the kind of thing for which macros are made. Listing 9.3 shows the same code, written using a macro instead of the string.

Listing 9.3

Using a macro

```
#import <Foundation/Foundation.h>

#define THE_KEY @"MY_IMPORTANT_DATA"

int main (int argc, const char * argv[])
{
    NSAutoreleasePool * pool = [[NSAutoreleasePool alloc] init];

    NSString *someValue = @"foobar";
```

continued

Listing 9.3   *(continued)*

```
    [[NSUserDefaults standardUserDefaults] setObject:someValue
                              forKey:THE_KEY];

    // do stuff...

    NSString *theValue = [[NSUserDefaults standardUserDefaults]
                              stringForKey:THE_KEY];



    [pool drain];
    return 0;
}
```

As you can see, at the top of this new source listing we are defining a macro called THE_KEY. This macro is being defined to be @"MY_IMPORTANT_DATA". Everywhere in the subsequent code where the words THE_KEY are located will be replaced with the string @"MY_IMPORTANT_ DATA" when the program is compiled. This will happen transparently as part of the compilation process but the end result is that this code, when compiled, will actually wind up being exactly the same as the listing that we saw previously. The only difference is that when you are writing the source code you can take advantage of Xcode's built-in code completion, and the compiler will detect if you have any instances of THE_KEY that were typed incorrectly. For example, if you accidentally wrote THE_KEY instead of THE_KEY, the compiler can check for that condition and issue an error.

Listing 9.4 shows another example where the program is taking different actions depending on whether the given macro value (DEBUGGING) is defined.

Listing 9.4

Optional compilation based on a macro

```
#import <Foundation/Foundation.h>

#define DEBUGGING 1

int main (int argc, const char * argv[])
{
    NSAutoreleasePool * pool = [[NSAutoreleasePool alloc] init];

#ifdef DEBUGGING
```

```
    NSLog(@"Debugging stuff...");
#else
    NSLog(@"Not debugging");
#endif

    [pool drain];
    return 0;
}
```

In this case, the code inside the main block is checking to see if a value has been set or the DEBUGGING macro. If this macro has been defined, in other words if it has any value at all, then it prints out the "Debugging stuff..." message. If the DEBUGGING macro has not been defined, then it prints out "Not debugging." This is really powerful because by using it, you can have certain code compile only when you are running in a debugging environment. For example, you might use this to cause your application to connect to a development server instead of your production server while you are testing.

One of the cool aspects of using macros in this way is that there are also flags that you can use as part of your compiler settings to cause these macros to be defined or undefined based strictly on your build settings. In other words, you can configure your build settings so that when you build your target for your debug environment you get this macro defined, and when you're building for release to your customers you do not. Again, remember that all of this expansion is actually happening at compile time. In addition to that, keep in mind that the expansion is happening in your source code at the location where you place the macro. This is difficult to explain, but easier with an example. Take a look at Listing 9.5.

Listing 9.5

An example of some macros which will give different values than you might expect

```
#import <Foundation/Foundation.h>

#define LOG_LINE NSLog(@"%s:%ld", __FILE__, __LINE__);

int main (int argc, const char * argv[])

{
    NSAutoreleasePool * pool = [[NSAutoreleasePool alloc] init];

    LOG_LINE
```

continued

Listing 9.5 (continued)

```
NSLog(@"%s %s", __DATE__, __TIME__);
LOG_LINE

    [pool drain];
    return 0;
}
```

In this code, I first defined a function called LOG_LINE. This function, when it is expanded in your code, turns into NSLog(@"%s:%ld", __FILE__, __LINE__);. This causes your program, when it runs, to log the filename and line number where the LOG_LINE function has been placed. The built-in macros __FILE__ and __LINE__ are provided by the compiler itself, and expand to the current source file name and the current line number. When you run this program notice that the line number changes between the two different calls to LOG_LINE. This is only possible because of this in-line expansion capability that macros have. Another illustration of this is shown by looking at the output of the line in between the LOG_LINE calls. The built-in macros __DATE__ and __TIME__ expand to the date and time that the preprocessor was run to compile this program. In other words, this is the date and time that your program was compiled. If you compile the program once and then run it multiple times, you'll find that the date and time shown here do not change on subsequent launches. This is because the date and time that are being expanded in your source code are effectively being hardcoded by the expansion of these macros in your code.

Listing 9.6 shows what this code might look like after the preprocessor expansion has already taken place.

Listing 9.6

Program with macros expanded

```
#import <Foundation/Foundation.h>


int main (int argc, const char * argv[])
{
    NSAutoreleasePool * pool = [[NSAutoreleasePool alloc] init];

    NSLog(@"Code/Macros/Macros.m:9");
    NSLog(@"%s %s", "May 18 2010",  "16:00:03");
    NSLog(@"Code/Macros/Macros.m:11");
```

```
    [pool drain];
    return 0;
}
```

Literally speaking, this is exactly what the preprocessor is doing. It takes your macros and expands them into whatever they are defined to be right inside your code.

You might notice that these particular macros are using double underscores at the beginning and end of the macro name. This is a standard that is reserved specifically for compiler-provided macros and not something that you should do in your code. You can use these macros — just don't use the double underscores in your own macro names.

Defining Macros

You begin a macro definition with the # symbol followed by the preprocessor directive and then any parameters to the directive such as the name of the macro and so on. Table 9.1 shows a listing of the most commonly used preprocessor directives.

Table 9.1

Directive	Purpose
#define	Used to define new macros such as constants and functions.
#ifdef	Begins an optional compilation block. If the parameter for the preprocessor directive is defined to be anything (even zero), then the code following the #ifdef up until a terminating #endif, #else, or #elif will be compiled and included in the application. If the parameter is not defined and an #else or #elsif block is provided, then the #else or #elsif block will be evaluated and if appropriate compiled and included in the application.
#undef	Removes a previously defined macro.
#import	Reads and includes another source file in this file. Guards against including the file multiple times automatically.
#include	Reads and includes another source file in this file. Does not prevent including a file multiple times.
#pragma	Special macro used for configuring the compiler and for annotations in the IDE.
#warning	Generates a compiler warning. Used to flag issues to the developer.
#error	Generates a compiler error.
#if	Begins a conditional compilation block similar to #ifdef, but relies on an expression (such as X > 10) which must evaluate to true in order to be considered true.
#else	Used after an #if or #ifdef to provide a conditional block to be compiled if the statement is false.
#elif	Used after an #if or #ifdef to provide an additional conditional block with an additional control statement to determine if it should be compiled.
#endif	Terminates an #if, #ifdef, #else, or #elif block.

For the purposes of this book, I will focus primarily on the `#define`, `#ifdef`, and other more commonly used preprocessor directives. The directives `#pragma`, `#warning`, `#include`, and `#error` are better served by viewing the GCC documentation.

NOTE

One very common use of the `#pragma` directive is in adding IDE directives to your code for use by the IDE in labels. Apple uses this extensively in its own templates. In many of their templates, you'll see the directive: `#pragma mark Something`. This will cause the IDE to display "Something" in the method name listing drop down list. Additionally, the special directive `#pragma mark –` causes a horizontal rule to be placed in the list.

Defining constants

The first type of macro that I showed you in this chapter was used for the purposes of defining a constant that would then be reused in multiple places in your application. Indeed, this is perhaps one of the most common uses of macros. I myself use macros in this form for defining keys for accessing `NSUserDefaults` just like they showed in the previous example.

To define a constant, you use the preprocessor directive #define followed by the name of the constant you are defining the value for. After the name, separated by a space, you then provide the value you want the preprocessor to expand your macro to in your source code. The preprocessor expands the macro by using all of the remaining text in your line until it encounters the end of the line.

In cases where you want to make a macro such as this and spread its definition out over multiple lines, you can do this by entering a backslash and then pressing enter. This causes the compiler to consider the next line to be part of the current line for the purposes of evaluating this macro.

Listing 9.7 shows an example of several different constants being defined using the `#define` preprocessor directive.

Listing 9.7

Defining constants with #define

```
#define FOO 1
#define BAR @"this is bar"
#define BAZ @"THIS IS A VERY LONG STRING \
AND IT CONTINUES DOWN HERE \
AND HERE."
#define BOZ BAR
```

An unspoken rule is to always name your macros using all capital letters. Doing this helps to distinguish macros in your source code from normal statements and makes your code easier to read. In the previous section, I mentioned that you should not use the double underscores for your own macro names. Additionally, you should not use underscores at the beginning or end of your macro names either because this is reserved for the compiler. It's perfectly safe to use underscores inside your macro names, and in fact, this is again another unspoken standard: separating multiple words in your macro names by using underscores instead of spaces since spaces are not legal anywhere in a macro name. Macro names must also begin with an alphabetic letter. Numbers are not allowed. You are free to use numbers after the first letter of the macro name but they cannot be used for the first letter.

As you found out in the previous section, macros can refer to other macros within their definition. In these cases, your macro will first be expanded to whatever you have defined, and then any macros inside of your macro definition will be expanded in place from there. For example, the macro BOZ above will ultimately expand to `BAR`, and then `BAR` will be expanded to `@"this is bar"`.

The exception to this rule is that macros are not recursive. Meaning, you cannot refer to the macro that you are defining in its definition. For example, the macro `#define FOO FOO` won't work.

Passing constants by compilation

I mention earlier in this chapter how you can define macros as part of your build settings. Listing 9.8 shows an example of an application that needs to be compiled to connect to a test server when it is being debugged and compiled to connect to the production server when it is not being debugged.

Listing 9.8

Conditional compilation based on build settings

```
#import <Foundation/Foundation.h>

int main (int argc, const char * argv[])
{
    NSAutoreleasePool * pool = [[NSAutoreleasePool alloc] init];

   NetworkConnection *conn = [[NetworkConnection alloc] init];
#ifdef DEBUGGING
   [conn connectToServer:@"http://develop.nowhere.com"];
#else
   [conn connectToServer:@"http://production.nowhere.com"];
```

continued

Listing 9.8   *(continued)*

```
#endif

    [pool drain];
    return 0;
}
```

Notice that the DEBUGGING macro is not actually being defined in this source file. In this particular case, I'm relying on the build settings to pass in that value when I do a debug build. If that value has been defined, then the application connects to the development server. If it is not, then it connects to the production server.

Figure 9.1 shows the build settings window and the parameter that you set in order to define values as part of your build settings.

The build setting that you use to define these preprocessor macros is the Preprocessor Macros setting. This particular setting takes a list of macro names and values separated by = . So, in other words, to define the preprocessor macro DEBUGGING, you would set this build setting to DEBUGGING=1 . The given value here, 1, is more or less just setting it to any value (even 0 would be OK) so that the #ifdef statement returns true. If we used a #if with an expression, like #if DEBUGGING > 10 then we could have variable levels of debugging based on the compilation flag.

By setting this build setting on the debug build, the DEBUGGING macro will be set when the source code is compiled. When you switch to the Release build, which does not have this setting, then the normal, production code will be compiled and included.

Using variables in macros

Although the syntactical capabilities of macros is much more primitive, macros are capable of taking parameters just like if when working with functions or methods. This enables you to create complex macros that actually do creative things with the contextual information available when the macro is being expanded.

For example, if you wanted to create a MAX macro to return the greater value of two parameters, you might create a macro such as Listing 9.9.

Listing 9.9

A macro for printing the value of a variable

```
#define MAX(X, Y) ((X) > (Y) ? (X) : (Y))
```

Figure 9.1

The build settings window.

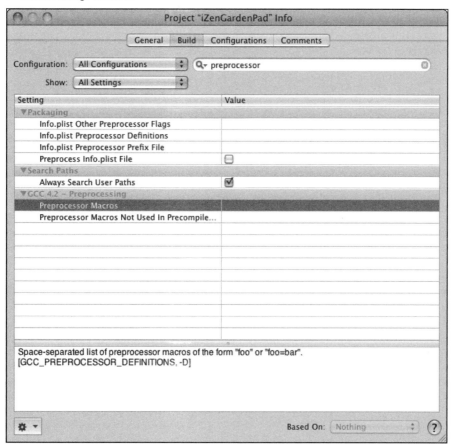

In this example, the MAX macro takes two arguments, X and Y. It then compares these two arguments by using the ternary operator. If X is greater than Y, it returns X, alternatively, if Y is greater than X, it returns Y.

When using parameters with a macro the parameters are specified inside parentheses just as if you were defining parameters for procedures. There are, however, a few subtle differences.

First, you do not need to provide a data type for the parameters. This code will not be compiled. Instead, the macro will be expanded where it is used in the parameters will be inserted directly into the expanded macro code. Therefore, variable types are not necessary here.

Secondly, the opening parenthesis of the parameter list must come directly after the name of the macro. Notice when we have been defining other macros, that the value that we are defining for the macro is separated from the macro name by a space. Therefore, if you were to put a space between the macro name and the opening parenthesis of the parameter list, the preprocessor would assume that the parameter list is the beginning of the macro value instead of part of the macro name.

Another subtle difference between procedures and macros with arguments is in the handling of the values inside the body of the macro value. Notice in the example above that there are a lot of extra parentheses being used in the body of the macro. Again, this has to do with the fact that the macro will be expanded in the code and that the values will be expanded inside the macro in the code. To illustrate this point, consider the expansion of the code `NSLog(@"Max Value: %ld", MAX( x & 20, 10 ));`. Without the additional parentheses, this might expand to `NSLog(@"Max Value: %ld", (x & 20 > 10 ? x & 20 : 10 ));`. In this case, order of operations dictates that the greater than comparison has higher precedence than the bitwise-AND operation and therefore would be performed on the 20 and the 10 rather than on x & 20 and the 10. By including the extra parentheses inside the body of the macro, you ensure that the order of operations is performed in exactly the way that you expect them to be. In other words, this code would actually expand to `NSLog(@"Max Value: %ld", ((x & 20) > (10) ? (x & 20) : (10)));`.

Using stringification

One of the macro tricks that I like to use in my own code is in logging values of particular variables as my application is running. Doing this can be useful because I can see what the state of my application is without necessarily stopping it in the debugger and looking at particular values one at a time.

To do this, I have to create a macro that takes a variable as a parameter. Because I might use this macro in multiple locations on different variables I also need to get the variable name and print it alongside the value of that variable. To do this, I use a special macro capability called stringification.

Stringification takes whatever code is passed to it and converts it to a C string by enclosing it in quotes. So, for example, if given `'x + 10'` as a parameter, it will turn it into `"'x + 10'"`. This makes it ideal for solving this kind of problem.

Listing 9.10 shows the macro as I would define it.

Listing 9.10

A macro to print the value of a variable

```
#define LOGVAR(var) NSLog(@"%s: %@", #var, var);
```

The key here is to prefix the variable name itself with a # symbol. This invokes the stringification.

If you use this macro in an application as shown in Listing 9.11, you can see that it will first print the name of the variable, and then it will print the value of that variable.

Listing 9.11

Using a macro to print the value of a variable

```
#import <Foundation/Foundation.h>

#define LOGVAR(var) NSLog(@"%s: %@", #var, var);

int main (int argc, const char * argv[])
{
    NSAutoreleasePool * pool = [[NSAutoreleasePool alloc] init];

    NSString *someVar = @"This is the value.";

    LOGVAR(someVar);


    [pool drain];
    return 0;
}
```

The `LOGVAR(someVar)` line gets expanded to something like Listing 9.12.

Listing 9.12

The expanded code

```
#import <Foundation/Foundation.h>


int main (int argc, const char * argv[])
{
    NSAutoreleasePool * pool = [[NSAutoreleasePool alloc] init];

   NSString *someVar = @"This is the value.";

   NSLog(@"%s: %@", "someVar", someVar);

    [pool drain];
    return 0;
}
```

NOTE
This code is deliberately simplistic for the purposes of example. In the case where you would actually want to create a macro like this you probably need to do something to determine the data type of the variable that's passed in so that you can use a correct format string when printing it out.

Handling conditional switching

You can choose to conditionally compile particular parts of your code by using the conditional preprocessor directives, #if, #ifdef, #ifndef, and their cohorts, #else, #elif, and #endif. You can optionally choose to include or not include entire chunks of your code based on whether something is defined, not defined, or whether an expression evaluates to true.

The first of these directives is the #if directive. The #if directive is used to allow or prevent a particular portion of your code from compiling based on the result of an expression. The expression can be any valid expression, using other macros, constants, variables from the code surrounding the macro expansion, or whatever. The key is that it must evaluate to true in order for the block following the #if directive to be compiled. You terminate the #if statement with a #end statement. If you want to provide an additional block of code to be compiled in the case that the expression evaluates to false, you put a #else directive inside the #if block, before the #end directive. Alternatively, you can place a #elif directive inside the #if block.

The #elif directive also takes an expression and will only compile the code between it and the next directive if that expression evaluates to true, just like the #if directive. Essentially, the whole #if, #else, #elif, #end construct is very similar to the if, else, construct, except that instead of affecting program flow during program execution, it affects what parts of your application are compiled. The #ifdef and #ifndef directives work just like #if, except that instead of using an expression, it simply tests to see if a value has been defined at all. In the case of #ifdef, the code is compiled if the value has been defined, and in the case of #ifndef, the code is compiled if the value is not defined.

Using built-in macros

GCC, the underlying compiler that Xcode uses to compile your code has a variety of built-in macros already available for your use. You've already seen some of them in use in the examples in this chapter. Macros like __FILE__, __LINE__, and others. To find out more information , visit the GCC documentation located at: http://gcc.gnu.org/onlinedocs/cpp/.

Summary

In this chapter, I've introduced you to the Objective-C preprocessor, a powerful tool which lets you write code that modifies your code as it compiles. Using it, you can do all sorts of things, from preventing syntax errors with constants, to printing out your variables, even to conditionally compiling portions of your code but not others. It's a tool that you'll probably not use often, but one which, when you need it, comes in very handy.

Handling Errors

Y ou hope that run time errors won't occur, but you know that they will. You try to code defensively, making sure to verify that the variables you are using have the values you expect. You write unit tests to make sure that any possible condition that could occur has been foreseen, and the solution to that problem is built into your application. You know that you can't foresee all problems, however. You know that no matter how hard you work to gird your application against the perils of the real world, as soon as your application is launched into real-world environments with real-world problems, such as limited memory, limited disk space, and users who interrupt your application at the worst time, you're going to run into problems. You're going to experience errors.

Thankfully, Objective-C has a variety of error handling capabilities built into it that you can leverage to write code that is robust, resilient, and stable. You can write applications that, when errors occur, bend rather than break.

In this chapter, I'm going to introduce you to the three major mechanisms built into Objective-C and the Foundation framework that will help you write code that will be brave in the face of these dangers, and which will "do the right thing" when presented with unforeseen problems. Before I begin, however, take a look at what kind of errors you might encounter in a typical application.

In This Chapter

Learning about different kinds of errors and how you should handle them

Using return codes to return status

Using exceptions for exceptional errors

Learning the proper way to use NSError

Classifying Errors

Errors that can occur in a typical, running program fall into three major categories.

The first category is the kind of error that simply consists of a success or failure condition. There is no additional information that can be gleaned about what happened, the operation simply succeeded or it didn't succeed. Typically, this is the most minor of errors, and is not the kind of error that drastically interrupts program flow. For example, if you are trying to gain access to a shared resource through a mutually exclusive lock, your program may try to gain access to the resource and fail because another program or part of your program are already accessing that resource. In this case, you want to know that accessing the resource failed, and you want to simply retry accessing the resource again. This category is a minor type of error condition. You know exactly what to do when the call fails and exactly what might have caused the failure.

Return codes are uniquely suited for this kind of error. Ideally, the return code can be as simple as a Boolean value. The return code can return YES if the call succeeded or NO if the call failed. In some languages that lack some of the more complex error handling mechanisms that I am about to introduce to you, error codes are the only option that you have for returning invalid conditions. In these languages, error codes are often overloaded with meaning. Often these languages require that the error code be set to particular values to mean particular error conditions. Typically, Objective-C does not do this because other mechanisms are in place that enable you to give better more descriptive error messages than plain old error codes provides.

The second category of errors is on the opposite spectrum from the first. This type of error, if not handled, causes data loss or an application failure. These errors are obviously much more serious than the first and consist of things like failure to open resources that are absolutely required for your application to continue running, consistency errors in your data storage, and so on. Imagine that these errors are so important that if you don't do something about them you would rather the application crash than continue running in order to avoid causing more damage than has already been done. These errors are, not to put too fine a point on it, exceptional conditions, so it makes sense that the error handling mechanism best suited to handling them are called Exceptions. Fortunately, errors of this kind are few and far between in Objective-C. Nevertheless, I show you how to handle them, and how to recover from them later in this chapter.

Finally, the third category of errors is somewhere in between the first two in terms of severity. This type of error is serious enough that you really need to pass more contextual information back up the stack to the person who is calling your function, but not so serious that it cannot be recovered from.

This is by far the most common type of runtime error that occurs in Objective-C programs. It's so common that Apple has provided a standardized error mechanism for handling these kinds of errors. It uses a combination of a return code to indicate success, and a specialized `NSError` object to provide contextual information in the case of failures. Working with `NSError` can be tricky, but by the end of this chapter you'll be able to handle errors such as this like a pro.

Understanding how to interrupt program flow

Knowing when to interrupt program flow is important.

Each of the three categories of errors I previously mentioned call for different design patterns in terms of how you handle interrupting program flow when the errors occur. When designing an API that has the potential to return an error, think of the users of the API and how the handling of the potential errors that can occur will impact the design of the code required to call your API. Ideally, you want to design your API so that the developer using it can do so while providing the smallest amount of infrastructure possible while at the same time being capable of capturing and handling any potential error conditions that might occur.

If your errors are minor and obvious and require little external (developer side) support or intervention, then you might consider using a return code to indicate that a particular call has failed. On the other hand, if the error condition that has occurred is so extreme that you absolutely have to completely bring the application to a halt in order to avoid more damage to the system, then using an exception may be the way to go. You have to assume that if the exception is not handled by users of your API that the application will crash, because that's exactly what an exception does. Looking at exceptions from this point of view, that is, by viewing an un-handled exception as a crash, really puts this sort of error condition into perspective and may help you to think about when exceptions are really justified (clue: very rarely).

Finally, for most other error conditions — the ones that fall between extremely minor and extremely serious — the NSError mechanism is probably the right choice. It communicates easily the fact that a call failed up the stack to the caller, but at the same time puts the responsibility for deciding how serious the error is where it belongs, in the hands of that very same caller.

Using the Different Mechanisms for Error Handling

So, let's get down to the nitty-gritty of how to use these three different error handling techniques. In the following sections, I cover how to use the three different error handling capabilities built into Objective-C, how they work in your code, and what you need to do to handle errors that occur in other people's code.

Using return codes

You've already seen how methods and procedures both have the capability of returning a value when they exit. You do this by using the return keyword. You declare the type of value that you return as part of your method signature and this determines what type of return value your method returns.

Using this return value to indicate failure or success is one of the oldest error handling mechanisms in programming languages. In the C programming language of which Objective-C is a derivative, seeing procedures that return an `int` return code to indicate different kinds of errors is very common. Typically these return codes would be mapped to error messages so that you could determine by looking at the value returned what the actual error was that occurred. Despite this ability to look up the error code, the error code itself was typically still just a number. This tended to be inconvenient, because different functions used different values to indicate different types of errors and looking them up meant looking at different tables of codes to error messages according to the procedure that you were using.

As a result, other error handling mechanisms were developed, and using return codes in this fashion fell by the wayside. Nonetheless, using return codes for simple errors is still certainly a worthwhile technique to understand and utilize. However, it's best when doing so to avoid the biggest problem with return codes, the lookup of codes to error messages, and instead stick with simple Boolean values, returning YES in the case of success or NO in the case of failure. This is generally the way that you see return codes used for error handling in Objective-C.

There are of course exceptions to this rule, for example, in cases where a method may be returning some value in the case of a successful call, sometimes the call will return nil instead of the expected value. Fortunately, `nil` and NO in Objective-C, when used as the control variable for an if statement and with the same result, they evaluate to false. Thus, you can treat these return values similarly when working with them.

Listing 10.1 shows an example of a class that is being used as a wrapper for a disk file. In this particular example, the expectation is that the data file on disk is there and readable. But what if it isn't? If the file doesn't exist, it can't be opened. In this particular case, the object method `-openFileAtPath:` will return nil.

Listing 10.1

Class definition for a file wrapper class

```
@interface FileWrapper : NSObject
{
    NSDictionary *contents;
}
-(BOOL)openFileAtPath:(NSString *)inPath;
@end;

@implementation FileWrapper

// dealloc and other stuff should be here...

-(BOOL)openFileAtPath:(NSString *)inPath;
{
```

```
    contents = [[NSDictionary dictionaryWithContentsOfFile:inPath]
                                        retain];
    if(!contents)
        return NO;
    return YES;
}

@end
```

The -openFileAtPath: method actually uses a method on NSDictionary that utilizes the exact same kind of error handling that I am illustrating here. In other words, the return value from the NSDictionary class method +dictionaryWithContentsOfFile: is normally an instance of NSDictionary. However, if the file does not exist, or it cannot be loaded as a property list file, then this method returns nil. The method shown in Listing 10.1 checks to see if the value returned from the NSDictionary method is nil. If it is, then it itself returns NO. Otherwise it returns YES.

Listing 10.2 shows the main function for a program that might be using this class.

Listing 10.2

Using the file wrapper class

```
int main (int argc, const char * argv[])
{
    NSAutoreleasePool * pool = [[NSAutoreleasePool alloc] init];

    FileWrapper *wrapper = [[FileWrapper alloc] init];
    if([wrapper openFileAtPath:@"..."])
    {
        // do stuff with the file here...
    }
    else
    {
        // tell the user the file couldn't be opened.
    }

    [pool drain];
    return 0;
}
```

As you can see, I've wrapped the call to `-openFileAtPath:` inside an if statement. If the call returns YES, that was a success, and I can do things with the file. Otherwise I have to tell the user that the file could be opened.

This example illustrates one of the problems with return codes in that you can't tell why the file couldn't be opened. All you know is that it couldn't. Ideally, you want to be able to tell the user exactly what happened, and why the file couldn't be opened. Maybe the file was missing, or maybe the user didn't have permission to open the file. The user has no way of knowing in this particular case.

That said, however, this is one of the simplest ways to indicate an error when one occurs.

Using exceptions

Moving now to the other extreme of error handling, the truly serious conditions, Objective-C provides an excellent facility for throwing and handling exceptions.

The Objective-C language provides several built-in directives specifically for exception handling. The act of signaling that an exceptional condition has occurred is known as *throwing* or *raising* an exception. Essentially, this consists of creating an instance of an `NSException` and then using the built-in Objective-C directive, `@throw`.

Once an exception is thrown, it will continue to travel up the call stack until it is caught. To catch an exception, you use the Objective-C directive @catch. The @catch directive can be used to catch specific subclasses of `NSException`, in the case where you may want to have special processing for particular kinds of exceptions or it can be written to catch all exceptions. Listing 10.3 shows the file wrapper example again but in this case if the file can't be opened, the `-openFileAtPath:` method throws an exception.

Listing 10.3

The -openFileAtPath: method using exceptions

```
-(void)openFileAtPath:(NSString *)inPath;
{
    contents = [[NSDictionary dictionaryWithContentsOfFile:inPath]
                                       retain];
    if(!contents)
    {
        if(![self fileExistsAtPath:inPath])
        {
            NSException *ex =
```

```
                    [NSException exceptionWithName:@"Error opening file"
                                            reason:@"File doesn't exist."
                                          userInfo:nil];
            }
            else if(![self hasPermissionForFileAtPath:inPath])
            {
                NSException *ex =
                [NSException exceptionWithName:@"Error opening file"
                                        reason:@"Permission error."
                                      userInfo:nil];
            }
            else
            {
                NSException *ex =
                [NSException exceptionWithName:@"Error opening file"
                                        reason:@"Unknown error."
                                      userInfo:nil];
            }
            @throw ex;
        }
    }
```

In this version of the -openFileAtPath: method, after I've determined that the file could not be opened, I then go through some of the typical reasons why it might have failed, and I craft an exception specifically to address each of those conditions. Once I have my exception built, I then throw the exception using the @throw directive.

In this particular case, I'm using the default NSException class to throw my exception. But if I wanted to be extra fancy, I could rewrite this method using a custom exception class for each of these different sorts of exceptional conditions.

An example of this is shown in Listing 10.4.

•

Listing 10.4

Throwing custom exceptions for different sorts of errors

```
-(void)openFileAtPath:(NSString *)inPath;
{
    contents =
        [[NSDictionary dictionaryWithContentsOfFile:inPath] retain];
    if(!contents)
```

continued

Listing 10.4   *(continued)*

```
    {
        NSException *ex;
        if(![self fileExistsAtPath:inPath])
        {
            ex = [FileMissingException
                        exceptionWithName:@"Error opening file"
                                   reason:@"File doesn't exist."
                                 userInfo:nil];
        }
        else if(![self hasPermissionForFileAtPath:inPath])
        {
            ex = [FilePermissionException
                        exceptionWithName:@"Error opening file"
                                   reason:@"Permission error."
                                 userInfo:nil];
        }
        else
        {
            ex = [NSException exceptionWithName:@"Error opening file"
                                        reason:@"Unknown error."
                                      userInfo:nil];
        }
        @throw ex;
    }
}
```

Notice that this method has had the return value removed completely. This is an example of code that returns successfully or not at all. In other words, if the file is able to be successfully opened, then the method returns successfully and everything works great. If an error occurs in opening the file, then an exception is thrown that will need to be caught by the caller.

CAUTION

I can't stress this enough, so I'll make the point again here: In this code, if the exception gets thrown and it is not caught by someone up the stack from this method, then the application will crash. So clearly, you would only want to use an exception in this manner if you knew that the failure was a critical problem for this application.

Because it's so important to catch these exceptions, take a look at how you do that. Listing 10.5 shows the updated main function for this application with proper exception handling code in place.

Listing 10.5

Handling the exception in the main function

```
int main (int argc, const char * argv[])
{
    int retCode = 0;
    @try
    {
        NSAutoreleasePool * pool = [[NSAutoreleasePool alloc] init];

        FileWrapper *wrapper = [[FileWrapper alloc] init];
        [wrapper openFileAtPath:@"..."];

        // do stuff with the file here...

    }
    @catch (NSException *e)
    {
        NSString *errorName = [e name];
        NSString *errorMsg = [e reason];
        NSLog(@"An error occurred: %@ - %@" , errorName, errorMsg);
        retCode = -255;
    }
    @finally
    {
        [wrapper release];
        [pool drain];
    }
    return retCode;
}
```

The way that exceptions work enables them to actually interrupt program flow no matter where it is in your application and then jump up the stack until the exception is caught.

Therefore, when there is the possibility for an exception to occur in a method that you're calling, you have to wrap the code that could throw an exception inside of what's called a try/catch block. In the code shown above, you can see that one of the first things that this program does is to use the @try directive. This begins a try/catch block. Once you use the @try directive, the code inside of the following code block (delimited by {}) will be executed just like normal until it either reaches the end of the code block, or an exception is thrown.

If an exception is thrown, program flow is interrupted immediately, and it jumps to the exception handlers that are designated by the @catch directive.

The @catch directives allow you to catch exceptions of particular types. When an exception occurs, the code jumps to the @catch directives and looks for the closest match to the exception that has been thrown. It then begins executing again the code inside of the catch block.

In this particular case, the catch block is simply printing out the error message and then setting the applications return code to an error status. By catching the generic NSException, as shown in Listing 10.5, you are effectively catching all exceptions.

You could even catch the id data type instead of NSException. This would enable you to catch any object that's thrown at all.

In cases like the earlier example where different kinds of exceptions are thrown for different kinds of error conditions, you would list separate catch blocks for each of the different kinds of exceptions that you needed to handle. An example of this is shown in Listing 10.6.

Listing 10.6

Catching different kinds of exceptions

```
int main (int argc, const char * argv[])
{
    int retCode = 0;
    @try
    {
        NSAutoreleasePool * pool = [[NSAutoreleasePool alloc] init];

        FileWrapper *wrapper = [[FileWrapper alloc] init];
        [wrapper openFileAtPath:@"..."];

        // do stuff with the file here...

    }
    @catch (FilePermissionException *e)
    {
        // ...
    }
    @catch (FileMissingException *e)
    {
        // ...
```

```
    }
    @catch (NSException *e)
    {
        // ...
    }
    @finally
    {
        [wrapper release];
        [pool drain];
    }
    return retCode;
}
```

When catching exceptions in this manner, you should list the exceptions in order from most specific to least specific, because the runtime will execute the first catch block match that it finds.

Because of the ability for an exception to interrupt program flow at any time, it can be difficult for your application to do appropriate cleanup of allocated memory and resources when an exception occurs. Fortunately, in addition to the try/catch constructs, there is an additional feature built into Objective-C exception handling, the @finally directive.

The @finally block works just like a @catch block except that it is always executed regardless of whether or not an exception occurs. This makes it the perfect place to clean up memory or free other resources that are allocated as part of the @try block. You can always rely on your @finally block being executed no matter what happens inside your try or catch blocks.

The advantages of this kind of error handling is that you can group your code and let it just run until something bad happens, and then handle that error condition. Additionally, errors can be very descriptive. You can put all sorts of things into the NSException object, and be as verbose as needed.

Try/catch/finally blocks can even be nested within each other in cases where you have complex processing requirements with complex error conditions. This allows you to have multiple levels of exception handling if needed.

NOTE
The use of exceptions for error handling in Objective-C is relatively rare compared to some other languages that use exceptions much more extensively. If you're coming from a language such as Java and are tempted to use exceptions yourself as extensively, I urge you to think twice, and instead, look at the next error handling mechanism that I'm going to visit, NSError.

NOTE
To cause the debugger to break when an exception is thrown, you can set a breakpoint in the Objective-C runtime method objc_exception_throw. If you do this, when an exception is thrown, it will trigger your breakpoint and stop your application. You have to be careful though, since some methods will throw and catch an exception without allowing it to pass up the stack. This is normal, and doesn't hurt anything.

Using NSError

When designing the Foundation framework, Apple recognized that they needed an error handling mechanism that retained the simplicity of a simple return code, but also provided a mechanism for specifying more information about what kind of error occurred. As a result, it began introducing a new error handling system called NSError. Listing 10.7 shows the file wrapper class, updated to use one.

Listing 10.7

File wrapper class using NSError

```
-(BOOL)openFileAtPath:(NSString *)inPath withError:(NSError **)outError;
{
    contents = [[NSDictionary dictionaryWithContentsOfFile:inPath] retain];
    if(!contents)
    {
        if(![self fileExistsAtPath:inPath])
        {
            NSDictionary *errorInfo =
            [NSDictionary dictionaryWithObject:@"File doesn't exist."
                                       forKey:NSLocalizedDescriptionKey];

            *outError = [NSError errorWithDomain:@"FileWrapper"
                                            code:404
                                        userInfo:errorInfo];
        }
        else if(![self hasPermissionForFileAtPath:inPath])
        {
            NSDictionary *errorInfo =
            [NSDictionary dictionaryWithObject:@"Permission Error."
                                       forKey:NSLocalizedDescriptionKey];

            *outError = [NSError errorWithDomain:@"FileWrapper"
                                            code:500
                                        userInfo:errorInfo];
```

```
    }
    else
    {
        NSDictionary *errorInfo =
        [NSDictionary dictionaryWithObject:@"Unknown error."
                            forKey:NSLocalizedDescriptionKey];

        *outError = [NSError errorWithDomain:@"FileWrapper"
                                code:501
                            userInfo:errorInfo];
    }
    return NO;
}
return YES;
}
```

NSError is a formalized design pattern that is being implemented across the Cocoa and Cocoa Touch frameworks.

To use it, you extend your method signature to take an indirect reference to an NSError object. This object is provided by the caller. An indirect reference is essentially a pointer to a pointer. In other words, it's a pointer that points to another pointer; in this case, it is a pointer to a variable allocated inside the stack of the caller. When you assign something to that variable, you dereference the indirect reference and thus are actually assigning to the variable to which it points.

NOTE
Some programmers will refer to indirect references as "pointer to a pointer", "pass by reference", or "a reference". I prefer the term "indirect reference" to distinguish it from a plain reference, which you might encounter when using Objective-C++. "Pointer to a pointer" would probably be the most accurate description, but I feel the phrase "pointer to a pointer" is confusing for new programmers.

This concept of an indirect reference probably sounds very confusing. If so, then good, you're perfectly normal. Fortunately, the underlying details are mostly unimportant as long as you understand the syntax that you have to use when creating and returning the NSError object.

When declaring the NSError indirect reference in your method's parameter list, you will declare it using the syntax " (NSError **) " . The double * signs mark this as an indirect reference.

Creating an NSError Object
Once inside your method, if an error occurs, before you return NO from the method, you must first create your NSError objects and assign it to the dereferenced NSError indirect reference. To do this, go ahead and create your NSError object just like you would normally, but

when assigning it to the passed in variable, you dereference the variable by using the dereference operator (*).So, in other words, to create and assign a new NSError object to the passed
in NSError indirect reference, you do something like Listing 10.8.

Listing 10.8

Assigning an NSError object to the passed in NSError indirect reference

```
*outError = [NSError errorWithDomain:@"FileWrapper"
                          code:404
                      userInfo:errorInfo];
```

The NSError factory method takes three parameters. The first is the error domain. This is a
string value used to indicate the subsystem from which the error has originated. Cocoa provides
several error domains itself, such as NSCocoaErrorDomain, NSPOSIXErrorDomain, and
so on. These are declared in the NSError.h header file. You can, and probably should, specify
your own error domain when creating your own instances of NSError. If you choose to do so,
the error domain string should be specified in reverse DNS notation, for example, com.
yourcompanyname.productname.classname.

The second parameter is the error code parameter. The error code is entirely application specific, and provides a means for you to specify a traditional error code as part of your error object.
How you choose to use the error code is up to you, but it must be an unsigned integer.

Understanding the NSError userInfo Dictionary

For the most part, the error code and the error domain are legacy parameters that are mostly
unused today. The real juice in the NSError object is in the userInfo dictionary. When creating the dictionary for this parameter, you can use several keys for different error information.
The keys are shown in Table 10.1.

Not all of these keys will always exist, and furthermore, users of the NSError class may add special domain-specific keys to the dictionary as well for the purposes of encoding data specific to
the error that has occurred.

The ability to encode all the information required for displaying an error message to the user,
the description, the error reason, a suggestion for how to recover, and even the buttons for the
dialog box, make it possible to even use the NSAlert class method +alertWithError: to display an
appropriate alert box with the appropriate buttons and text fields with the data from the
NSError object.

Table 10.1

Key	Purpose
NSLocalizedDescriptionKey	A localized description of the error condition, such as "File could not be opened because it does not exist." Also accessible via the `NSError` object method `-localizedDescription`.
NSLocalizedFailureReasonKey	A localized reason for the error, such as "File does not exist." Also accessible via the `NSError` object method `-localizedFailureReason`.
NSLocalizedRecoverySuggestionErrorKey	A localized description of what the user might do to try to resolve the problem. Also accessible via the `NSError` method `-localizedRecoverySuggestion`.
NSLocalizedRecoveryOptionsErrorKey	An array of strings to be used for buttons in a dialog box when presenting the error to the user. The first string will be used as the right most button, and then sequentially left from there.
NSRecoveryAttempterErrorKey	An object which conforms to the `NSErrorRecoveryAttempting` protocol, which can be used to attempt to recover from the error. (Mac OS X only)
NSUnderlyingErrorKey	Another `NSError` object representing the actual underlying error.

Working with a recovery attempter

The recovery attempter is a little-known and rarely used component of NSError. Available only on Mac OS X, it provides an object that can be used to automatically attempt to recover from the error that has occurred.

The object provided must conform to the NSErrorRecoveryAttempting protocol, which defines two methods, -attemptRecoveryFromError:optionIndex: which is invoked exclusively in applications using a modal, non-document centric user interface, and -attemptRecoveryFromError:optionIndex:delegate:didRecoverSelector:contextInfo: which is invoked by applications with a document-centric user interface.

Recovery attempters work hand-in-hand with the OS X responder chain. To cause the recovery attempter to be used, you call either -presentError: or -presentError:modalForWindow:delegate:didPresentSelector:contextInfo: on any object in the responder chain. These two methods correspond to presenting an error for a modal application in the former case, and a document-based application in the latter case. When you call them, they will present an alert to the user, displaying the information from the NSError. When the user clicks a button, the appropriate recovery attempt method will be called on the recovery attempter, passing the index of the clicked button as the optionIndex parameter.

The `-attemptRecoveryFromError:optionIndex:` method returns a BOOL value if the error is able to be recovered from. The `-presentError:modalForWindow:delegate:didPresentSelector:contextInfo:` method is expected to call the selector provided on the delegate object. That selector should take a form similar to Listing 10.9.

Listing 10.9

The recovery attempter callback function

```
- (void)didPresentErrorWithRecovery:(BOOL)didRecover
                        contextInfo:(void *)contextInfo;
```

Again, recovery attempters are rarely used, and probably not something you'll typically run into in your code. Nonetheless, it's an interesting feature of NSError.

Working with NSErrors in methods

Returning to the file wrapper example, in order to take advantage of this new NSError code, you'd have to change the main block to look something like Listing 10.10.

Listing 10.10

Using a method with NSError

```
int main (int argc, const char * argv[])
{
    NSAutoreleasePool * pool = [[NSAutoreleasePool alloc] init];

    FileWrapper *wrapper = [[FileWrapper alloc] init];

    NSError *error = nil;

    if([wrapper openFileAtPath:@"..." withError:&error])
    {
        // do stuff with the file here...
    }
    else
    {
        // tell the user the file couldn't be opened.
        // here you have the error object filled in.
        showErrorToUser(error);
    }

    [pool drain];
    return 0;
}
```

The important changes here center around the fact that you can now check the return code of the `-openFileAtPath:withError:` method. If it's NO, then the error object should now contain an initialized `NSError` object containing everything you need to display an error to the user.

CAUTION

Some code examples with `NSError` call for you to set `NSError` to `nil`, and then check to see if `NSError` has been initialized to determine if an error occurred. This is absolutely wrong. There are parts of Cocoa that do manipulate the `NSError` object even though they succeed. The correct pattern to use with `NSError` is as shown here. Check the return code of the method, and if it's NO or `nil`, then check the error object for more information.

This method of error handling is the best of all worlds. It's simple and informative, and it doesn't force the user to handle the error. It provides enough flexibility for the user of the API to do the right thing while not pretending to know better than her.

Summary

Error handling is a vital part of being an effective programmer, so it's good that Objective-C gives you enough tools to handle error conditions gracefully and correctly. You have the tools available to you. Use them.

Using the Foundation Framework

Understanding How the Frameworks Fit Together

When working with Objective-C on MacOS X, iPhone, and iPad, the reusable libraries provided by the operating system are typically packaged as frameworks. These frameworks bundle together header files, documentation, and dynamic libraries to present a package containing all of the information and data necessary for using the code within them.

How exactly frameworks are implemented is relatively platform specific. A framework could be packaged as a dynamic library like the one I just described, as is the case in MacOS X, or it could be a static library, as is the case occasionally on Linux or BSD. Because of the platform centric nature of the framework bundle itself, a detailed explanation of how to build a framework is beyond the scope of a language-centric book such as this one. However, that said, it is important that you understand what some of the key frameworks that are typically used with Objective-C are and what they provide. Therefore, this chapter focuses on giving you an overview of the available frameworks on some of the platforms upon which you can build your Objective-C programs. For reasons that will become obvious later, writing a strictly language-centric Objective-C book without including extensive coverage of at least the Foundation framework is almost impossible. Because of this, the remainder of this part of the book focuses on discussing some of the details of this key component.

In This Chapter

Explaining frameworks

Learning where Foundation fits into other frameworks

Learning how to add frameworks to your projects

Understanding the Foundation Framework

You may not know it, but you have already been using frameworks in your applications if you have been following along with the example code from this book. Every example application that's been shown so far has been a Foundation application, which means that it links with the Foundation framework.

Most languages have a *standard library*. The C programming language for example has the C. standard library. C++ extends the standard library to also include a standard template library. Java also has a standard library, and so on. In most cases, these standard libraries are specified as providing certain functionality, but implementation is left to the platform vendors.

Objective-C as a language does not specify a standard library as such, but over time, the Foundation framework has evolved into the closest thing to a standard library that Objective-C has. It provides many of the same facilities — strings, collections, I/O, and so on that the standard libraries of these other languages provide.

Though originally developed and supported by NeXT/Apple for NeXTstep and Mac OS X, it has become the gold standard by which other platforms must adhere to in order to realistically be considered a viable Objective-C platform. Foundation itself is a huge library, and a comprehensive list of every class and method that Foundation provides is way beyond the scope of what would be practical here. To give you just a taste of what's available as part of this library, however, I have listed many of the more commonly used classes in Table 11.1.

Table 11.1

Class	Purpose
NSArchiver/NSUnarchiver	Used for serializing and deserializing objects that conform to the NSCoder protocol.
NSArray/NSMutableArray	Ordered collections.
NSAutoreleasePool	Implements the auto release pool used in retain count and memory management.
NSBundle	Provides a dramatic interface for application bundles.
NSCalendar	Provides classes for dealing with calendars.
NSData	A class whose purpose is for storing generic data.
NSDate	A class for creating and manipulating dates.
NSDateFormatter	Provides localization and formatting for dates.
NSDictionary/NSMutableDictionary	An associative collection.
NSLock	Thread locking.
NSError	Used to store error information.
NSException	The base class for exceptions.
NSEnumerator	Used for the purposes of enumerating over a collection.
NSFileHandle	A wrapper class for dealing with file I/O.

Class	Purpose
NSFileManager	A class which encapsulates operations related to the file system such as creating directories and so on.
NSGarbageCollector	A class for interacting in an object-oriented manner with the garbage collector.
NSSet/NSMutableSet	An unordered set collection.
NSNotification/NSNotificationCenter	Provides a means for sending and receiving arbitrary notifications through the runtime.
NSObject	The base class or all other classes.
NSTask	A class for interacting with operating system processes.
NSThread	A class for creating and interacting with threads.
NSURL	A class which encapsulates uniform resource locators.
NSURLConnection	Networking classes enabling connection to resources located on the Internet utilizing supported protocols.
NSString/NSMutableString	The Objective-C string class.

Perhaps the most important class that Foundation provides is NSObject, from which every other class in Objective-C inherits. In fact, it is NSObject which provides much of the functionality that we take for granted as part of Objective-C, things like Key Value Coding, reflection, and some aspects of dynamic dispatch. Without Foundation, Objective-C would be an absolutely crippled language. The two go hand in hand.

Foundation is extremely comprehensive. For the most part, before considering inventing some low-level class yourself, check first to see if it already exists in Foundation. More than likely, it does.

Even now, I find myself discovering new things in Foundation and other frameworks, and constantly being surprised at all the unusual edge cases Apple has anticipated. For a full listing of everything in the Foundation, or any other Apple framework, visit the Apple documentation at http://developer.apple.com.

Exploring other frameworks

The Foundation framework does not stand alone on MacOS X. Apple provides many additional frameworks as part of the standard platform as well as hundreds of frameworks that you can download from third parties. Among the Apple provided frameworks are things like AppKit, which provides the classes necessary for building GUI applications on MacOS X, UIKit which provides the classes needed for building GUI applications on iPhone and iPad, and a slew of other frameworks which provide functionality specific to things such as network services, graphics, and so on. For the purposes of this book, we will focus exclusively on Foundation. This framework easily has the greatest cross-platform support of any of the frameworks on MacOS X. It is available in the official Apple versions on MacOS X, iPhone, and iPad, and in the form of open source third-party implementations on Linux, BSD UNIX, and even Windows. One type of implementation enables you to develop your application by using Xcode on MacOS X, and cross compile to build an executable for Windows. In many ways, the Foundation framework provides greater portability and power than some standard libraries that have been built specifically for that purpose.

For now, however, since Apple platforms are by far the most popular platforms for Objective-C developers at this time, I focus primarily on features available there.

Using Frameworks in Your Projects

Though it is specific to MacOS X, I am going to visit, briefly, the subject of using frameworks in your own projects so that you'll know how to handle them when you need to.

Frameworks provided by Apple are typically installed in the directory that you installed Xcode, by default /Developer. Under this directory, you'll find a directory called Platforms. Inside the Platforms directory, you'll find a directory for each of the different development platforms for which you have an SDK installed. For example, if you have installed the iPhone SDK, then you will see directories corresponding to iPhone OS. If you have not, then you will only see directories corresponding to MacOS X.

Inside of the SDK directory, you'll find a path leading to System/Library/Frameworks It is within this directory that all of the frameworks for this particular platform in this particular SDK located.

Adding frameworks

Adding a framework to your project is very straightforward. You simply right-click or option click the target to which you intend to add the framework, and choose Add ⇨ Existing Frameworks. Doing this brings up the framework selection dialog box, as shown in Figure 11.1.

This dialog box enables you to select from the list of installed frameworks whichever framework you wish to link with your currently selected target.

Figure 11.1

The framework selection dialog box.

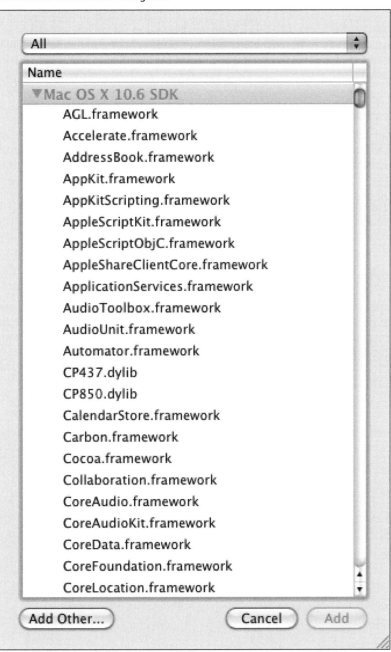

Including the headers

Remember that simply linking with the framework is not enough to enable you to actually use the classes and code contained within it. You also need to be sure to include the appropriate header files into your source file. Recall when you learned about importing header files that you tell the compiler to search the linked framework directories by enclosing the name of the header file you are importing in <>. Doing so causes the compiler to search the system including directories as well as any framework directories.

Considering garbage collection

An important consideration when linking with third-party frameworks is to ensure that the framework in question supports the memory management model that you have selected for your project. Not all frameworks support both garbage collection and reference counted memory management. So be sure when you are reviewing the documentation for the framework that you intend to link to your project that you are linking with the correct version of that framework for the memory management system that you have selected. Linking with the incorrect version will cause a compilation error.

Summary

In this chapter, I have introduced you to the concept of frameworks and also talked about the Foundation framework which serves as the closest thing to a standard library that Objective-C has. The remainder of this part of the book will utilize the Foundation framework extensively and it is important that you have this conceptual introduction to the framework and what it provides. Now that you have this background information, you'll be better prepared for the detailed coding examples to come.

Using Strings

A ny good standard library needs a great string class, and Objective-C with Foundation is no exception. In fact, the foundation framework comes with an excellent string class, NSString. Like many of the low-level core classes in Foundation, an immutable version of NSString, as well as a mutable version called NSMutableString exists. These two classes give you a tremendous amount of functionality when working with string values.

Understanding the String Declaration Syntax

Although NSString and NSMutableString have many types of initializers and factory methods available, strings are such a commonly used class in Objective-C, a special language construct has been created explicitly for the purposes of declaring a string easily. This construct is shown in Listing 12.1.

Listing 12.1

The Objective-C NSString shortcut syntax

```
NSString *someString = @"this is a string";
```

Essentially, the compiler knows that any time it encounters @ and then a string contained within double quotes, it should create a static const NSString object to contain the string provided.

Any two declarations of the exact same string value, even if stored in different variable names, point to the same object. Therefore, you can use these strings for keys, for example, where the equality of the string as compared to another instance of that string will be considered to be equal, both using the -isEqual: object method as well as the == operator, which will compare the value of the pointers.

To illustrate this, look at Listing 12.2.

Listing 12.2

Examining string constant equality

```
NSString *string1 = @"this is a string";
NSString *string2 = @"this is a string"; // same object as string1
NSString *string3 = [NSString stringWithString:string1]; // makes new

assert(string1 == string2); // true
assert([string1 isEqual:string2]); // also true
assert([string1 isEqual:string3]); // true
assert(string1 == string3); // false
```

Most often, you declare strings using the Objective-C string construct, but numerous initializers and factory methods are available on the `NSString` and `NSMutableString` classes. Some of the more common ones are shown in Table 12.1.

Table 12.1 NSString and NSMutableString factory methods.

Method	Purpose
+string	Constructs a new empty string.
+stringWithFormat:	Constructs a new string using the printf-style format specifier given and any arguments required by the format specifier.
+stringWithCharacters:length:	Constructs a new string containing length characters retrieved from the C. style array provided.
+stringWithString:	Constructs a new string with the value of the given string.
+stringWithCString:encoding:	Constructs a new string using a C. style string by converting it using the specified encoding.
+stringWithUTF8String:	Constructs a new string using a C.-style string encoded with UTF-8 string encoding. This is equivalent to calling +stringWithCString:encoding: using NSUTF8Encoding for the encoding parameter.
+stringWithContentsOfFile:encoding:error:	Constructs a new string containing the contents of the file specified using the encoding provided.

Method	Purpose
+stringWithContentsOfURL:encoding:error:	Constructs a new string containing the contents of the resource specified by the URL. The resource will be downloaded using the specified protocol, and decoded using the provided encoding. This call will block while the resource is downloading.
+stringWithContentsOfFile:usedEncoding:error:	Constructs a new string containing the contents of the file specified. Will attempt to automatically detect the type of file encoding used and inform the caller of the type of encoding detected via the usedEncoding out parameter.
+stringWithContentsOfURL:usedEncoding: error:	Constructs a new string containing the contents of the resource specified by the provided URL. Will download the resource, and attempt to detect the type of file encoding used and inform the caller of the encoding type via the usedEncoding out parameter.

Each of these also has an initializer version that can be used if you prefer to create your strings that way.

NOTE

The term "factory method" refers to class methods that can be used to construct an object using particular arguments.

Using format strings

One of the more commonly used factory methods is the +stringWithFormat: factory method, which utilizes a printf style format string and a list of arguments to construct the string. (I use format strings in many of the examples of this book. Every time you see a call to NSLog, you see an instance of a format string.) Listing 12.3 shows an example of a format string used with a call to NSLog.

Listing 12.3

The format string in NSLog

```
NSLog(@"The age of the employee named %@ is %ld", [employee name], [employee age]);
```

The use of @"" indicates the format string is an instance of NSString. When creating a format string, you use a special combination of percent signs and characters to indicate particular parameters that will be substituted into the string when it is passed to the object that is using the string. The format string contains three kinds of components, the first is the format specifiers. A format specifier is a special combination of characters, beginning with a %, followed by one or more numbers and letters specifying the format of the argument to be substituted into the format string at runtime. You can use a format specifier to insert anything from an object, to an integer, or a float. A format specifier can also specify how the argument is formatted when placed into the string. For example, to construct a format specifier to insert a floating-point value with two decimal places after it, you use a format specifier, such as `%.2f`. The different characters used for the format specifiers are extensive and comprehensive, and could probably fill a book this size with their complexity and quirks. Therefore, I won't go into a great amount of detail about all of them. I encourage you to read the Apple documentation on format strings.

That said, however, there is one format specifier which I would like to address specifically. It is the format specifier `%@`. This specifier is special to Objective-C. It is intended to be used in conjunction with object arguments. What it does is cause the format string to take the object passed as an argument for that format specifier and call the method `-description` on that object in order to get a string representation of that object. Most foundation classes have a `-description` method that returns something sensible for the class in question. `NSString's -description` method actually returns the string itself. `NSArray's -description` method returns a string that shows a stringified representation of the contents of the array. The default `NSObject` implementation of `-description` returns a string, which shows the pointer address of the object. If you create a custom class, and you want to use this feature of format strings with your class, be sure to override the `-description` method accordingly.

The second type of component that can be used in a format string is called an escape sequence. You use escape sequences to insert special, nonstandard characters into the string. The first letter of an escape sequence is always a backslash character followed by a character that tells the compiler what type of special character you wish to insert. For example, to insert a carriage return character into the string, you use the escape sequence `\r`.

The most commonly used escape sequences are \n to insert a newline, \r for a carriage return, \" for a double quote, and \t for a tab character. Because of the use of the \ character to begin an escape sequence, the escape sequence \\ also inserts just a \ character.

Finally, the third type of component you can use in a format string is essentially anything that doesn't fall into the first two component categories. These characters are simply passed straight through into the final result.

When a format string is interpreted, it goes through the format string, and for each format specifier that it encounters, it looks for a following argument to the function for which this format string is an argument itself. It then substitutes the value of that argument into the result string and performs whatever conversion the format specifier indicates. To give you an idea of exactly how this works, take a look at Listing 12.4.

Listing 12.4

Using format strings

```
NSString *str;

NSString *cardName = @"Ace";
NSString *cardSuit = @"Spades";

str = [NSString stringWithFormat:@"The winning card is %@ of %@.",
                                  cardName, cardSuit];
// str is "The winning card is Ace of Spades."

   str = [NSString stringWithFormat:@"You have %ld gold!",
                                     [player goldAmount]];
// str is "You have 1000 gold!"

   str = [NSString stringWithFormat:@"Your change is: $%.2f.", change];
// str is "Your change is $2.43
```

Notice that the arguments passed when working with format strings are passed using an unusual syntax. The format string allows you to pass a variadic argument list to the +stringWith Format method. The count of arguments is determined by how many format specifiers are provided.

NOTE

To ensure your code is 64-bit safe, it's generally considered a best practice to use the %ld format specifier when working with integers. When using NSInteger as the type for your integers, it will automatically change with the architecture from 32-bit to 64-bit. Using %ld for your format specifier insures that the format string will work with either 32-bit or 64-bit NSIntegers, regardless of their size.

Working with Other NSString Methods

Using format strings allows you to create strings in a much more flexible fashion than if you simply had to append them together. Various applications for format strings are available aside from simply constructing new strings. For example, you can also append a formatted string, as shown in Listing 12.5.

Listing 12.5

Appending a formatted string

```
NSMutableString *str = [...];

[str appendFormat:@"Your change is: %.2f.", change];
```

You can also split a string into separate components by using the method –components SeperatedByString:. This method will search for instances of the given string within the receiver, and then returned and NSArray containing the parts of the string separated by that string. Listing 12.6 shows example of this.

Listing 12.6

Splitting a string into its components

```
NSString *str = @"This is a string of words.";

NSArray *words = [str componentsSeperatedByString:@" "];

// words is now [@"This", @"is", ... ]
```

Similarly, the corollary to this is the NSArray method –componentsJoinedByString: which will do the opposite operation. It will take an array of strings and combine them into a single string with each component separated by the given string.

You can perform string searching and replacement using methods like –rangeOfString: to find the range of a given string within the receiver, or –stringByReplacingOccurrences OfString:withString: to do string replacement. NSString even has some limited regular expression matching support as well.

Overall, NSString is an amazingly powerful and comprehensive class with a lot of functionality much more than can be covered here. My advice is to visit the NSString documentation, and review all the methods it provides you.

Using NSString categories

Because NSString is such a comprehensive class already, Apple has chosen to extract into separate category files that are used in conjunction with NSString. These are the NSString (AppKitAdditions) and NSString(UIStringDrawing) categories. These are not strictly part of the Foundation framework; however, they are part of the GUI toolkit frameworks Cocoa, and Cocoa Touch. They provide methods used for drawing strings on windows and views. Because they are not part of Foundation, I won't cover them here, for more information on them, please visit the Apple Documentation, or pick up one of the other books in this series on those subjects.

Summary

The NSString and NSMutableString classes are a vital component of Objective-C. I could write chapters and chapters about all of the different methods and how you can use them in your code. However, the best thing you can do is simply to be familiar with the NSString and NSMutableString class documentation. Usually, if there's something you need on NSString, the functionality is going to be there. You just need to find it.

Working with Collections

While Foundation provides you with tons of classes for all kinds of purposes, it's worthwhile to visit a few of the most fundamental classes in depth because of the extent to which you are likely to use them in your applications.

Among those fundamental classes is the group of classes known as collections. A collection is a class which manages a group of objects. Every good language has a good collections API and Objective-C is no exception. The Foundation framework contains classes for dealing with arrays, dictionaries, hash tables, sets, and so on. These classes provide a comprehensive toolset for managing and manipulating groups of objects for almost any circumstance. Additionally, thanks to a small sprinkling of syntactical sugar as part of the language, dealing with enumerating, filtering, and sorting with these collection classes is simple and intuitive.

Working with Arrays

The first collection class that I want to introduce you to is NSArray. The NSArray class is used for managing an ordered collection of objects. An ordered collection of objects is a grouping of objects that is expected to be maintained in the order in which they were stored. Typically, an ordered collection of objects is accessed either through enumeration or by index.

To create an NSArray, you can either use an initializer, or you can use one of its numerous class factory methods. Listing 13.1 shows an example of creating a new NSArray.

In This Chapter

Learning to use collections

Understanding mutability versus immutability

Using specialized collections

Enumerating the members of a collection

Sorting and filtering collections

Using blocks with collections

Listing 13.1

Creating a new NSArray

```
NSArray *array = [NSArray arrayWithObjects:@"foo", @"bar", @"baz", nil];
```

The NSArray class is immutable — once it is created, you cannot modify its contents. However, because Objective-C provides no mechanism for ensuring the immutability of the objects inside an array, if you access an element of an array, those objects can be modified.

NOTE

Elements in collection classes do not need to be the same type. You can mix them at will.

You can access the count of the elements inside the array using the –count method, which returns an NSInteger.

You can access the elements of NSArray sequentially by using fast enumeration, indexed access, or by using an NSEnumerator object. Examples of all three of these are shown in Listing 13.2.

Listing 13.2

Accessing the elements of an array sequentially

```
NSArray *array = [NSArray arrayWithObjects:@"foo", @"bar", @"baz", nil];

// fast enumeration

for(NSString *item in array)
{
    NSLog(@"%@", item);
}

// indexed access
```

```
for(NSInteger n = 0; n < [array count]; n++)
{
    NSLog(@"%@", [array objectAtIndex:n]);
}

// using an NSEnumerator

NSEnumerator *enumerator = [array objectEnumerator];
NSString *item = nil;
while((item = [enumerator nextObject]))
{
    NSLog(@"%@", item);
}
```

Accessing an individual element of an NSArray is done by using the method -objectAt
Index: which returns an individual element at the given index. NSArray also provides the
convenience method -lastObject: which returns the last element of the array. To find the
index of a specific element, you can also use the method -indexOfObject:, which sends
the -isEqual: message to each of the elements of the array, and returns the first element
which returns YES. Both of these are shown in Listing 13.3.

Listing 13.3

Accessing individual elements.

```
NSArray *array = [NSArray arrayWithObjects:@"foo", @"bar", @"baz", nil];

NSString *item = nil;

item = [array objectAtIndex:1]; // item is now 'bar'

item = [array lastObject]; // item is now 'baz'

NSLog(@"%ld", [array indexOfObject:@"foo"]); // yields 0
```

CAUTION

`NSArray` as well as all collections in Objective-C is zero based. This means the first element starts at index 0, and the last element has an index of one less than the length of the array. If you try to access an element outside of these index boundaries, you will get an exception.

In addition to the methods that return individual items at individual indexes, you can also use other methods that return groups of objects based on ranges of indexes. These methods, such as `–objectsAtIndexes:` and `–indexesOfObjects:` work similarly to the methods that are used for accessing individual elements, except that they take an `NSIndexSet`, specifying the items you want. These calls return a new `NSArray` containing the subset of objects matching the indexes passed in. Listing 13.4 shows examples of these methods.

Listing 13.4

Accessing groups of elements

```
    NSArray *array = [NSArray arrayWithObjects:@"foo", @"bar", @"baz", nil];
NSRange range;
range.location = 1;
range.length = 2;

NSIndexSet *indexSet = [NSIndexSet indexSetWithIndexesInRange:range];

// this should get indexes for [@"bar", @"baz"]
NSArray *subItems = [array objectsAtIndexes:indexSet];
```

The access time for an element of an `NSArray`, while not strictly specified as such, can be assumed to be at worst, O(lg N), but is often O(1) for most operations. Linear search operations can have a worst-case complexity of O(N*lg N).The `NSArray` class is useful for storing virtually any collection of Objective-C objects, including objects that are not of the same class. However, `NSArray` is incapable of holding either nil values, structs, or scalars. If you feel the need to store a nil value in an `NSArray`, instead consider using an instance of `NSNull`. This class was made specifically for cases where you needed to store a "non-value" in a container class. When it comes to storing structs, you should wrap the struct in an `NSValue`. The same goes for storing scaler values, `NSNumber` provides a convenient wrapper object which you can use to store a scalar value.

Using dictionaries

The next collection class that I'd like to talk about is `NSDictionary`. The `NSDictionary` class provides a container for an associative collection of objects. *Associative* collections refer to collections that contain both keys and objects which must be associated to each other. To access a given element of the collection, you request the element by asking for the object associated with a given key.

Often, instances of NSString are used as the keys for the dictionary. This is not a requirement. The objects used as keys can be of any type, provided they implement the NSCopying protocol and are unique. The dictionary determines uniqueness via the NSObject method -isEqual: versus other keys in the dictionary, and will throw an exception if you attempt to create a dictionary with two keys that are the same.

Like NSArray, NSDictionary can be initialized either by using an initializer or by using one of the numerous NSDictionary class factory methods. Listing 13.5 shows several examples of how to create instances of NSDictionary.

Listing 13.5

Creating instances of NSDictionary

```
NSDictionary *dict;

    // normal initializer...

dict = [[NSDictionary alloc] initWithObjects:@"foo", @"bar", @"baz"
                              forKeys:@"one", @"two", @"three"
                                count:3];

// factory method

dict = [NSDictionary dictionaryWithObjects:@"foo", @"bar", @"baz"
                            forKeys:@"one", @"two", @"three"
                              count:3];

// this one reads in a plist file and uses it to create the dict...

dict = [NSDictionary dictionaryWithContentsOfFile:@"something.plist"];

// just like the NSArray...

dict = [NSDictionary dictionaryWithObjectsAndKeys:
        @"foo", @"one",
        @"bar", @"two",
        @"baz", @"three",
        nil];
```

You can access individual elements of an NSDictionary by using the object method -objectForKey:, which retrieves the object associated with the given key. Listing 13.6 shows an example of this operation.

Listing 13.6

Accessing an individual elements of an NSDictionary

```
NSLog(@"%@", [dict objectForKey:@"one"]); // prints 'foo'

NSLog(@"%@", [dict objectForKey:@"two"]); // prints 'bar'
```

Just like when using the NSArray class, there are variants of this method which take as parameters, multiple keys to access multiple objects at once. One variant of these calls is the -objects ForKeys:notFoundMarker:, which calls for an object that will be returned in the event that a given key is not found. Listing 13.7 shows an example of this method in use.

Listing 13.7

Using the method -objectsForKeys:notFoundMarker:

```
NSArray *keys = [NSArray arrayWithObjects:@"one", @"ten", @"two"];

NSArray *items = [dict objectsForKeys:keys notFoundMarker:[NSNull null]];

// items now contains [@"foo", NSNull, @"bar"]
```

As is the case with NSArray, nil values, structures, and scalars cannot be stored as objects in an NSDictionary. You need to wrap them, instead, by using NSNull, NSValue, or NSNumber, respectively.

In addition to being able to access individual elements of an NSDictionary by key, you can also retrieve all keys in the dictionary or all objects in the dictionary by using the methods -allKeys or -allObjects, respectively. Both of these methods return an instance of

NSArray which can then subsequently be used in the same patterns as NSArray for the purposes of enumeration. That is, you can enumerate over all of the keys, or all of the objects in an NSDictionary by enumerating over these arrays using a for loop, a while loop, and so on. Listing 13.8 shows an example of doing this.

Listing 13.8

Enumerating over the keys and objects in NSDictionary

```
// these two have the same output
// iterating the objects...
NSArray *objects = [dict allObjects];
for(NSString *obj in objects)
{
    NSLog(@"%@", obj);
}

// default is to iterate the keys
for(NSString *key in dict)
{
    NSLog(@"%@", [dict objectForKey:key]);
}
```

In addition to using the -allKeys method to get an array you can use iteration to loop over the dictionary's values using the -allObjects method. Just iterating using the dictionary itself as the iteration object as shown here allows you to loop over the keys as well.

Finally, you can also retrieve a sorted array of keys in an NSDictionary by using the method -sortedKeysUsingSelector:. I cover more about sorting collections shortly, so I won't discuss this method here other than to simply inform you that it exists.

Like NSArray, NSDictionary cannot contain nil keys or objects, and it cannot contain scalars or structs.

NSDictionary is usually implemented internally as a hash table. Therefore, access by key to a given object is typically going to be O(1). Again, this is not specified explicitly, so, your mileage may vary.

Working with sets

The NSArray class provides a collection for use with an ordered collection of objects, and the NSSet provides a class for working with unordered collections of objects. Using an NSSet, you can store objects that do not have to be stored in a particular order. The fact that an NSSet is unordered enables it to be slightly faster when accessing individual elements, though they cannot be accessed by index or key.

Again, creating an NSSet is done by using either an initializer or one of the numerous NSSet class factory methods. Listing 13.9 shows how to create an NSSet using a factory method and how to manipulate the members of the set.

Listing 13.9

Creating an NSSet

```
NSSet *set = [NSSet setWithObjects:@"foo", @"bar", @"baz"];

NSLog(@"%@", [set member:@"foo"]); // outputs foo

NSLog(@"%@", [set anyObject]); // prints one of them, no idea which

NSLog(@"%@", [set allObjects]); // [@"foo", @"bar", @"baz"]

NSLog(@"%ld", [set containsObject:@"baz"]); // prints '1'
```

Object stored in an NSSet must respond to the NSObject methods –isEqual: and –hash. If the –hash method of an object stored in an NSSet depends on the internal state of the object, the stored object must not change while it is in the set.

Accessing objects in the set can be done by using the methods –allObjects, which returns an array containing all of the objects in the set, –anyObject which returns a non-deterministic object from the set, or –member: which returns the member of the set that matches the passed in parameter determined by using the method –isEqual:. Finally, the method –any Object returns a non-deterministic member of the set.

You can iterate over the objects of the NSSet by using fast enumeration or an NSEnumerator.

Listing 13.10 shows accessing objects in an NSSet and enumerating over an NSSet.

Listing 13.10

Operations on an NSSet

```
NSSet *set = [NSSet setWithObjects:@"foo", @"bar", @"baz"];

NSLog(@"%@", [set member:@"foo"]); // outputs foo

NSLog(@"%@", [set anyObject]); // prints one of them, no idea which

NSLog(@"%@", [set allObjects]); // [@"foo", @"bar", @"baz"]

NSLog(@"%ld", [set containsObject:@"baz"]); // prints '1'

for(NSString *item in set)
{
    NSLog(@"%@", item);
}

NSEnumerator *enumerator = [set objectEnumerator];
NSString *item = nil;
while((item = [enumerator nextObject]))
{
    NSLog(@"%@", item);
}
```

Foundation also provides a subclass of NSSet called NSCountedSet. This nifty class allows you to add the same object to the set multiple times. The NSCountedSet keeps track of how many times you added a given object, but only actually stores the object once. It keeps a running count of the number of times the given object is added to the set and requires an equal number of -removeObject: calls to actually remove the object.

NSCountedSet's implementation of the -count method returns the number of distinct objects, not the total number of times all objects were added to the set. In order to access the count for a given object, you can use the method -countForObject:.

Understanding mutability

Each of the collection classes that I've introduced you to so far have been immutable. After you create the collection, you cannot add objects to or remove objects from the collection. Collections wouldn't be particularly useful if you were limited to adding or removing objects from them.

Therefore, Foundation also provides mutable versions of all of these classes. The names of the mutable versions of the classes are NSMutableArray, which corresponds to NSArray, NSMutableDictionary, corresponding to NSDictionary, and NSMutableSet that corresponds to NSSet. Each of these classes provides additional methods, in addition to the read-only methods of their immutable counterparts for the purposes of adding, removing, and replacing objects within the collections.

NSMutableArray provides the method -addObject: for placing an object at the end of the array, -insertObject:atIndex: for inserting an object at a specific index, -removeLast Object for removing the last object in the array, -removeObjectAtIndex: for removing an object at a given index, and -replaceObjectAtIndex:withObject: for replacing a given object at a specified index with another object. Listing 13.11 shows some examples of using these methods on an NSMutableArray.

Listing 13.11

Manipulating the elements of an NSMutableArray

```
NSMutableArray *array = [NSMutableArray array];

[array addObject:@"foo"];
[array addObject:@"baz"];
[array insertObject:@"bar" atIndex:1];
// now [@"foo", @"bar", @"baz]

[array removeLastObject];
// now [@"foo", @"bar"]

[array removeObjectAtIndex:0];
// now [@"bar"]

[array replaceObjectAtIndex:0 withObject:@"boz"];
// now [@"boz"]
```

There are naturally plural forms of each of these methods that perform the same operations with arrays of objects or ranges of indexes.

Similarly, NSMutableDictionary provides methods for manipulating its contents as well. For example, to add an object into the dictionary, you use the method -setObject:forKey:. To remove an object, you use the method -removeObjectForKey:. Listing 13.12 shows an example of manipulating an NSMutableDictionary.

CAUTION

Calling −setObject:forKey: with a key that already exists in the dictionary will replace the old object with the new one.

Listing 13.12

Manipulating the elements of an NSMutableDictionary

```
NSMutableDictionary *dict [NSMutableDictionary dictionary];

[dict setObject:@"foo" forKey:@"one"];
[dict setObject:@"bar" forKey:@"two"];
[dict setObject:@"baz" forKey:@"three"];

// dict now contains all three objects and keys

[dict removeObjectForKey:@"two"];

// dict now only has foo and baz in it
```

Finally, NSMutableSet provides similar functionality with the methods −addObject:, and −removeObject:. Additionally, it also provides specialized methods for adding and removing groups of objects. −unionSet:, for example adds all the objects from another set to the receiver. Similarly, −minusSet: removes a set of objects from the receiver.

Understanding Collections and Memory Management

You have to be careful when working with collections in a non-garbage collected memory environment. When an object is removed from the collection, it is released. This has several implications for you as a developer.

First and foremost, because the collection will be retaining objects that are added to it, you do not need to retain those objects outside of the collection if you don't have some other good reason to do so. You can assume that by placing the object into the collection, that the collection then owns it. When the collection is deallocated, it sends a release to each of the objects in the collection, so you do not need to be concerned about the potential for memory leaks, because the collection fulfills that part of the memory management contract.

Secondly, because objects are released when removed from a collection, the possibility that a given object that you intend to continue to use but which is being removed from a collection, may be released without your being aware of it. Listing 13.13 shows an example of this problem when using an NSMutableArray.

Listing 13.13

Error when removing an object from an NSMutableArray

```
NSMutableArray *array = [NSMutableArray arrayWithObjects:@"foo",
                        @"bar", @"baz", nil];

NSString *item = [array objectAtIndex:1];

[array removeObjectAtIndex:1]; // item is released here.

NSLog(@"%@", item); // error!!
```

The error in this code occurs because although you have retrieved the object from the array, you have not retained it. As long as you do not remove the object from the array, it is still retained by the array and therefore can be manipulated at will. However, if you remove the object from the array, it is immediately released. Therefore, accessing the method on the object as shown here causes an error.

The correct way to write this code is to retain the object that you have retrieved from the array prior to removing it from the array. Listing 13.14 shows the same code corrected.

Listing 13.14

The correct way to remove an object you wish to continue using

```
NSMutableArray *array = [NSMutableArray arrayWithObjects:@"foo",
                        @"bar", @"baz", nil];

NSString *item = [array objectAtIndex:1];

[item retain]; // keep it around!
```

```
[array removeObjectAtIndex:1]; // item is released here.

NSLog(@"%@", item); // OK

[item release]; // remember to release it since you retained it!
```

Obviously, when working in a garbage collected environment, these types of problems do not occur.

Using specialized collections

A few collection classes serve specific narrow purposes. Although they are rarely used, it's nice to know that they exist, if you need them; these are `NSPointerArray`, `NSHashTable`, and `NSMapTable`. They are primarily used in garbage collected environments for specialized collections requiring weak relationships.

Each of them provides an interface that is similar to, but does not inherit from a specific type of collection. `NSPointerArray` for `NSArray`, `NSHashTable` for `NSSet`, and `NSMapTable` for `NSDictionary`.

Because of their similarity of purpose and their rarity of use, I won't belabor this subject by going into a great amount of detail on every one of these, however, it can be useful to look at one of these three, `NSPointerArray`, for the purposes of example since the design pattern used in its construction is similar enough to the other two as to not require additional explanation.

The class `NSPointerArray` is probably one of the most powerful of these specialized collection classes. It specifies an `NSArray` like interface but allows for the insertion of null values and arbitrary pointers. Additionally, by specifying certain options when creating an instance of `NSPointerArray`, you can configure your array to have specific memory management policies with regard to the objects stored within it. For example, you can specify that objects that get reclaimed by the garbage collector get replaced by a NULL value. To do this, you create a zeroing weak memory configuration by using the `NSPointerFunctionsZeroingWeakMemory` option.

You specify the options for your instance of `NSPointerArray` when you create it using the methods `-initWithOptions:` or `-initWithPointerFunctions:`. When using the method `-initWithOptions:`, you are specifying that the array that you are creating will obey the policies set forth by the options that you are passing as a parameter. The options, which are specified using a bitwise-or, set specific policies or "personalities" for the array. For example, to create an array to store standard C-style strings that require `strcmp` to compare them and `malloc`/`free` for memory management, you do something like Listing 13.15.

Listing 13.15

An NSPointerArray to store C strings

```
NSPointerArray *array = [[NSPointerArray alloc] initWithOptions:
                (NSPointerFunctionsCStringPersonality|
                          NSPointerFunctionsMallocMemory)];
```

You can only specify one such personality option and one such memory option for a given instance.

Alternatively, for maximum flexibility, you can use the initializer `-initWithPointer Functions:` that allows you to specify an instance of `NSPointerFunctions` as a parameter. This class encapsulates the functions that will be used by the array for operations, such as hashing, equality finding, storage, and deletion. Each of these different operations has a corresponding function that you can configure by using an instance of this class. When you pass this instance to the `NSPointerArray`, it will then use the functions that you have defined when objects are inserted, removed, and so on, in place of the normal retain, release, and other methods that would be used in a normal `NSArray`.

The cases when you actually need to use `NSPointerArray` are probably few and far between. However, it is available as a tool if you need it.

Enumerating

The elements of a collection can be iterated over by using fast enumeration or by using an `NSEnumerator`. By using fast enumeration, you simply use a standard for loop. Enumerating in this way over an `NSArray` or `NSSet` enumerates over each element of the collection. Using fast enumeration on an `NSDictionary` enumerates over its keys.

Listing 13.16 shows each of these three collection types being enumerated.

Listing 13.16

Enumerating over collections using fast enumeration

```
NSMutableArray *array = [NSMutableArray arrayWithObjects:@"foo",
                        @"bar", @"baz", nil];
```

```
for(NSString *item in array)
{
    NSLog(@"%@", item);
}
```

Alternatively, you can use "old style" enumeration, using `NSEnumerator`. In this method, you acquire an `NSEnumerator` for your collection and then call the `NSEnumerator` object method `-nextObject` repeatedly until you receive a `nil`, which indicates the end of the collection. This is shown in Listing 13.17.

Listing 13.17

Enumerating the collections using NSEnumerator

```
NSEnumerator *enumerator = [array objectEnumerator];
NSString *item = nil;
while((item = [enumerator nextObject]))
{
    NSLog(@"%@", item);
}
```

There is also a reverse enumerator that you can access, which will enable you to iterate over the elements of the container in reverse. This can actually be used both in the traditional while loop as well as using fast enumeration, as shown in Listing 13.18.

Listing 13.18

Enumerator Tricks

```
NSEnumerator *enumerator = [array reverseObjectEnumerator];
NSString *item = nil;
while((item = [enumerator nextObject]))
{
    NSLog(@"%@", item);
}
```

continued

Listing 13.18 *(continued)*

```
for(item in enumerator)
{
    NSLog(@"%@", item);
}
```

This also works for forward enumerators, but because that's the standard behavior for fast enumeration, that is rarely used.

Changing the contents of a collection while enumerating is dangerous and will cause the enumeration to become invalid and cause an error. Therefore — don't do it.

Sending Messages to Elements

Another common requirement is to loop over the elements of a collection, calling some method on each of them. This is accomplished via the object methods `-makeObjects PerformSelector:` and `-makeObjectsPerformSelector:withObject:`. These methods take a selector object, which specifies the method to be called on each of the objects in the collection. In the case of the latter method, a parameter, given as the object parameter, is also passed to each of the method calls.

Listing 13.19 shows an example of using this method to iterate over a collection of items in a game engine, updating their positions. In this case, the game state object is passed to each element so that it can use it.

Listing 13.19

Making all objects of a collection perform some action

```
NSArray *gameObjects = [...];

GameState *gameState = [...];

[gameObjects makeObjectsPerformSelector:@selector(updatePosition:)
                            withObject:gameState];
```

This causes each element of the array to receive a call to `-updatePosition:` with the parameter gameState.

Sorting and Filtering

`NSArray` and `NSMutableArray` benefit from a plethora of sorting and filtering capabilities. `NSArray`, because of its immutability, has methods that allow you to retrieve a copy of the array, sorted or filtered, whereas `NSMutableArray` allows you to also sort the array in place. For the purposes of discussion here, I focus primarily on `NSMutableArray`, but you should know that you can access any of the non-mutating methods through `NSArray` as well.

Sorting an array can be done with the methods `-sortUsingDescriptors:`, `-sortUsing Function:context:`, or my personal favorite, `-sortUsingSelector:`, each of which takes a different type of sorting object as an argument to use for performing the sort.

The first of these, `-sortUsingDescriptors:` takes an instance of `NSSortDescriptor` as an argument. To create one of these, you specify the key path of the property upon which you want to sort the objects, whether this sort will be ascending or descending, and finally, if you choose, a selector which will be called using the property as arguments to do the comparison. If no selector is provided, the default is to use the standard `-compare:` selector.

In other words, take for example if you have an array of `Employee` objects, and you wanted to sort them based on employment date. The property that you would actually be sorting by in this case would be the employment date property, and you could perform this sort by using something like the code shown in Listing 13.20.

Listing 13.20

Sorting an array of employees using -sortUsingDescriptors:

```
NSMutableArray *employees = [...];

NSSortDescriptor *descr =
[NSSortDescriptor sortDescriptorWithKey:@"employmentDate"
                              ascending:YES];

NSArray *descriptors = [NSArray arrayWithObject:descr];

[employees sortUsingDescriptors:descriptors];
```

In this example, I'm only using a single descriptor, but you can also sort by multiple criteria by providing multiple descriptors. The parameter is an array, so you simply put them all into an `NSArray` and call the method.

The second of these methods `-sortUsingFunction:context:` It is for use when you need to perform your compare by using a function pointer. The function pointer that is passed as the argument to this method should be of the form `NSInteger comparisonFunction (id obj1, id obj2, void *)`. Its first two arguments are the two objects being compared. Its third argument is the context information, which is passed unchanged from the additional parameter provided to the method. This technique is useful when you need to pass some kind of additional external information to the comparison. You would do this by passing it as the contextual information pointer. Listing 13.21 shows an example sorting an array using this technique.

Listing 13.21

Sorting an array using a function

```
NSInteger sortByEmploymentDate(id employee1,
                               id employee2,
                               void *ctx)
{
    return [[employee1 employmentDate]
            compare:[employee2 employmentDate]];
}

NSMutableArray *employees = [...];

[employees sortUsingFunction:sortByEmploymentdate context:nil];
```

The third technique, using the method `-sortUsingSelector:` takes a selector object as a parameter. When used, the array iterates over all the elements of the array calling the given selector as a comparison method. The selector in question is expected to be implemented as an object method on the class of all of the elements of the array. It takes as an argument another element of the array and returns an `NSComparisonResult` specifying `NSOrderedSame`, `NSOrderedAscending`, or `NSOrderedDescending`, depending upon whether the receiver of the method and the past in object are equal, ordered ascending, were ordered descending relative to each other. Listing 13.22 shows the same employee array sort being done by using this technique. In this example, I'm showing the `Employee` class as well, to demonstrate how you might create the method that's being called.

Listing 13.22

Sorting the employee array using -sortUsingSelector:

```
@interface Employee
{

}
-(NSComparisonResult)compareEmploymentDate:(Employee *)other;
@end

@implementation Employee

-(NSComparisonResult)compareEmploymentDate:(Employee *)other;
{
    return [[self employmentDate] compare:[other employmentDate]];
}

@end

[employees sortUsingSelector:@selector(compareEmploymentDate:)];
```

Again, each of these methods sorts a mutable array in place. The NSArray class provides corresponding, non-mutating methods for each of these via the -sortedArrayUsingSort Descriptors:, -sortedArrayUsingFunction:context:, and –sortedArrayUsingSelector: methods, respectively.

 NOTE

You can also sort arrays using blocks, which I detail in the next section.

To filter an array, you use the method –filterUsingPredicate:, which takes an NSPredicate object as a parameter. The NSPredicate object allows you to specify via a simple query language, conditions to be met for the purposes of filtering the array. You specify the conditions of the query by using a query string. The query language used with NSPredicate is similar to but not a direct derivative of SQL. It allows you to specify things such as "first Name == 'John'", or "birthDate >= '01/01/2001'". In each of these cases, the named property is compared against the value given by using the operation specified, and if it logically returns true if the object is included in the result set. If it logically returns false, then the object is filtered.

So, to filter the array from the previous examples for all employees that have been at the company more than 5 years ago, you might do something like Listing 13.23.

Listing 13.23

Filtering an array

```
NSPredicate *predicate = [NSPredicate
                     predicateWithFormat:@"employedForYears >= 5"];

NSArray *seniorEmployees = [employees filterUsingPredicate:predicate];
```

The assumption here is that you have created an object method on the Employee class that calculates the number of years employed and it's looking for all employees for which that returns 5 or greater.

Using Blocks with Collections

NSArray also has the ability to do transformations using blocks. I showed you this briefly back in the section about blocks, but for the sake of thoroughness, I'll discuss it again here. Using the method -enumerateObjectsUsingBlock:, which takes a block as a parameter and executes the block, passing each element of the array to it as the iteration proceeds. The other form of this method, -enumerateObjectsWithOptions:usingBlock: takes an options parameter, which allows you to specify how the enumeration will be done. This parameter is a bitwise or'd value which can be one or both of the flags NSEnumerateConcurrently or NSEnumerateReverse, which specify that theta enumeration occurs in parallel or in reverse, respectively. In Chapter 5, I showed you how to iterate over the items in an array by executing a block. Here, in Listing 13.24, we cut right to the chase and use the -enumerateObjects UsingBlock: method to perform the same operation.

Listing 13.24

Performing a map operation on the elements of an NSArray

```
__block NSMutableArray *result = [NSMutableArray array];

void (^theBlock)(id obj, NSUInteger idx, BOOL *stop) =
^{
```

```
    [result addObject:transformObj(obj)];
}

[array enumerateObjectsUsingBlock:theBlock];
```

When this completes, the result array should contain all the elements of the original array but with whatever transformation the `transformObj` function is doing.

To do the same, but only over a subset of the array, you can use the method `-enumerate ObjectsAtIndexes:withBlock:`. You can also access a subset of the array by using the method `-indexesOfObjectsPassingTest:`. This convenient method allows you to pass a block to which each object will be given. If the block returns `YES`, then the object's index will be included in the returned array, otherwise it will not. This makes filtering a breeze with blocks.

Another method of performing a similar procedure might be to use the object methods `-makeObjectsPerformSelector:` or `-makeObjectsPerformSelector:with Object:`, which perform an enumeration of the elements of the array and call the given selector on each object. The disadvantage of this method as opposed to the ones that take blocks is that the selector has to be defined on the class of the objects in the array. This can be difficult in some cases, and might even force you to make a category to extend third-party classes for this purpose.

Summary

Collection classes are a vital part of any standard library. Objective-C, fortunately, has an excellent group of collection classes that make working with groups of objects easy. With `NSArray` for ordered collections, `NSDictionary` for associative collections, and `NSSet` for unordered collections, you have all the tools you need.

Using NSValue, NSNumber, and NSData

As I highlight in Chapter 13, when working with collections, collections are capable of storing only valid Objective-C objects. Collections are incapable of storing scalars, structures, or other arbitrary low-level data. This is an inconvenience, but one that the designers of the Foundation framework anticipated and solved.

In order to store scalars and structures in collections, you need to use a class wrapper for these values. In other words, a class that enables you to store the value inside of an object. The Foundation framework provides three primary classes for this purpose, NSValue, NSNumber, and NSData.

The NSValue class is the simplest of these classes, providing a low-level interface for the arbitrary storage of virtually any C datatype. For example, you can store structures within it, you can store ranges within it, and so on. Once the data is stored within the NSValue instance, you can then use the instance of NSValue in a collection object. Because NSValue is relatively low level, it does not provide some of the conveniences of higher-level abstractions. Its purpose is to be flexible but it is limited in its capabilities because it can only store simple stack-allocated data. NSNumber is a subclass of NSValue. It provides a higher level abstraction to the NSValue data encoding system specifically for the purposes of storing numbers. It provides numerous factory methods for various scalar types to make creation and manipulation of the NSNumber objects easier. Using NSNumber is generally easier than using NSValue directly, and you should prefer it when possible.

I mentioned that NSValue is capable only of storing simple, stack allocated data. In fact, it is possible to store references to dynamically allocated data within an NSValue as well. You can use this as a means to keep track of dynamically allocated data in collections. However, when doing this, you must also have other code in place to keep track of the actual data itself so that you can allocate it and deallocate it. Managing memory manually like this can be inconvenient. Fortunately, there is a third class which enables you to wrap

In This Chapter

Boxing Datatypes for
Use in Collections

Working with
NSNumber, and NSValue

Using NSData and
NSMutableData

arbitrary dynamic data as well. This class is the NSData class. This class provides an object-oriented interface for a dynamically allocated byte buffer. You can use it to store any arbitrary chunk of bytes either directly or by copying the bytes from an allocated buffer. You can also use it to write that data out to disk as well.

Using NSValue and NSNumber

Now that I've introduced you to each of these classes, in the next sections, I show you how to use them. I start with the NSValue and NSNumber classes, and then proceed on to NSData and NSMutableData.

Wrapping arbitrary datatypes with NSValue

I mentioned before that NSValue is used for storing arbitrary data types. To create an NSValue, you provide it with a pointer to the value that you want to store, and a C string indicating the data type. Telling the NSValue instance about the type of the data is important because that tells it how many bytes it needs to read in order to get all of the data. Fortunately, Objective-C provides a special directive, @encode() that returns the appropriate encoding for a given type for your platform. Listing 14.1 shows how to create an NSValue using an arbitrary structure, passing the address of the structure instance for the pointer to the value, and using the @encode() directive to find the appropriate datatype.

Listing 14.1

Creating an NSValue for an arbitrary structure

```
typedef struct
{
    int someMember;
    float someOtherMember;
} MyDataType;


MyDataType item;
item.someMember = 10;
item.someOtherMember = 500.3;
NSValue *boxedStruct = [NSValue value:&item
                        withObjCType:@encode(MyDataType)];
```

This technique can be used with any structures that you create or any of the structures provided by the frameworks. For example, you could just as easily use the exact same code as above to encode an `NSRect` or an `NSSize`, both of which are foundation structures.

`NSValue` can also store integers, floats, and so on as well although `NSNumber` is probably a better choice when dealing with those particular types of values.

You can also store pointers to dynamic data inside an `NSValue`. To do this, you store the address of the pointer, as shown in Listing 14.2.

Listing 14.2

Storing pointers to dynamic data in NSValue

```
char *foo = malloc(1024);

NSValue *boxedPointer = [NSValue value:&foo
                         withObjCType:@encode(char **)];
```

An important thing to understand here is that what you are actually storing is the pointer itself and not the data. Therefore, you need to make sure that dynamically allocated data is not freed after storing it in the `NSValue`.

Wrapping numbers with NSNumber

For a higher-level abstraction when dealing with numbers, such as ints, floats, and the like, the `NSNumber` class provides some additional factory methods and accessors that automatically do the type conversion and determination for you. Using `NSNumber` is as simple as calling the appropriate factory method with your value. Listing 14.3 shows a few examples.

Listing 14.3

Creating NSNumbers

```
int someNumber = 110;
float someFloat = 500.3;
NSNumber *theNumber = [NSNumber numberWithInt:someNumber];
  NSNumber *theFloat = [NSNumber numberWithFloat:someFloat];
```

Doing arithmetic with NSDecimalNumber

Though you can easily get at the underlying value stored inside an NSNumber for the purposes of mathematical operations, sometimes you may want to just perform simple operations by using the NSNumber object. For this, Foundation provides the NSDecimalNumber class.

The NSDecimalNumber class is a subclass of NSNumber that provides methods for performing simple, base-10 arithmetical operations. It has various methods such as -decimalNumber ByAdding:, -decimalNumberBySubtracting:, -decimalNumberByRaising ToPower:, and so on. These methods make it easy to use NSArray methods such as −make ObjectsPerformSelector:withObject: to do math operations on all members of a collection.

N O T E

NSDecimalNumber is immutable, so all the math operations reviewed here return their result as a new NSDecimalNumber.

To see an example of how you might use these methods to give a bonus to all the employees in an employee dataset, take a look at Listing 14.4.

Listing 14.4

Giving a flat $5000 bonus to all employees

```
NSArray *employees = ...;
  [employees
makeObjectsPerformSelector:@selector(addToSalary:)
withObject:[NSDecimalNumber numberWithFloat:5000.0]];
   // the implementation of addToSalary: might be this...

  -(void)addToSalary:(NSDecimalNumber *)inRaise
  {
     self.salary = [self.salary decimalNumberByAdding:inRaise];
  }
```

Because NSDecimalNumber is capable of storing very large values (up to 38 digits x 10^+/- 128) it can also be convenient for some very large number calculations, however, using the C-level scalar values directly, rather than through NSDecimalNumber will almost always be faster, so choose this method with care. Generally speaking, this is for use with collections exclusively.

Using NSData and NSMutableData

When working with chunks of binary data, foundation provides you with the NSData and NSMutableData classes to be used for an object-oriented interface in manipulating that data. These classes can manage the allocation and deallocation of buffers and also provide an object wrapper for the purposes of storing the data in collection classes. They also provide an interface for writing data to files and transmitting data through socket communication.

Creating NSData objects

You can create NSData objects either by using an existing low-level data structure that you have previously allocated or by copying data from any of the other types of Objective-C objects that support the NSCopying protocol.

To create an NSData object using raw bytes from a C data structure, you use the factory method +dataWithBytes:length:, which takes a pointer to a data buffer and then copies the bytes from that data buffer into the NSData object. If you prefer to access the bytes inside the buffer directly, without copying them, you can use the factory method +dataWithBytes NoCopy:length:, which also constructs an NSData object but without copying the data, thus resulting in an NSData object with a buffer directly accessing the raw memory that you provide. In this case, the bytes provided must have been allocated by using malloc because the NSData object when released will free the bytes using the free function. Because NSMutableData allows you to make modifications to the data within it, doing so while pointing to an externally allocated buffer would lead to problems, therefore, when using NSMutableData, the object will copy the bytes regardless of whether you specify whether or not to copy them. Listing 14.5 shows an example of creating an NSData object using a preallocated buffer of bytes.

Listing 14.5

Creating an NSData object

```
char *buf = malloc(1024);

NSData *data = [NSData dataWithBytes:buf length:1024];
```

One of the more common uses for NSData objects is to access the bytes stored in files or resources on the Internet. You can easily create an NSData object with the contents of a file by using the factory method +dataWithContentsOfFile:, which takes the path to the file that you want to read as its parameter. To do the same thing but with a resource from the Internet, you use the factory method +dataWithContentsOfURL:. This method will access the Internet using the provided protocol from the provided URL and download the resource and make the raw data of that resource available as the raw data of the NSData object. As usual, as in most cases with these kinds of convenience methods, the download process will block the current thread until it completes so use this method with caution. NSData also provides methods for writing data to disk using the methods -writeToFile:atomically: and -writeToURL:atomically:. The latter of these methods only supports writing to local file URLs. Each of these takes as a secondary parameter one which specifies whether to write the file atomically. In cases where the data that you are writing is especially large, it may be possible for your application to terminate in the middle of writing the data. This can result in a corrupted file on disk. The atomic parameter specifies that the file will first be written to a scratch file and when the file operation is complete the scratch file will then be copied over to the final location. By using this flag, you know that your original file will only be overwritten if the replacement file has been able to be completely written successfully.

Accessing the raw bytes in an NSData object

The NSMutableSet class provides an object-oriented interface for an NSData object containing bytes that you want to be able to manipulate. You can add bytes to it by using the methods -appendBytes:length: and -apendData:; you can replace bytes using the method -replaceBytesInRange:withBytes:; and you can also truncate or expand the NSMutableData buffer by using the method -setLength:. If you want to simply zero out a particular portion of the buffer (setting it's bytes to 0's) you can use the method -resetBytesInRange:. This provides you with all the tools you need to manipulate raw data from files and structures at will. Listing 14.6 shows how you can use this capability to read a file from disk, modify specific bytes, and then write it back out to disk. In this case, the file in question is a legacy game data save file, which uses a hard-coded file format wherein particular values are stored at particular locations in the data.

Listing 14.6

Modifying the raw bytes of a game save file

```
int goldOffset = 617; // at location 617 in the file
int goldLength = 4; // 4 bytes are used for storing the gold

  NSRange goldRange = NSMakeRange(goldOffset, goldLength);
  NSMutableData *gameData = [NSMutableData dataWithContentsOfFile:@"..."];

  [gameData replaceBytesInRange:goldRange withBytes:newGoldValue]; [gameData
  writeToFile:@"..." atomically:YES];
```

As you can see, NSData makes a very convenient low-level interface for accessing raw data. It also provides a convenient wrapper for storing that data inside collection classes as well, just like with NSNumber and NSValue.

Summary

The purpose of this chapter was to introduce you to a few classes that make working with non-standard Objective-C data easier. They are particularly convenient when working with collections, which as you saw in Chapter 13 work only with Objective-C objects. These classes provide a very simple wrapper for that low level data so that you can then use them in collection classes and leverage the object-oriented capabilities of Objective-C with them. We live in a world filled with edge conditions and legacy data. Objective-C provides one of the cleanest, most integrated interfaces for that legacy data of any language out there. Its C language roots make it especially well suited to this task.

Working with Times and Dates

Working with dates on computers is traditionally a complex proposition. Dates, despite appearances, are not nearly as simple as they might seem. They're filled with exceptions and edge conditions, such as leap years, calendar changes, and so on. A comprehensive consideration of the subject reveals that even taking into consideration these exceptions, there are still issues surrounding questions of how far back your calendar should go and what to do with dates that fall before that boundary, and so on. The CE/BCE standard which we are accustomed to is really a fairly ineffective kludge.

If you need more proof of how difficult working with dates can be, recall the Y2K problem that the computing industry experienced at the beginning of this century. Naïve programmers had previously thought that they could represent the year in dates using only two digits. When the century mark rolled over, millions of lines of code had to be rewritten.

Even now, we face future problems with dates due to the fact that most computers store their dates using 32-bit integers as a count of seconds since January 1, 1970. Unfortunately, this counter will roll over sometime in the year 2032. Although that may seem far away, I remind you that programmers said the same things about the year 2000 when they were writing their two-digit year handling code.

Even if you ignore some of these larger questions, there is still the very practical point of how to handle dates and times properly in your application. For example, how do you handle determining the duration of a week in hours. Your first response to that maybe simply to multiply the number of hours in a day by seven. This would be a typical, albeit naïve response. But what if one of those days is the day upon which we change from daylight savings time to standard time, or vice versa? Now your calculation has suddenly become incorrect.

These kinds of problems are very common in software development and have resulted in some very high profile bugs that cost millions of dollars in public relations damage and problems for customers. Don't be that programmer.

In This Chapter

Manipulating dates with NSDate and NSCalendar

Working with time intervals

Localizing dates

In this chapter, I introduce you to the NSDate class, which is used for constructing and manipulating data objects within your applications. I also introduce you to the NSCalendar class that allows you to specify the rules that are used in calculating dates. Finally, I'm going to introduce you to the NSDateFormatter class, which allows you to convert a date value into something that you can display to the user. These three classes, when used together, form an effective tool kit for all of your date handling needs. Using them is the preferred method of manipulating dates in Objective-C applications.

Constructing Dates

NSDate is the class that encapsulates a given instant in time. It includes both the date and time. It can be used to represent the current time, by constructing a new NSDate object by using the class method +date, or you can construct an NSDate object representing any time in the past or future by constructing one using an NSTimeInterval. Listing 15.1 shows how to create an NSDate object representing the current time. It actually shows two different methods, the first using the +date factory method and the second using the standard initializer.

Listing 15.1

Constructing an NSDate object

```
NSDate *now = [NSDate date];
NSDate *alsoNow = [[NSDate alloc] init];
```

Working with Time Intervals

An NSTimeInterval represents a slice of time in seconds. By using it, you can construct dates relative to other dates. For example, you can construct an NSDate object which represents "30 minutes from now" by constructing an NSDate object using the initializer –init WithTimeIntervalSinceNow: and passing the number of seconds in 30 minutes as the parameter.

When representing time measurements in the future, the NSTimeInterval from now to that future time is represented as a positive integer. In other words, five seconds in the future is represented as the NSTimeInterval 5. Similarly, to represent a time in the past, you use a negative integer as your NSTimeInterval. So, to represent five seconds ago in the past you would create an NSTimeInterval with a value of -5. You can manipulate and create new dates relative to any other date by adding positive or negative NSTimeIntervals to that date. This is shown in Listing 15.2.

Listing 15.2

Creating dates with time intervals

```
NSDate *now = [NSDate date];
NSDate *anHourAgo = [now dateByAddingTimeInterval:-3600];
NSDate *anHourFromNow = [now dateByAddingTimeInterval:3600];
```

Comparing dates

You can compare dates to determine whether one or the other is earlier, later, equal, or to determine how much of a time interval exists between two dates.

To find out the time interval between two dates, you use the method `-timeIntervalSinceDate:`. You call this method on one of your dates, passing another day as the parameter. This method returns the time interval between the two dates. Just like when constructing a new `NSDate` object, the `NSTimeInterval` that is returned will be positive if the receiver of the call is after the given parameter and negative if the receiver is before the parameter. There is also the shortcut method `-timeIntervalSinceNow`, which simply gives you the time interval between the receiver and the current time. Listing 15.3 shows some examples of these methods in use.

Listing 15.3

Calculating the time interval between different dates

```
NSDate *now = [NSDate date];
NSDate *anHourAgo = [now dateByAddingTimeInterval:-3600];
NSTimeInterval timeBetween = [now timeIntervalSinceDate:anHourAgo]; // 3600
```

Additionally, the `NSDate` class also provides the methods `-laterDate:`, `-earlierDate:`, and compare: for the purposes of comparing dates. In the case of the methods `-laterDate:` and `-earlierDate:`, these methods return the later or earlier, respectively, date of the two dates being compared. Meanwhile, the `-compare:` method returns a standard `NSComparisonResult`, and is useful when sorting dates. Listing 15.4 shows these methods in action.

Listing 15.4

Comparing dates

```
NSDate *now = [NSDate date];
NSDate *anHourAgo = [now dateByAddingTimeInterval:-3600];
assert([now laterDate:anHourAgo] == now); // true
assert([now earlierDate:anHourAgo] == anHourAgo); // true
assert([now compare:anHourAgo] == NSOrderedDescending); // true
```

Using NSCalendar

Although it can be useful to construct an NSDate for a specific instant in time using an NSTime Interval, more often you will want to construct an NSDate for a specific day or a relative time based on calendar representations of time rather than the number of seconds. Not only is this easier to think of conceptually, it is also often more accurate and less prone to error. These are the cases where the edge conditions in calendar manipulation are most likely to bite you.

The Foundation framework provides the NSCalendar class for exactly this purpose. It provides a mechanism for specifying dates using more natural date components, such as day, month, week, and so on. It does this not only for the Gregorian calendar as we use it today, but also for specialized calendars, such as Hebrew calendars, Islamic calendars, Buddhist calendars, and so on. In this way, it also provides a powerful localization tool for delivering a rich localized experience for your users.

To construct a new NSDate object for a given day of a given month, you first construct an NSDateComponents object, and use it to set whatever parameters you want to include. You then construct an NSCalendar for the calendar in which you are trying to construct the date. Using these two together, you can then create the NSDate object representing the day you're looking for. Listing 15.5 shows how to do this.

Listing 15.5

Constructing an NSDate using NSDateComponents and NSCalendar

```
NSDateComponents *components = [[NSDateComponents alloc] init];
[components setMonth:4];
[components setDay:13];
[components setYear:2010];

NSCalendar *currentCalendar = [NSCalendar currentCalendar];
NSDate *date = [currentCalendar dateFromComponents]; // 04/13/2010
```

Similarly, if you want to construct a date representing "One week ago" you can do so using something like Listing 15.6.

Listing 15.6

Working with relative dates

```
NSCalendar *calendar = [NSCalendar currentCalendar];
NSDateComponents *components = [calendar components:(NSYearCalendarUnit |
                                                     NSMonthCalendarUnit |
                                                     NSDayCalendarUnit)
                                           fromDate:today];
[components setWeek:([components week] - 1)];
NSDate *oneWeekAgo = [calendar dateFromComponents:components];
```

You can even convert a given date from one calendar to another by passing an NSDate object created in one NSCalendar to another. Listing 15.7 shows how this is done.

Listing 15.7

Converting dates between calendars

```
NSDate *today = [NSDate date];
NSCalendar *calendar = [NSCalendar currentCalendar];
NSDateComponents *components = [calendar components:(NSYearCalendarUnit |
                                                     NSMonthCalendarUnit |
                                                     NSDayCalendarUnit)
                                           fromDate:today];
NSCalendar *japaneseCalendar =
[[[NSCalendar alloc] initWithCalendarIdentifier:NSJapaneseCalendar];
NSDate *inJapan = [calendar dateFromComponents:components];
```

Using these techniques, the dates that you construct will take into account all of the idiosyncrasies of the calendar. For example, it will handle things like leap year and daylight savings time automatically for you.

Working with time zones

One other fairly common item when working with dates and times is the matter of time zones. Foundation provides the NSTimeZone for the purposes of enabling you to specify the time zone in a given address calendar object. Just like specifying different calendar types, the time zone of the given `NSCalendar` can affect the calculated time of a given instant compared to the same time in another region. In other words, this moment in time one week ago in a different time zone would actually be a different time in terms of hours than the same time in your current time zone.

`NSTimeZone` also provides a list of all the time zones it knows about by using the class method `+knownTimeZoneNames`. You can use this class method to present a list of time zones to the user.

You create an `NSTimeZone` object by specifying the time zone name as a parameter to the factory method `+timeZoneWithName:` or by specifying the abbreviation of that time zone by using the factory method `+timeZoneWithAbbreviation:`. These are shown in Listing 15.8.

Listing 15.8

Creating NSTimeZone objects

```
NSTimeZone *est = [NSTimeZone timeZoneWithAbbreviation:@"PST"];

NSTimeZone *azZone = [NSTimeZone timeZoneWithName:@"America/Arizona/Phoenix"];
```

After you have constructed these objects, you can use them in conjunction with your `NSCalendar` object. If you do not explicitly set the time zone on your calendar, it uses the system's default time zone. But if you want your times to be in a particular time zone, you can set the time zone on the `NSCalendar`, and then any dates you get from that calendar will be adjusted accordingly.

Using NSDateFormatter

Most of the time, when working with dates, you wind up representing those dates to the user as a string. Just like when working with dates themselves, numerous edge conditions need to be accounted for when doing date to string conversions. Aside from simple standard localization issues, such as getting the month and day names correct for the users region, consider that there are different formats at different dates can be represented using. For example, a day of the week can be represented as its full name, Tuesday, as an abbreviated version, Tue, or just a letter T. Months are even more complicated. They can be represented as a full name, September, an abbreviation, Sept. or a number, 9. In the U.S. dates are typically represented as MM/DD/YYYY, whereas in Europe, they are represented as DD/MM/YYYY. As you can see, the potential variations are infinite.

To handle all of the complications in formatting dates, Foundation provides you with the NSDateFormatter class. This class allows you to specify the type of behavior you require and then converts the given NSDate object into a string representation of that date matching the behavior you requested. For example, to display a date using the short, numeric-only style, such as 09/20/10, you would use the NSDateFormatterShortStyle, as shown in Listing 15.9.

Listing 15.9

Formatting the date for short numerical format

```
NSDate *date = [NSDate date];
NSDateFormatter *f = [[NSDateFormatter alloc] init];
[f setDateStyle:NSDateFormatterShortStyle];
NSString *dateStr = [f stringFromDate:date]; // yields MM/DD/YY
```

This goes both ways, in that you can also use an NSDateFormatter to convert a natural language string representing a given date to an actual NSDate object. This example is shown in Listing 15.10.

Listing 15.10

Converting a natural language string into an NSDate object

```
NSDateFormatter *f = [[NSDateFormatter alloc] init];
[f setDateStyle:NSDateFormatterShortStyle];
NSDate *date = [f dateFromString:@"02/25/10"];
```

Constructing an NSDateFormatter for virtually any date format that you need to work with is impossible, but typically you will use one of the standard sets of formatters that are provided by the system.

Summary

Working with dates is a complex subject filled with details that can trap the unwary developer. Over the years, Apple and others have put a lot of thought and care into the NSDate and NSCalendar classes to make dates less of a problem for developers. You should avoid manipulating dates manually, and instead use these classes. Doing so saves time.

Exploring Advanced Topics

Multiprocessing with Threads

Threads. Probably no other computing subject strikes more fear and trepidation into the hearts of experienced programmers. It should. Threads cause bugs that are difficult to track down, difficult to reproduce, and maddeningly frustrating to fix. At the same time, however, they promise to unlock more of our multicore computing potential than any other modern software technology. This dual nature makes them a complex subject worthy of an entire chapter dedicated to handling them properly.

Every program has at least one thread, usually called the main thread. The main thread begins execution in your main function and then is responsible for executing the rest of your application code unless you explicitly create another thread.

Conceptually, you can think of a thread as a single line of execution through your application by which instructions are executed sequentially. When you create another thread, you actually have two separate threads of execution, running through your application in parallel. If your application is running on a single core, single CPU machine, your threads may appear to be running simultaneously, however, they are actually given different time slices on the CPU. On the other hand, if your application is running on a multicore, or multi-CPU machine, then it is entirely possible for two threads in your application to actually be executing simultaneously.

When two threads are executing simultaneously in this manner, it is possible that the two threads may both try to access the same chunk of memory at the same time. When this occurs, the exact behavior is undefined and as a result, this can cause an error in your program. This circumstance is called an unsafe thread condition. These circumstances only occur when the code which is executing is written without thread safety in mind.

To prevent these kinds of circumstances, you have to prevent one thread from accessing the same memory or data that another thread is accessing at the same time. This is called making your code *thread safe*. It is vitally important that whenever you use threads you make sure that all of the code that you write is thread safe. Debugging problems in threads is extremely difficult because often the bug only occurs in very specific very narrow race conditions. This means that a bug might appear on a particular user's computer because of the speed and configuration of their computer and never show itself on your computer. Additionally, because the debugger specifically can stop your application at particular points and because it narrows the execution of your application down to a specific thread, threading bugs often won't show up in a debugger at all. It is because of these issues that threading bugs are sometimes known as *"heisenbugs"*. They get this nickname because you know that they occur, but when you try to observe them they disappear.

Many developers see all of the wonderful thread related tools that they have available in Objective-C, and their first reaction is to think that somehow threads are going to solve all of their design problems. It can be very tempting to fire off threads into the background for various tasks, leaving your main thread free to handle user interface interaction; but doing this is a bad idea. Even in cases like network code, where other languages might encourage you to use threads to prevent blocking I/O, 99 percent of the time, when it comes to Objective-C, using a thread is going to be the wrong tool for the job. Using threads is a technique that should be reserved for narrow requirements, for example situations where you have CPU intensive calculations. Even in these cases, properly written, thread-safe code can be in danger of being blocked by shared resources such as GUI interaction. These problems can cause multithreaded code to, in some cases, actually be slower than the single-threaded alternative.

Objective-C provides a variety of tools for creating and manipulating threads as well as for writing thread safe code. In this chapter, I review some of the key technologies that are required for writing thread-safe code, and then introduce you to some of the classes that make creating and using threads in Objective-C simple.

CAUTION

One note of warning, the Cocoa UI frameworks (UIKit and AppKit) are not, in fact, thread safe. Any interaction with any GUI element in your application at any time must always be done on the main thread. If you must update a GUI element from a background thread, you can dispatch a method to be called on the main thread by using the `NSObject` method `-performSelectorOnMainThread:withObject:...` methods to do so.

CAUTION

A common bug which some programmers encounter is in the use of notifications using `NSNotificationCenter`. Notifications are sent on the thread upon which they are posted. This means that if you post a notification from a background thread that then updates a GUI component, you are in danger of a thread safety issue. Therefore, take care when working with notifications in a threaded application.

Synchronizing Code

The key to writing thread-safe code is to remember that no thread is ever safe reading or writing a particular chunk of memory that might simultaneously get written to by another thread. If the memory that is being read or written to is also simultaneously changing from underneath the thread, the behavior of the application is undefined. Anything could happen. So the key then is to ensure that when you are writing to a particular block of memory or variable that no other thread will be able to read from it until you are finished.

The most common way to prevent another thread from accessing memory that you're writing to while you're writing it is the use of a mutually exclusive lock, or mutex.

Using Locks

A mutually exclusive lock, or *mutex,* is an object which prevents the simultaneous access of a common resource (usually memory). It's called a mutually exclusive lock because it locks out access to the resource and allows exclusive access to only one thread at a time.

The Objective-C foundation framework provides two main types of mutually exclusive locks. The first, and simplest, is the NSLock class. The NSLock class represents a simple mutex that you can instantiate and then lock prior to writing to a particular variable or memory location. Other threads, which want to write to or read from the same variable, should attempt to lock the same NSLock object before initiating their data access. Attempting to lock the NSLock blocks the thread until the lock is unlocked and can be locked again. In this way, the attempt to lock the NSLock will prevent access to the data until the first thread is finished with its access.

To create an instance of an NSLock, you simply instantiate one using the standard alloc/init pattern. Listing 16.1 shows an example of how you do this. Typically, you hold the instance of your NSLock as a member variable of whatever class is accessing the data. It is important that the lock be maintained and available as a variable that both threads can access so that they can acquire the lock accordingly.

Listing 16.1

Creating an instance of an NSLock

```
-(id)init
{
    if((self = [super init]))
    {
        lock = [[NSLock alloc] init];
    }
    return self;
}
```

Typically, you would create your instance of NSLock as I've shown here in the initializer of the class. Then, within the accessors of the data that you want to protect, you would simply acquire a lock on the NSLock instance before attempting to access the data. Listing 16.2 shows an example of some accessors written using this technique.

Listing 16.2

```
-(void)setSomeVar:(id)inValue
{
    [inValue retain];
    [lock lock];
    id originalValue = someVar;
    someVar = inValue;
    [lock unlock];
    [originalValue release];
}

-(id)someVar
{
    id ret = nil;
    [lock lock];
    ret = [someVar retain];
    [lock unlock];
    return [ret autorelease];
}
```

Remember that attempting to lock an instance of NSLock, which is already locked results in your thread blocking until the lock can be acquired. If this presents a problem, NSLock provides two convenience methods for you to help. The first is the -tryLock method. This method attempts to acquire a lock, but if it cannot, it immediately returns with a result of NO. If it is able to acquire the lock, it returns a result of YES. This can be convenient to use in cases where you may want to attempt to acquire a lock before doing something, but if you can't acquire the lock, you can perform some other operation while waiting to attempt again.

The second convenience method that NSLock provides is the -lockBeforeDate: method. Just like the -tryLock method, this one also returns a Boolean, yes or no, depending on whether or not he was able to lock the instance of NSLock. In this case, however, this method will block for a period of time until the date specified. When this method expires, if it has not been able to achieve the lock, it will return NO.

The biggest problem with NSLock is that if you mistakenly attempt to lock a lock already locked by the thread from which you are attempting to lock it again, this results in what's known as "deadlock." Because the act of attempting to lock the lock will block the current thread, you can wind up in a situation in which you are waiting for a lock to be unlocked but it will never get unlocked because the thread responsible for unlocking it is the thread which is waiting for it to be unlocked. This may sound incredibly contorted and complex, but this does in fact happen in complex applications.

To solve this problem, there is another kind of lock called `NSRecursiveLock`. This lock keeps track of the thread which has locked it, and if that thread attempts to lock it again, it simply returns immediately. You do not need to be concerned about accessing the data which you are yourself locking from your existing thread. Therefore, attempting to lock a lock which you already have a lock on doesn't make any sense. Using an `NSRecursiveLock` in these cases resolves this problem.

Using the @synchronize keyword

Using locks is a simple and efficient way to ensure that your code is thread safe. However, you may find, after you've written a certain amount of `NSLock` based code, certain patterns begin to emerge.

The first pattern is that you often want to lock access to specific variables, or all member variables of a particular object, and so you have instances of locks that are associated with these specific variables. Often, you have a lock that uses a member of a given class as its lock object. You might lock this lock whenever you need to access any of the data in that class. Alternatively, you might have particular locks associated with particular variables, and you want to make sure that you lock those locks whenever those particular variables are accessed. In other words, you are trying to protect the coupling between the data. Ideally, you'd like to have some kind of language construct that enabled you to express this relationship in your code.

The second pattern that tends to emerge when working with thread locks is the fact that it is easy to forget to unlock your locks. When this occurs, you wind up with deadlock situations that can really ruin your day. This can be especially problematic when exceptions are introduced, causing situations where normal execution of the call stack might be interrupted. Because of these problems, Objective-C introduced a built-in language directive called `@synchronized`. This directive provides a built in low-level mutually exclusive lock mechanism which also includes specific scoping and variable parameters. What this means is that the `@synchronized` directive gives you the ability to specify a lock for a specific variable and to specify that lock exists for a particular scope of code. Listing 16.3 shows an example of the `@synchronized` directive in use.

Listing 16.3

Using @synchronized

```
-(void)setSomeVar:(id)inValue
{
    [inValue retain];
    @synchronized(someVar)
    {
```

continued

Listing 16.3   *(continued)*

```
        id originalValue = someVar;
        someVar = inValue;
        [originalValue release];
    }
}
```

As you can see, the @synchronized directive takes a single parameter, specifying the variable upon which the lock is intended. Additionally, it takes a block of code, specified within curly braces, that specifies the scope within which the lock will be locked. Essentially, you can think of this as a scoped lock. The lock exists only within the scope of the code bracketed within the curly braces.

Often, the @synchronized directive is used with the self variable to specify that an entire object is locked within the scope of the @synchronized block. Listing 16.4 is an example of this.

Listing 16.4

Using self as the variable to be synchronized.

```
-(void)setSomeVar:(id)inValue
{
    [inValue retain];
    @synchronized(self)
    {
        id originalValue = someVar;
        someVar = inValue;
        [originalValue release];
    }
}
```

One nice feature about @synchronized is that, because it specifies the scope of the lock, if anything, including an exception, causes it to exit that scope, the lock is released.

Using @synchronized rather than NSLock or NSRecursiveLock is considered to be the more modern and more correct form of ensuring thread safety. When possible, you should use this technique in your applications.

NOTE

The immutable Foundation classes, such as `NSString`, `NSArray`, `NSDictionary`, and `NSSet`, are naturally thread safe because they cannot be modified once created. However, the variable you store them in is not, and therefore should be protected with a lock if you will be modifying it.

Understanding atomicity

Another tool available to you for ensuring that your code is thread safe relates to the use of properties. The atomic property flag specifies that no matter how many threads may be accessing a given property, setting or getting its value, you'll always get a "whole" value, versus a partial value. Essentially, it ensures that the accessor created by the `@synthesize` directive for your property utilizes an `@synchronized(self)` block within the generated accessor prior to assignment or retrieval of the value. When you specify the `nonatomic` flag, no such `@synchronized` block is used.

By specifying the `atomic` flag (which is the default), you are specifying that the property accessor itself is thread safe. Which is to say, if two threads are simultaneously accessing that particular member variable through its property accessors, the operations will be thread safe. However, it does not ensure thread safety across your entire object or across subsequent calls to multiple different accessors on the same object. To do this, you would need to implement some form of object-wide lock.

Using NSThread

There are several different ways of creating new threads in Objective-C. The first of these is using the `NSThread` object.

Creating threads

To use the `NSThread` class to create a thread, you can either use the factory method `+detachNewThreadSelector:toTarget:withObject:`, or you can use the standard initializer, `-initWithTarget:selector:object:`. In the case of the former method, the thread will be created and launched running the code provided by the selector and target. In the case of the latter method, the thread will be initialized but won't actually be launched until you call the `-start` method. Listing 16.5 shows an example of creating a thread using the factory method.

Listing 16.5

Creating a new thread

```
[NSThread detachNewThreadSelector:@selector(work:)
                toTarget:self withObject:someData];
```

In this case, the selector that we are calling is the `-work:` method which is defined on the current object from where this method is being called (in other words self). The `-work:` method takes one argument. We provide this argument with the `someData` parameter. What this code will actually do is create a new thread, in that thread will then call the `-work:` method on self, passing the `someData` parameter to it. Once the thread is launched, the method returns.

Manipulating Running Threads

After a thread has been created and detached, it will continue to run until the selector used to launch the thread exits. If you need to have control over stopping the thread, you should typically include a check inside the run loop of the selector for some variable that you will set in your main thread. In other words, if you take for example a case where you want to have some job running continually in the background until the user pushes a stop button, you need to have some variable that can be set on the foreground thread and checked in the background thread. An example of this is shown in Listing 16.6.

Listing 16.6

A typical background thread run loop

```
-(void)work:(NSDictionary *)somData
{
    while([self continueRunning])
    {
        // do some work...

        [self doSomethingWith:someData];
    }
}
```

In this particular case, this is a relatively brute force technique. There's nothing occurring outside of this method, and nothing tricky going on with the run loop.

There are some rare cases where you may want to allow the run loop of the current thread to actually get some processing time inside your thread. For example, some classes, such as `NSURLConnection,` can be scheduled to run on the current run loop rather than launching their own threads.

To make sure that these classes and methods get appropriate time on the run loop, you need to make sure that you give the run loop an opportunity to run inside your thread run loop. Listing

16.7 shows another example of a background thread run loop that is actually also giving the current threads run loop an opportunity to run if there is anything that needs to be done.

Listing 16.7

A run loop which also allows the current thread run loop to run

```
-(void)work:(NSDictionary *)somData
{
    while([self continueRunning])
    {
        // do some work...

        [self doSomethingWith:someData];
        [[NSRunLoop currentRunLoop] runUntilDate[NSDate date]];
    }
}
```

You don't have to give it a lot of time to run, you simply have to say `runUntilDate`, and pass the current date. If anything needs to be processed, this will give it an opportunity to do so. Specifying a later date would only cause the current thread to block at that location until that date with the run loop running in the background. If nothing needed to be done on the current run loop, then it would do nothing but sleep.

NOTE

The assumption I make in Listings 16.6 and 16.7 is that the `continueRunning` property has been declared to be atomic. This insures thread safety for setting and retrieving the value in this thread and the main thread.

Accessing the main thread

I mention previously that the Cocoa GUI frameworks are not thread safe. If you need to access any GUI elements from your background thread, you must do it through the main thread. It cannot be done on your background thread. Obviously, this would be a huge limitation if you couldn't access the main thread from your background thread. Fortunately, Objective-C provides methods that allow you to access the main thread from your background thread very easily.

If you can imagine that the work that we're doing in our background thread needs to compute some kind of value and then update a GUI component to display that value as it's being calculated. To do this, from your background thread you simply use the NSObject method -performSelectorOnMainThread:withObject:waitUntilDone: This method takes three parameters. The first is the name of the selector to call. This selector will be called on whatever object the -performSelector method is being called on. The second parameter is an optional object that will be passed to the method that's called. Finally, the third parameter specifies whether you want the current thread to block until the method that you're calling on the main thread has completed. Listing 16.8 shows an example of this method in action.

Listing 16.8

Updating a GUI element from a background thread

```
-(void)doSomethingWith:(NSDictionary *)someData
{
    NSValue *calculatedValue =
            [someObject calculateValueFromData:someData];
    [self performSectorOnMainThread:@selector(updateGui:)
                        withObject:calculatedValue
                      waitUntilDone:NO];
}
```

Crossing threads using perform selector

In addition to causing the main thread to perform certain actions within its own context, there can be cases where you need to communicate from the main thread to your background threads as well. Just like when working with updating GUI components or otherwise communicating with the main thread, NSObject also provides methods for performing selectors on a specific background thread. The method you use for this is -performSelector:onThread:waitIntilDone: This works the same way as the previous method, except that instead of executing the selector on the main thread, it executes the selector on the provided thread.

Using NSOperation and NSOperationQueue

NSThread is a powerful class and it gives you a great way to create and manage threads at a low level. However, when it comes to innovation, NSThread is essentially using the same technology that has been used for creating threads for the last 40 years. Recently, Apple added some new threading capabilities to Objective-C.

Managing threads in this way can be difficult and error prone. The most complicated aspect of managing threads manually is the fact that the ideal number of threads for your application varies depending on how many other system threads are currently running as well as how many cores exist on the machine you're running on. In an ideal world, you want to spawn just the right amount of threads to take advantage of 100 percent of your CPU resources. Knowing how many threads would achieve this goal is difficult for you, the programmer. Recently, Apple added some new threading capabilities to Objective-C to address exactly this conundrum. The centerpiece of this new threading model is called Grand Central Dispatch.

Grand Central Dispatch is centered around the classes NSOperation and NSOperationQueue. These two classes together provide a high-level object-oriented abstraction for dealing with threads as individual atomic tasks.

The core class of this suite of classes is NSOperation. The NSOperation class provides a base class for you to inherit from for the purposes of defining a task to be executed on a background thread. You can think of an NSOperation object as an instance of a task that you want to perform. You inherit from the NSOperation class and create your own custom operation class. You then instantiate this custom operation class and hand the operation off to an NSOperationQueue which is responsible for managing the operation. NSOperation Queue will even spawn whatever necessary threads are appropriate for having that task operate in the background. The NSOperationQueue, under the covers, leverages Grand Central dispatch and launches an appropriate number of background threads to handle however many operations you feed to it. Operations can be configured with dependencies such that a given operation will not be started until all of its dependencies have already been completed. Additionally, the queues can be configured to run in parallel or to execute their operations serially.

CROSS-REFERENCE

Chapter 5 also discusses some of the low level Objective-C functions you can use for interacting with Grand Central Dispatch.

NOTE

Some developers who are new to Objective-C mistakenly think that NSOperationQueue is a useful tool for simply serializing tasks one after another on the current thread. This is incorrect. NSOperationQueue is really better used in association with background threads. This is its default operation.

Creating operations

NSOperation and NSOperationQueue are ideally suited to tasks that are "embarrassingly parallel." These are tasks which have no real dependencies, but which consist of CPU bound calculations. These kinds of tasks can run on multiple core CPUs very effectively. Imagine for example, an application that performs a certain graphic effect on a series of photos. To create an NSOperation to do this you would first subclass NSOperation and create your own custom operation class, as shown in Listing 16.9.

Listing 16.9

A custom NSOperation subclass

```
@interface PhotoBlurOperation : NSOperation
{
    NSImage *photo;
    NSString *photoPath;
}

-(id)initWithImageAtPath:(NSString *)pathToImage;
-(void)blur;

@end

@implementation PhotoBlurOperation

...

-(void)main
{
    if(![self cancelled])
        photo = [NSImage imageAtPath:photoPath];
    if(![self cancelled] && [self photo])
        [self blur];
    if(![self cancelled])
        [photo writeToOutputPath:...];
}

@end
```

This is an incredibly simple example, and obviously I'm not giving you the details of the blur here, but the basics are the same regardless of how complicated your operation will be. The important point to understand here is that the main entry and exit point of your operation is the main method implemented in your NSOperation subclass. This is where the thread that is spawned to handle your operation will begin executing and when your main method exits the thread also exits. Threads cannot be forcibly terminated, instead, if an NSOperation needs to be canceled, the cancelled property will be set to YES. You are expected in the implementation of your main method, as well as any other lengthy methods inside of your operation, to periodically check the cancelled property to determine if your NSOperation has been canceled. If it has, you are expected to clean up any work that you have begun and attempt to exit your main method as soon as possible. In Listing 16.9, for example, you would be expected to check the canceled property regularly in the blur method, perhaps as you looped over sections of the image.

Adding operations to queues

After you have created instances of your operations, you then submit those operations to an NSOperationQueue. The NSOperationQueue is what will manage the threads that are spawned that are then responsible for running the operations that you have provided to it.

Following our image blur example, imagine that you have a directory of images that you want to blur. You might load up all of the files from that directory, create blur operations for each one of them, and then feed them to an NSOperationQueue to perform the actual blur. Listing 16.10 is an example of adding operations to a queue.

Listing 16.10

Adding operations to a queue

```
-(void)processDirectoryOfFiles:(NSString *)inDirectoryPath
{
    NSArray *filesInDirectory = [...]; // get listing of files.

    queue = [[NSOperationQueue alloc] init];

    for(NSString *imagePath in filesInDirectory)
    {
        PhotoBlurOperation *op = [[PhotoBlurOperation alloc]
                            initWithImageAtPath:imagePath];
        [queue addOperation:op];
    }
}
```

After an operation is added to the queue, it remains in that queue until it is finished executing or it has been cancelled.

Manipulating queue parameters

As each operation is added to the queue, the queue begins pulling off operations to process. NSOperationQueue, in conjunction with GCD will automatically configure an appropriate number of threads to handle your operations based on the current system status. If you want to manually configure the number of threads it will use, you can use the property maxConcurrentOperationCount. Setting this property limits the number of threads the queue will use. If you configure this to 1, you are, in effect, creating a serial queue.

NSOperationQueue has other methods that allow you to determine the status of the queue. You can find out how many operations are in the queue waiting to execute by calling the method -operationCount. You can also access the operations themselves from the method. If you want to block your current thread until a queue has finished all of its work, you can use the method -waitUntilAllOperationsAreFinished.

Using other kinds of operations

In addition to being able to inherit from NSOperation, and create your own operations, Foundation also provides you with two other built-in NSOperation subclasses. NSInvocationOperation for creating an operation that calls a given method on an already existing object, and NSBlockOperation that takes a block which will be executed as part of the operation main method.

NSInvocationOperation is convenient for cases in which you have code which already does the task at hand, but is part of an already existing class. It can be inconvenient to refactor that code and put it into an NSOperation. NSInvocationOperation allows you to simply call a given method in-situ. For example, imagine if you had a category on NSImage which did the blur operation for you. You could create operations to blur your images by doing something similar to Listing 16.11.

Listing 16.11

Using an NSInvocationOperation

```
-(void)processDirectoryOfFiles:(NSString *)inDirectoryPath
{
    NSArray *filesInDirectory = [...]; // get listing of files.

    queue = [[NSOperationQueue alloc] init];

    for(NSString *imagePath in filesInDirectory)
    {
```

```
        NSImage *image = [NSImage imageAtPath:...];
        NSOperation *op = [[NSInvocationOperation alloc]
                            initWithTarget:image
                            selector:@selector(blur)
                            [object:nil];
        [queue addOperation:op];
    }
}
```

CAUTION

In this example, this would take a lot more memory, since you're loading all the images ahead of time. For this reason, this example a poor one to follow verbatim.

The purpose is simply to show how to use NSInocationOperation.

As you can see, you can create an NSInvocationOperation and cause it to call blur on the image object and add it to the operation queue just like the NSOperation subclasses.

NSBlockOperation is convenient if the operation you want to perform can be easily expressed as a code block. Listing 16.12 shows the same blur operation using an NSBlockOperation.

Listing 16.12

Using NSBlockOperation

```
-(void)processDirectoryOfFiles:(NSString *)inDirectoryPath
{
    NSArray *filesInDirectory = [...]; // get listing of files.

    queue = [[NSOperationQueue alloc] init];

    for(NSString *imagePath in filesInDirectory)
    {
        NSOperation *op = [NSBlockOperation blockOperationWithBlock:^
            {
                NSImage *image = [NSImage imageAtPath:imagePath];
                [image blur];
            }];

        [queue addOperation:op];
    }
}
```

If necessary you can add multiple execution blocks to a single `NSBlockOperation` by using the method `-addExecutionBlock:`. The operation will execute each block in sequence and will not be considered complete until all blocks have been executed.

CAUTION

Some calls that take blocks as parameters will automatically execute the block in a background thread. This is not always documented. Therefore, you should always assume that any block you pass to an API you didn't write will be executed in another thread and should be written with thread safety in mind. This includes being careful not to mutate objects outside the block that you may have access to.

Summary

All of the thread tools I have shown you in this chapter give you tremendous power when it comes to building applications that take advantage of multi-processor and multi-core machines. As always, with great power comes great responsibility, and you have to make sure you architect your applications appropriately when using these tools.

When possible, if you have the choice, I encourage you to use single-threaded designs in your code rather than introducing threads. Use threads only when it is absolutely appropriate for your problem domain.

When you do use threads, use the highest level of abstraction that will accomplish your goals, and, as always, be sure to use appropriate thread locking and synchronization to prevent multiple threads from stomping on each other in memory. This chapter has provided you with all the tools you need to write high performance multi-threaded applications in Objective-C.

Objective-C Design Patterns

One of the joys of developing with Objective-C and the Foundation framework is the fact that its designers have fully embraced the most modern of software development methodologies when thinking about engineering the API and language. Indeed, some experts argue that these methodologies even originated with Objective-C.

Among the methodologies that are well represented in Objective-C and Foundation is the concept of design patterns. In fact, evidence shows that the first implementation of many of the common design patterns that we use in programming today actually originated in the Objective-C community. Though they may not necessarily be called by their modern names, "Chain of Responsibility", "Observer", and so on, there can be no mistaking that the Objective-C versions of these common (today) design patterns are well represented in the Objective-C language.

In this chapter, I show you how to implement some of the more common design patterns in Objective-C. Objective-C, Foundation, and Cocoa leverage design patterns heavily within their respective APIs; therefore, you will encounter design patterns in Objective-C regularly. It can be useful to understand how these design patterns are implemented, specifically in Objective-C, because the implementation in a dynamic compiled language such as Objective-C can sometimes be slightly different than its implementation in a more strictly typed language, such as C++ or Java.

In This Chapter

Understanding design pattern usage in Objective-C

Learning how to make a singleton in Objective-C

Delegating responsibility using delegates

Observing changes using notifications

Recognizing Patterns in Solutions

Have you ever noticed that over time, the same kinds of problems tend to appear in your application development over and over again in different projects? You might be working away, and find yourself faced with a particular programming circumstance that closely, but not exactly, matches a scenario that you just previously dealt with elsewhere. Perhaps the problem was close to another problem but not close enough that you could exactly reuse the code that you used in the previous solution. A *design pattern* is a generalized, reusable solution to a specific programming problem that can be reused and reapplied within the scope of widely varying application architectures. Typically, experienced developers find themselves faced with the same general types of problems within the context of different applications. Often, the solution to these general problems can be applied in these different contexts, leveraging the knowledge and code that already exists. Typically, this is not a case where you reuse the code exactly from a previous solution, but instead, you use the same ideas that you used to solve the problem previously.

As an example of a typical design pattern, imagine a situation where you might have two objects, object `Foo` and object `Bar`. `Bar` wants to be notified whenever a particular event occurs inside of object `Foo`. How would you approach this problem?

What you might do in this circumstance is give `Foo` a reference to the `Bar` object such that whenever the event in question occurs, it knows to then call a method on `Bar` to tell `Bar` about it. This is a very common problem and a very common solution. The two of these together make up a design pattern. In fact, this particular design pattern is called the Delegate design pattern. `Bar` is becoming the delegate to the object `Foo`.

There are usually two different states where a developer recognizes that it would be appropriate to use a particular design pattern. The first is in the design phase of an application. Studying design patterns can be useful because it enables developers when discussing abstract ideas about application design to have a sort of "lingua franca" with which to discuss particular solutions. In other words, instead of going to the trouble of describing the details of a given solution a developer, you can simply say, "Here we will use a Delegate to address this particular problem." The other developer knows immediately what you're talking about and could probably implement the solution with no additional information. This makes design patterns an absolutely vital tool in the expert developer's arsenal.

The second place that design patterns typically come up is when a developer is busy working away at a particular problem. The developer often finds himself faced with complex problems, which on the surface require complex solutions.

Design Patterns train your mind to immediately respond with the correct solution to whatever programming problem is at hand.

Because of these reasons, a detailed study of Design Patterns is almost always a good use of your time. If possible, you should strive to study design patterns by using resources specific to the language that you are using. In other words, study design patterns in Objective-C and Cocoa. However, there are probably more resources available for the generic study of Design Patterns using pseudocode than there is specific to Objective-C. Do not let this discourage you. Most of these resources are just as applicable in Objective-C.

In the next few sections, I review how to implement a few specific design patterns specifically in Objective-C. This discussion is not a comprehensive listing of all of the design patterns in Objective-C, but it should be enough to get you started and help you understand how

Objective-C differs from other languages in its implementation of these particular patterns. My goal here is not a full catalog of patterns, but instead a sampling of patterns that are particularly illustrative, and which will help you approach other design pattern books more comfortably as an Objective-C programmer.

Describing Design Patterns in Objective-C

Most design pattern books follow a specific format in the description of their patterns. Typically, these books begin by stating a particular type of problem. They then follow the problem statement with a description of the solution, including code for the solution, and then finally a discussion about the solution. For the purposes of the design patterns I am going to discuss here I intend to follow this pattern.

Using Singletons

Problem

You need to ensure that there is one and only one instance of a particular class in your application and provide a global point of access to it. This may be due to design constraints or for the purposes of controlling access to a finite resource.

Solution

The solution to this problem is called a singleton. A singleton is a class that ensures that you cannot create more than one instance of it. Normally, this is accomplished by creating a single instance of that class the first time the constructor for your class is called. Subsequent calls to the constructor check for the existence of the global instance, and if it exists, returns a reference to the global instance rather than creating a new one.

Implementing a singleton in Objective-C consists of several steps. First, you have to create the global instance. The global instance is typically stored in a global variable. One important aspect of this global instance is that you should be sure to set the instance to nil. You will later be checking whether this variable is set to nil when your initializer is called. Listing 17.1 shows a typical declaration of a global singleton instance. Typically, this declaration is put into the implementation file for the class that you are turning into a singleton.

Listing 17.1

The global instance definition

```
static MyClass *instance = nil;
```

After you have created the place to store your global instance, you need to provide global access to that instance through a factory method which checks for the existence of the instance, and if it does not exist creates it. This is shown in Listing 17.2.

Listing 17.2

The singleton factory method

```
+(MyClass *)sharedInstance;
{
    @synchronized(self)
    {
        if(!instance)
            [[self alloc] init];
    }
    return instance;
}
```

This method is declared as a class method so that it can be accessed from the class itself. When it's called, it first checks to see if the instance variable has been initialized. If it has not, then it initializes the instance variable. Finally, it returns the global instance.

The place where the actual initialization of the global instance variable occurs is in the +allocWithZone: method, which is ultimately what's called when you call the last method +alloc. This method is shown in Listing 17.3.

Listing 17.3

Initializing the global instance

```
+(id)allocWithZone:(NSZone *)inZone;
{
    @synchronized(self)
    {
        if(!instance)
        {
            instance = [super allocWithZone:inZone];
```

```
            return instance;
        }
    }
    return nil;
}
```

Using this method rather than the factory method to verify and initialize the global instance ensures that even if someone attempts to create an instance of your singleton using the standard +alloc and -init methods, they will still receive the global instance and not a new copy.

You should implement some methods in order to ensure the safety of the global instance. For example, you should also implement the method -copyWithZone:. This method is called when your object receives a call to the method -copy. Normally, this is expected to make a copy of your object as well as all of its attributes. By overriding this method, you can instead simply return yourself, or in other words, since it would only ever be called on the global instance, you are in fact simply returning a pointer to the global instance. Listing 17.4 shows how you would implement this method.

Listing 17.4

Implementing -copyWithZone:

```
-(id)copyWithZone:(NSZone *)inZone;
{
    return self;
}
```

In a non-garbage collected, retain count memory model, you should also override the appropriate methods to repent your global instance from being released. Therefore, you need to override the methods -retain, -retainCount, -release, and -autorelease. Each of these should be overridden with the intent to prevent your object from being retained, or released. You will only ever have one instance of this object, and it should only ever have a retain count of one

Listing 17.5 also shows all four of these methods as they should be implemented on a singleton.

Listing 17.5

Implementing memory management methods

```
-(id)retain;
{
    return self;
}

-(unsigned)retainCount;
{
    return NSUIntegerMax;
}

-(void)release;
{
    //  empty
}

-(id)autorelease;
{
    return self;
}
```

Essentially, each of these methods is being overridden to do simply nothing. Once you've implemented your singleton, to use it, you simply use the global factory method. The first time you access it, the global instance will be initialized. All subsequent calls to the factory method will return that original instance. Because you've overridden all of the memory management methods, any attempt to retain or release that object will simply do nothing.

NOTE
The methods described here for implementing a singleton in Objective-C are what I would call the "safe" methods. In other words, if you are distributing your code to third parties who might misuse your singleton, the techniques shown here are the safest. In the discussion section on this design pattern, I will also show you a shortcut "unsafe" version, which you can also use at your discretion.

Discussion

Foundation, Cocoa, Cocoa Touch, and many other frameworks that are used in conjunction with Objective-C make extensive use of singletons. Most often, these are used in cases where the object in question is encapsulating access to a resource for which there can only ever be one instance of it. For example, the NSNotificationCenter has a singleton at its heart. Similarly, in Cocoa Touch the UIApplication, for which there is only ever one application that you might be running in, also has a singleton.

Singletons are one of the most powerful and most commonly used design patterns. They are often used in places where developers might be tempted to use a global variable. The advantages of the singleton over a global variable are that the singleton allows you better control over exactly when the global instance is created, and also insures that there can only ever be one global instance. Without Singletons, it might be possible for some part of your application to reinitialize the global instance. Singletons prevent that.

The technique that I showed you previously for creating a singleton is considered to be the "safe" technique. If you are a developer of a library for third-party consumption, or if you are working on a team where you cannot be certain that users of your API will understand that your object is a singleton and that it does not need to be released or retained and so on, I recommend using this technique for your singletons.

However, if you are a solo developer developing your code for yourself, and you feel confident in the fact that you know better than to release your Singleton prematurely, then a simpler version of the singleton pattern is shown in Listing 17.6.

Listing 17.6

The cheaters version of a singleton

```
static MyClass *instance = nil;

+(id)sharedInstance;
{
    if(!instance)
    {
        instance = [MyClass new];
    }
    return instance;
}
```

This is really all you need to do to implement an unsafe singleton. All the other methods that I described are really there to prevent you from hurting yourself with your own code. Some things that are notably absent here are things such as, overriding the memory management methods, thread safety, and so on. The key here is that you have to know as a user of this singleton that it is, in fact, a singleton and must not be released or retained. Additionally, you need to be sure that when you are initializing your global instance that you are doing it before you launch any external threads. Although reading the contents of the instance variable from multiple threads at once is safe, it would not be safe to write to it. Therefore, you need to make sure that your first access to the shared instance method is done prior to the creation of any threads that might need to access the global instance.

If you are sure that you can match all of these requirements, then this is a much simpler version of the singleton implementation. Generally speaking, this is the implementation that I use in my code.

The study of this particular design pattern in Objective-C is useful because of its use of the factory method for its implementation. Objective-C uses factory methods more than almost any other language that I know. Therefore, the use of a factory method to access the singleton is virtually second nature to most Objective-C developers. Sometimes, when working with other languages, you have to go out of your way to prevent the developers from simply creating an instance of your object using a standard constructor. You have to document the factory method, and post warnings in all of your code to ensure that the developers use the factory method. Most experienced Objective-C developers look first at the factory methods for ways to construct new objects because typically the factory methods are more convenient than using the standard initializes. Additionally, if you follow the "safe" singleton implementation, Objective-C provides you with sufficient tools to prevent the unwary developer from accidentally deallocating the singleton and causing bugs.

Delegating responsibility

Problem
You have two objects, one of which needs to be notified of state changes in the other. Alternatively, one of the objects would like to give responsibility to another object for determining changes in behavior at runtime.

Solution
The solution to this problem is the delegate pattern. The delegate pattern defines a solution wherein one object holds a reference to another object. The referenced object implements a previously determined interface, which is used to inform the referenced object of changes within the referencing object. Not only can this pattern be used to tell the referenced object about state changes within the referencing object, but it can also be used to delegate responsibility to the referenced object or for making decisions on behalf of the referencing object at runtime.

For example, given our two objects Foo and Bar, Foo might choose to delegate responsibility to Bar for the purposes of determining how to behave in the event of an error. When an error condition occurs, the Foo object tells its delegate, Bar, that the error has occurred, and Bar is given an opportunity to intervene.

Implementing the delegate pattern in Objective-C consists of creating a protocol defining the delegate interface, creating a delegate object, which implements the protocol, and including a reference to the delegate object within the delegating object. Listing 17.7 shows an example of the protocol and implementation of the delegating object. In this case, MyClass is the object

that will be delegating responsibility to the delegate. The protocol for the delegate is called
`MyClassDelegate`.

Listing 17.7

The delegate protocol and the interface for the delegating class.

```
@protocol MyClassDelegate
-(void)requiredMethod;

@optional
-(void)somethingOptional;

@end

@interface MyClass
{
    id<MyClassDelegate> delegate;
}
@property (assign) delegate;
@end
```

As you can see, the `MyClass` instance holds a reference to the delegate, which is defined to
implement the `MyClassDelegate` protocol.

In order for this to work, you must have previously set the delegate object on `MyClass` to an
instance of an object that implements the delegate protocol. A very important caveat when
working with Objective-C and delegates, is that in Objective-C, your delegate must be specified
as an assigned property so that it is not retained. Doing this helps to avoid circular references in
cases where the delegate object may have created the delegating object. If the delegating
object retains the delegate, then this circular reference would cause neither object to be able to
be deallocated.

As a corollary to this, when the delegate object is deallocated, it should also be sure to remove
itself as a delegate so that the delegating object no longer has a dangling reference to it. If you
fail to do so, this will cause an error when the delegating object attempts to make calls on the
delegate since it no longer exists.

When an event occurs which the delegate would be interested in, the `MyClass` instance must
call the appropriate delegate method. An example of this is shown in Listing 17.8

Listing 17.8

Calling a delegate method

```
@implementation MyClass
-(void)doSomethingUseful
{
    // ... useful things ...

    // now we want to notify the delegate

    [delegate requiredMethod];
}

-(void)doSomethingElse
{
    if([delegate respondsToSelector:@selector(somethingOptional)])
        [delegate somethingOptional];
}
@end
```

In the case where you want to use one of the optional protocol methods, you first have to determine if the delegate implements that method. You do this by using the NSObject method -respondsToSelector:, which will tell you if the object responds to the given method name. This is important. If you don't check to see if the delegate implements the optional method before calling it and if the delegate has chosen not to implement that method, you will get an error.

Discussion

The Delegate pattern is another extremely common and useful pattern used in Objective-C, Foundation, and Cocoa. Throughout the frameworks, it's used in cases where reusable components need information from your application code in order to deal with runtime implementation details. Additionally, developers often use this pattern in cases where they might be passing off control to another component and they want to be "called back" when the subordinate component has completed whatever processing was necessary.

As I mentioned in the chapter on protocols, protocols can be used to provide a convenient mechanism for defining an agreed-upon interface. This makes them an ideal tool for use in the Delegate pattern. When creating reusable components, you can define a delegate protocol for that component. Users of that component can then pick and choose the methods they need to implement based on the information they require or the information they need to provide. Recall that protocols can specify both required and optional methods. If a particular delegate behavior is required by your class, then be certain to use required methods on the delegate protocol. Alternatively, if a given behavior is optional, use optional methods.

The Delegate pattern is useful to study in Objective-C because it illustrates the power of both protocols and dynamic typing. The delegate object can be any class that implements the delegate protocol. This makes this pattern uniquely useful in Objective-C. Additionally, Objective-C's verbose method naming standard and named parameters makes the protocol definition a self-documenting contract between the delegating object and the delegate. This is tremendously powerful in terms of documenting behavior. It is for this reason that I specifically chose this particular design pattern to highlight here.

Notifying objects of changes

Problem
You need to notify multiple objects of changes in state.

Solution
The Delegate pattern is an excellent choice in cases where you have a one-to-one relationship between the delegating object and the delegate. But what about circumstances where you need to notify multiple observers of your state changes? In these cases, instead of implementing a one-to-one relationship such as the Delegate pattern, you want to implement something like the Observer pattern.

The Observer pattern defines a pattern wherein objects may register with another object as an observer of that object. Once an object has registered as an observer, then any events that the Observer is interested in will be sent to the Observer when they occur.

The implementation of the Observer pattern in Objective-C is done using the `NSNotificationCenter` class. This class provides a global dispatch system for observers and events. Observers can register with the `NSNotificationCenter` to observe specific events in the system. Observable objects, when these events occur, can then post notifications to the `NSNotificationCenter`. When they do, any observers of those notifications will then be notified, and can take whatever action they deem appropriate.

Implementing the Observer pattern by using the `NSNotificationCenter` consists of two parts.

First, your observable object must be prepared to post notifications to the `NSNotification Center` whatever observable events occur. To do this, the object accesses the global `NSNotificationCenter` singleton, and uses the method `-postNotificationName: object:userInfo:`. This method takes an `NSString` parameter specifying the name of the notification to be sent, followed by the object sending the notification and an optional `user-Info` object. An implementation, showing posting and notification is shown in Listing 17.9

Listing 17.9

Posting a notification

```
#define MY_FANCY_NOTIFICATION @"MY_FANCY_NOTIFICATION"

@implementation Bar

-(void)someMethod;
{
    ...
    [[NSNotificationCenter defaultCenter]
            postNotificationName:MY_FANCY_NOTIFICATION
                          object:self
                        userInfo:nil];
}

@end
```

Typically, the notification name is defined as a const `NSString`, such that it can be used as shown here and so that it leverages Xcode's code completion.

On the Observer side, the observer simply needs to register with the `NSNotification Center` as an observer. When it does so, it specifies the name of the notifications it wishes to observe as well as, optionally, what object it wishes to observe. When the given object posts that particular notification, the Observer will receive that notification. If the observer specifies nil for the object parameter, it will receive notifications from all objects posting the given notification. Listing 17.10 shows an observer registering for a given notification.

Listing 17.10

Registering as an observer

```
-(void)viewDidLoad;
{
    [[NSNotificationCenter defaultCenter]
                addObserver:self
```

```
            selector:@selector(stuffChanged:)
                name:MY_FANCY_NOTIFICATION
              object:nil];
}
```

When adding your object as an observer, you must provide a selector which will be called when the notification is received. In this case, the selector being specified is the -stuffChanged: method. This method must be specified to take a single parameter. When it is called the parameter that is passed will be an instance of NSNotification. This object contains information about the notification, what object posted the notification, and the userInfo object that was specified by that object when the notification was posted. Listing 17.11 shows the implementation of the -stuffChanged: method.

Listing 17.11

Implementation of the -stuffChanged: method

```
-(void)stuffChanged:(NSNotification *)inNotification;
{
    Bar *bar = (Bar *)[inNotification object];
    [bar askSomeQuestion];

    NSString *someData = [[inNotification userInfo] objectForKey:@"somedata"];
    [self doSomething];
}
```

Finally, an important part of being an observer is making sure that you remember to remove yourself as an observer when you are being deallocated. Failure to do so may cause an error, because you're object is no longer valid but it is still referenced in the NSNotification Center. To remove yourself as an observer from NSNotificationCenter, you call the object method -removeObserver:.

Listing 17.12 shows an implementation of a dealloc method where the object is removing itself as an observer from the NSNotificationCenter.

NOTE
You need only call this method once for any given observer. Even if you are observing multiple notifications that may be received from multiple different observable objects, using this call to remove yourself as an observer will remove you as an observer completely for all notifications.

Listing 17.12

Removing yourself as an observer.

```objc
@implementation Foo

-(void)dealloc;
{
    [[NSNotificationCenter defaultCenter] removeObserver:self];
    [super dealloc];
}

@end
```

Discussion

The `NSNotificationCenter` provides the implementation of the Observer pattern in Objective-C. It enables objects to post notifications about changes in their state and then allows any objects which wish to be notified of those changes to observe for those notifications. The `NSNotificationCenter` allows multiple objects to observe notifications and also allows multiple objects to post a given notification. In this way, it provides a many to many relationship between observers and notifiers. One question that you might be asking would be when to use `NSNotificationCenter` versus the delegate pattern. Firstly, you should use the `NSNotificationCenter` whenever there might be multiple parties interested in the information that you are sending the notification about. The delegate pattern really only works in a one-to-one relationship. You may be connected to implement an array of delegates when working with the delegate pattern to overcome this limitation. Instead of doing this, you should consider using the `NSNotificationCenter`.

Another case where the `NSNotificationCenter` makes a bit more sense than using a delegate is in cases where the Observer and the observed object are far away from each other in your code. In other words, if the observer and the thing that you want to observe are in totally different subsystems, and getting references from one side of your application to the other presents challenges, the `NSNotificationCenter`, being a global singleton, provides a convenient interface between those two objects. There are some limitations when working with the `NSNotificationCenter`, specifically, it's really only designed for passing around simple data. It does not allow for the complex definition of delegate protocols and so on which make working with delegates so convenient. You are limited, as far as the data passed during the notification process to the object and the userInfo dictionary. This doesn't mean that it is impossible to send complex data, simply that it is not as convenient as the delegate protocol is.

NOTE
Another big limitation with notifications vs. delegation is that delegates can have a return value from their methods while notifications cannot.

The Observer pattern and its Objective-C implementation, the `NSNotificationCenter`, presents an interesting design pattern to study in Objective-C because of the fact that it is implemented almost entirely through the framework classes rather than through implementation details of the Objective-C language itself. In other words, the fact that this design pattern is implemented simply by using a standard class, `NSNotificationCenter`, and some standards agreed upon between the observed object and the observers make this an interesting pattern to study. Consider the idea that as you discover design patterns in your own code, you might be able to leverage your knowledge of this pattern and how it is implemented to create more reusable components yourself, which can be integrated into your own code as easily.

Summary

In this chapter, I have shown you how to implement three different design patterns in Objective-C. This is by no means a comprehensive listing of the vast catalog of potential design patterns available. My intent was simply to introduce you to a representative few design patterns so that you could get a feel for how Objective-C as a language impacts the implementation of those design patterns as compared to C++ or Java. My recommendation, for further research on the subject, is to pick up a book on design patterns. There are several available, including at least one which specifically addresses design patterns in Cocoa. No matter how you approach design patterns, I do suggest that you make an effort to study them.

Reading and Writing Data with NSCoder

M any modern languages include the ability to encode objects into data, which can be archived to disk or sent over a network connection. This process is known as serialization. The idea is that in cases where you want to send an object from one process to another, either via disk or via network, you need a mechanism that freezes the object in place, including all of its data in a platform agnostic form so that it can be thawed and reconstituted by the recipient of the object and have all of its data intact.

Objective-C uses a suite of classes and protocols to implement serialization. The centerpiece of the Objective-C serialization system is the NSArchiver and NSUnarchiver classes. Using them, you feed them objects which conform to the NSCoding protocol, and they take the objects and serialize the objects to a data format which is transferable to disk or over the network.

So to use Objective-C serialization, the first thing you need to do is implement the NSCoding protocol on your objects.

Implementing the NSCoding Protocol in Your Objects

The NSCoding protocol defines two methods that must be implemented on your object in order to be NSCoding compliant. The first is the -encodeWithCoder: method. This method is called by the archiver when it needs to serialize your object. It takes an NSCoder as a parameter. \NSCoder is an abstract base class. Typically the actual objects that will be passed to you will be instances of NSArchiver or NSKeyedArchiver. Using the NSCoder, you then archive the member variables of your object into it.

Encoding objects

To serialize your member variables into the NSCoder, you use the methods on the instance of NSCoder which has been passed into your -encodeWithCoder: method. NSCoder provides a variety of methods for the purposes of encoding basic types as well as

In This Chapter

Learning about serialization

Implementing the NSCoding protocol

Using NSArchiver and NSUnarchiver to archive objects to disk objects. To encode an object into an `NSCoder`, you use the `NSCoder` methods `-encode Object:` or `-encodeObject:forKey:`. Not all `NSCoder` instances work the same. Some support keyed archiving and some do not. To determine if your instance of `NSCoder` supports keyed archiving, use the method `-allowsKeyedCoding`. This method returns `YES` if the instance of `NSCoder` supports keyed archiving. Any object which supports the `NSCoding` protocol can be encoded using the `-encodeObject...` methods. Most low level Foundation classes such as `NSString`, `NSArray`, and `NSDictionary` all do. An example implementation of an `-encodeWithCoder:` method encoding objects is shown in Listing 18.1.

Listing 18.1

A simple -encodeWithCoder: implementation

```
@interface MyClass : NSObject <NSCoding>
{
    Foo *memberVariable;
    Bar *anotherVariable;
    NSArray *someMemberArray;
}

@end

@implementation MyClass

...

-(void)encodeWithCoder:(NSCoder *)inCoder
{
    if([inCoder allowsKeyedCoding])
    {
        [inCoder encodeObject:memberVariable forKey:@"memberVariable"];
        [inCoder encodeObject:anotherVariable forKey:@"anotherVariable"];
        [inCoder encodeObject:someMemberArray forKey:@"someMemberArray"];
    }
    else
    {
        [inCoder encodeObject:memberVariable];
        [inCoder encodeObject:anotherVariable];
        [inCoder encodeObject:someMemberArray];
    }
}

@end
```

If the coder does not allow keyed coding, the variables will be encoded in the order you feed them to the NSCoder. Thus, it's important that they also be unencoded in the same order, so your unarchiving code will need to know that order as well. For this reason, using a keyed archiver is usually preferable to a non-keyed one.

Keyed archiving is considered the more "modern" form of archiving. So if you do not need backwards compatibility with non-keyed archivers, you can safely implement this code to only encode using keys.

NOTE

Be sure to state that you are implementing the NSCoding protocol as part of your interface declaration.

Encoding basic types

Basic scalars like ints, floats, and structs can also be encoded using NSCoder by using the methods defined on it such as -encodeDouble:forKey:, -encodeInt:forKey:, and so on. If you extended the class from the last example to include some scalars and structures, you might change the -encodeWithCoder: method to look like Listing 18.2.

Listing 18.2

```
@interface MyClass : NSObject <NSCoding>
{
    Foo *memberVariable;
    Bar *anotherVariable;
    NSArray *someMemberArray;
    NSRect aRect;
    int aNumber;
}

@end

@implementation MyClass

...

-(void)encodeWithCoder:(NSCoder *)inCoder
{
    if([inCoder allowsKeyedCoding])
    {
        [inCoder encodeObject:memberVariable forKey:@"memberVariable"];
        [inCoder encodeObject:anotherVariable forKey:@"anotherVariable"];
        [inCoder encodeObject:someMemberArray forKey:@"someMemberArray"];
```

continued

Listing 18.2   *(continued)*

```
        [inCoder encodeRect:aRect forKey:@"aRect"];
        [inCoder encodeInt:aNumber forKey:@"aNumber"]
    }
    else
    {
        [inCoder encodeObject:memberVariable];
        [inCoder encodeObject:anotherVariable];
        [inCoder encodeObject:someMemberArray];
        [inCoder encodeRect:aRect];
        [inCoder encodeInt:aNumber];
    }
}

@end
```

NSCoder has a variety of these methods available. See the NSCoder documentation for more information.

Working with object graphs

Because of the way the NSCoding protocol works, it's expected that any given object will encode its member variables, and each of them will encode their member variables, and so on. So the nice thing about NSCoder is that you only really need to worry about encoding your own state. Assuming all your member variables also implement the NSCoding protocol, you can encode them "opaquely" and not have to think about what's inside them.

That said, you might need to be concerned about circular references. NSCoder does not do any kind of circular reference checking, so if you have a circular reference in your code, it may cause issues for archiving. Another gotcha that can sometimes catch programmers unaware is the fact that only the data itself, and not the pointers and addresses of objects, are archived. Meaning, an archived object pointer, when unarchived, will be different from the original pointer. Therefore, when unarchiving things, you may need to manually reconnect your references in order to fully complete your object graph.

Using other types of data

In cases where you have data that doesn't neatly fit into one of the scalar types or into an object, you may need to encode that data using NSData boxing. To do this, you simply box your data into an NSData object, and then encode the NSData object using the NSCoder method -encodeDataObject:. An example of this is shown in Listing 18.3.

Listing 18.3

Encoding a malloc'ed memory block in your NSCoder

```objc
@interface MyClass : NSObject <NSCoding>
{
    Foo *memberVariable;
    Bar *anotherVariable;
    NSArray *someMemberArray;
    NSRect aRect;
    int aNumber;
    char *buf;
}

@end

@implementation MyClass

// buf might be allocated using malloc(1024) etc...

...

-(void)encodeWithCoder:(NSCoder *)inCoder
{
    if([inCoder allowsKeyedCoding])
    {
        [inCoder encodeObject:memberVariable forKey:@"memberVariable"];
        [inCoder encodeObject:anotherVariable forKey:@"anotherVariable"];
        [inCoder encodeObject:someMemberArray forKey:@"someMemberArray"];
        [inCoder encodeRect:aRect forKey:@"aRect"];
        [inCoder encodeInt:aNumber forKey:@"aNumber"]
        NSData *bufData = [NSData dataWithBytes:buf length:1024];
        [inCoder encodeObject:bufData forKey:@"someData"];
    }
    else
    {
        [inCoder encodeObject:memberVariable];
        [inCoder encodeObject:anotherVariable];
        [inCoder encodeObject:someMemberArray];
        [inCoder encodeRect:aRect];
        [inCoder encodeInt:aNumber];
        NSData *bufData = [NSData dataWithBytes:buf length:1024];
        [inCoder encodeDataObject:bufData];
    }
}

@end
```

Decoding objects

The other side of the NSCoding protocol is used to decode objects that have been encoded. There's a special initializer provided specifically for this purpose called -initWithCoder:, it is the only initializer that requires that you **not** call the designated initializer when you use it. An implementation of this method for decoding our example is shown in Listing 18.4.

Listing 18.4

An example of -initWithCoder:

```
-(id)initWithCoder:(NSCoder *)inCoder
{
    if((self = [super init]))
    {
        if([inCoder allowsKeyedCoding])
        {
            memberVariable =
                    [[inCoder decodeObjectForKey:@"memberVariable"]
                            retain];
            anotherVariable =
                    [[inCoder decodeObjectForKey:@"anotherVariable"]
                            retain];
            someMemberArray =
                    [[inCoder decodeObjectForKey:@"someMemberArray"]
                            retain];
            memberVariable =
                    [[inCoder decodeObjectForKey:@"memberVariable"]
                            retain];
            aRect = [inCoder decodeRectForKey:@"aRect"];
            aNumber = [inCoder decodeIntForKey:@"aNumber"];
            NSData *bufData = [inCoder decodeObjectForKey:@"someData"];
            buf = malloc(1024);
            [bufData getBytes:buf length:1024];
        }
        else
        {
            memberVariable = [[inCoder decodeObject] retain];
            anotherVariable = [[inCoder decodeObject] retain];
            someMemberArray = [[inCoder decodeObject] retain];
            memberVariable = [[inCoder decodeObject] retain];

            aRect = [inCoder decodeRectForKey:@"aRect"];
            aNumber = [inCoder decodeIntForKey:@"aNumber"];
            NSData *bufData = [inCoder decodeDataObject];
```

```
            buf = malloc(1024);
            [bufData getBytes:buf length:1024];
        }
    }
    return self;
}
```

CAUTION

The -initWithCoder: method is specified as part of the NSCoding protocol. If the object you are inheriting from implements the NSCoding protocol, you should call [super initWithCoder:...] here instead of [super init]. In this case, the class inherits from NSObject, which does not implement that protocol. The same goes for the -encodeWithCoder method. It should also call -encodeWithCoder on the superclass if the super-class implements the NSCoding protocol.

Of special note, make sure you are retaining the objects you get back from NSCoder. They follow the same retain/release rules as you would use elsewhere. Your scalars and structs, however, do not need to be retained because they're not objects.

Using NSArchiver and NSUnarchiver

After your objects support the NSCoding protocol, you can archive them and unarchive them using NSCoders. The most common NSCoders are NSArchiver and NSKeyedArchiver, and the corresponding decoding classes, NSUnarchiver and NSKeyedUnarchiver. Again, NSArchiver is considered more of a legacy class, so I'll focus here on NSKeyedArchiver.

To archive an object graph using NSKeyedArchiver, use the class method +archived DataWithRootObject:, which will return an NSData with all the data from the root object on down archived within it. Alternatively, you can also use the factory method +archive RootObject:toFile: to directly write that data to a file. Listing 18.5 shows this in action.

Listing 18.5

Writing data to disk

```
-(void)writeDataToPath:(NSString *)inPath
{
    [NSKeyedArchiver archiveRootObject:objects toFile:inPath];
}
```

When this is called, NSKeyedArchiver will start with the root object you have provided, and call -encodeWithCoder:, passing itself as the coder, then take the data it gets back from that and write it out to disk. Because -encodeWithCoder: called -encodeWithCoder: on all the sub-objects of the root object, they'll all get encoded into the file. Reading data from an archive is similarly simple. To do so, you use the NSKeyedUnarchiver method, +unarchiveObjectWithData:, to decode from an NSData object, or +unarchive ObjectWithFile:, to decode from a file. This is shown in Listing 18.6.

Listing 18.6

Reading data from disk

```
-(void)readDataFromPath:(NSString *)inPath
{
    objects = [[NSKeyedUnarchiver
                unarchiveObjectWithFile:inPath] retain];
}
```

Again, here NSKeyedUnarchiver will open the file and call initWithCoder on the root object in that file. This causes all of the subobjects in the object graph to be thawed out again.

Working with Archiver File Formats and Legacy Data

The archives written by NSKeyedArchiver can be either XML or Binary. To configure the file format, use the method -setOutputFormat: on the NSKeyedArchiver object you create before writing the data to disk. (This will require you to use the standard alloc/init method for creating the archiver). You can set this value to NSPropertyListXMLFormat_v1_0 for XML or NSPropertyListBinaryFormat_v1_0 for binary formats. Binary formats tend to be slightly faster and smaller than XML, but are, of course, less portable.

The NSCoder system is designed for modern object graphs made up primarily of Objective-C objects. If you have legacy binary file formats, you can always fall back to using standard C file I/O routines to read and write them.

Summary

Object serialization in Objective-C is easy to use and powerful. You can use it for saving your application state to disk or you can use it to send data over a network connection to another process. In this chapter I've shown you how to make your objects compatible with the NSCoding protocol, and also how to read and write your object graphs to disk using the NSKeyedArchiver and NSKeyedUnarchiver classes. Together, these will give you the tools needed to leverage serialization in Objective-C.

Using Objective-C on Other Platforms

Although by far the best platforms for coding Objective-C are the ones that come from Apple, they are, by no means, exclusive. Objective-C has quite an extensive history on other platforms such as Linux, BSD, and even Windows. Depending upon your exact needs, you'll find that there are open source communities that support these alternative platforms quite well. In this chapter, I'd like to give you a brief introduction to some of these other platforms and tell you where you can find more information about them.

The biggest challenge when looking at Objective-C on other platforms is in the support of the frameworks that make Objective-C powerful. Porting the actual Objective-C language is a reasonably trivial affair. Since the GNU compiler collection (gcc) began including support for Objective-C, it has become available on virtually all of the platforms that gcc supports. However, porting the core frameworks is a much more daunting task.

To be sure, the Foundation framework has the greatest cross-platform support. Since I have focused almost exclusively on the foundation framework in this book, that means that any of the examples in this book should, with a few exceptions, compile and run on any of these other platforms.

When it comes to Cocoa and some of the other higher-level frameworks, they are generally not available on other platforms. There are exceptions to this rule, but to be perfectly honest, you need to be very careful when thinking about working with the GUI frameworks if your code needs to run on platforms other than OS X.

That said, the best support for all of the frameworks that are typically used with Objective-C come from two primary projects. They are GNUstep and Cocotron. These two open source projects take drastically different approaches to their portability technique, but the end result is the same in both cases, the ability to write and compile Objective-C code with Cocoa and Foundation support on Linux, Windows, BSD, and other platforms.

In This Chapter

Using Objective-C on Windows, Linux, and other platforms

Understanding Objective-C framework maturity

Working with Other Libraries

Using GNUstep

The first and oldest of these projects is the GNUstep project, which can trace its history all the way back to the original NeXTstep days. In fact, this project was originally developed to provide an open source alternative to the closed source NeXTstep platform. In that regard, it has done a decent job of re-creating the NeXTstep desktop environment, including the icons, the file browser, the mail client, and so on. See Figure 19.1.

Figure 19.1

The GNUstep environment running on Unix.

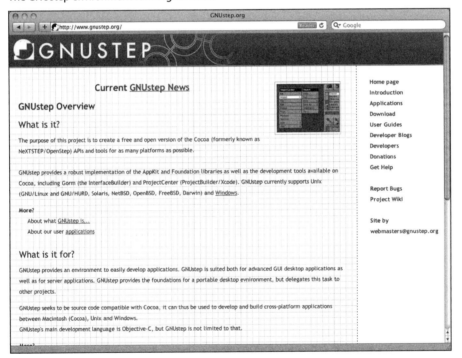

Because of its extensive history, the GNUstep project has some of the best support for Foundation and Cocoa. However, because their goal was really to replicate the NeXTstep environment, rather than emulating either MacOS X or the native widget set of the platform upon which applications run, they actually include an entire NeXTstep widget set instead. This means that if you choose to use this project to port your GUI application to Windows, your application will actually look like a NeXTstep application when it runs on Windows. This includes everything right down to the types of menus used. Additionally, there are issues related to the filesystem required for running GNUstep applications. At last check, in order to run a GNUstep application on Windows, you had to have a full-on GNUstep filesystem installed as well as numerous support libraries.

All this can be disconcerting for a typical user. For the purposes of completeness, I will mention here that there have been efforts over the last few years to add skinning support to the GNUstep project. This would enable you to at least create an application for windows and then skin that application with the Windows widget set. In other words, the GNUstep project is working on its portability when it comes to graphical applications, and improving it over time, but it's not perfect yet. All that said, when it comes to the Foundation framework, the GNUstep project has some of the best, most extensive support available anywhere. I would say that if your application is a commandline application, such as a server, and your intent is to port the application to Windows or Linux, that the GNUstep project will very likely enable you to do exactly that. Arguably, a good way to leverage existing Objective-C code that's been written on MacOS X and which you want to port to Windows might be to port the backend, underlying non-GUI code using Objective-C and GNUstep. You can then write a native GUI that runs on top of that backend code, communicating with it using interprocess communication or linking with it as a library. By doing this, you get the best of both worlds. You get to port your business logic code, while still providing a familiar native user interface to the user.

For more information about the GNUstep project visit their website at http://www.gnustep.org.

Using Cocotron

Another more recent attempt at cross-platform Objective-C has been the creation of the Cocotron project. The Cocotron project has taken a different approach with regard to porting applications to platforms other than MacOS X. Cocotron provides a cross compiler environment for Xcode so that you can cross compile your application inside Xcode on your MacOS X desktop. Using this cross compiler, you can build for Windows, Linux, or other desktop UNIX. The applications cross compiled in this manner look, feel, and behave exactly like native applications.

The way the Cocotron project works is by leveraging the Xcode ability to have multiple toolchains and SDKs installed and usable for compiling your code. The same technology that lets you click a button and compile your code for iPhone OS or Mac OS X allows Cocotron to work its magic.

Cocotron is an ideal solution if you feel most comfortable with MacOS X and Xcode as your development environment. It allows you to do all of your development on MacOS X and then simply change your SDK and recompile your application for your target platform.

As if this capability weren't enough, Cocotron also has some of the best third party support for the Cocoa and Foundation frameworks. Its implementation is good enough that there are actually commercial quality applications that use Cocotron today to simultaneously deploy on MacOS X and Windows.

The biggest areas that Cocotron tends to lag behind are in networking, threading, and some higher level framework support. These are being actively worked on however, and if you have a sufficient budget, you can even contract the Cocotron maintainers for the purposes of improving specific parts of the libraries, which your application requires.

Figure 19.2 shows an example application written using Cocotron running on Windows and MacOS X.

Figure 19.2

An application written using Cocotron.

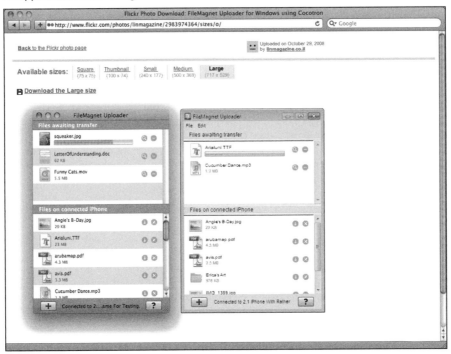

If you have an adversity to developing on MacOS X as your primary development environment, Cocotron is probably not for you. However, if your goal is simply to port an existing application from MacOS X to Windows with as little effort as possible, Cocotron might be a good choice. At the very least, I would say, download the project and try compiling your application with it. It will probably take you less than a day, and it will tell you reasonably quickly whether your application is among those that can be easily ported using this project.

For more information on the Cocotron project you can visit the Web site at `www.cocotron.org`.

Using other open source libraries

Cocotron and GNUstep are not the only open source alternatives to Apples Objective-C frameworks. There are other implementations available, but most of them are limited in scope or no longer maintained. My suggestion, when considering writing in Objective-C on platforms other than Mac OS X or iPhone is to evaluate the two projects I have mentioned here and see if they will suit your needs. If so, then you're in luck!

Looking Toward the Future

One of the reasons that I wanted to write this book is because I feel that Objective-C is an underappreciated language. Its cousins, C++, Java, and others tend to receive much more attention. I think one of the reasons that this is so is because, traditionally, Objective-C has only been useful for developing on MacOS X.

With the advent of the iPhone and now the iPad, Objective-C has received a tremendous amount of new attention and has been experiencing unprecedented growth in terms of new users learning the language. This has been both a blessing and a curse.

It is a blessing because it ensures that the platform will survive for many years to come, but it is also a curse because it demonstrates the lack of adequate standardization and documentation for this outstanding language.

Unlike C and C++, Objective-C does not have an ISO standards body driving its specification. Some would argue that this is actually a good thing. In fact, that may be one of the reasons that Objective-C is as elegant and perfectly suited to its task as it is. However, the problem is that due to this lack of standardization, there is very little adoption of Objective-C outside of its core platforms. This means that these new developers who are coming to the platform will be limited in the future to developing only on MacOS X or iPhone OS.

No one knows what the future may bring in terms of new hardware and new platforms. When learning a language, you are making an intellectual investment in that language and in the platforms upon which that language runs. In order to ensure that an investment in Objective-C is an investment which will pay dividends long into the future, we need to push Objective-C as a language beyond its core platforms. It needs to gain greater support and greater adoption on other platforms such as UNIX and Windows. I can't say that I advocate an Objective-C ISO standardization, but I would definitely like to see improvements in third party project support on these platforms.

To be sure, some of the projects that I introduced you to in this chapter have these ideals as their goals. That's excellent, and we should help support and promote those projects even if they are not on platforms that we ourselves may favor. Keeping Objective-C alive and a viable programming environment for different platforms helps to make your investment here more valuable in the future.

Summary

In this chapter, I've introduced you to a couple of open source projects which enable you to compile and run your Objective-C applications on platforms other than MacOS X or iPhone OS. Though they are not perfect, they are good, and improving, and in the future they may provide viable development platforms. Even today, there are some developers who are using these third-party projects for porting commercial applications. In cases where developers run into difficulties using these third-party projects for porting, they can also work with the maintainers of the projects to help improve those projects. If possible, I encourage you to do this as well. Not only does it help in improving language support on these alternative platforms it also can help improve your understanding of the language as well. One of the best learning environments is in working with existing code and trying to improve it.

By encouraging a thriving alternative platform ecosystem for Objective-C, we help ensure that our intellectual investment will continue to repay us long into the future.

Index

SPECIAL CHARACTERS AND NUMERICS